Civil Wars and Foreign Powers

Civil Wars and Foreign Powers

Outside Intervention in Intrastate Conflict

Patrick M. Regan

Ann Arbor

THE UNIVERSITY OF MICHIGAN PRESS

First paperback edition 2002
Copyright © by the University of Michigan 2000
All rights reserved
Published in the United States of America by
The University of Michigan Press
Manufactured in the United States of America
⊖ Printed on acid-free paper

2005   2004   2003   2002   4   3   2   1

A CIP catalog record for this book is available from the British Library.

Library of Congress Cataloging-in-Publication Data

Regan, Patrick M.
    Civil wars and foreign powers : outside intervention in intrastate conflict / Patrick M. Regan.
      p.   cm.
    Includes bibliographical references and index.
    ISBN 0-472-11125-6 (alk. paper)
    1. Peacekeeping forces.   2. Civil war.   3. Military policy—Decision making.
  4. International relations—Decision making.   I. Title.

JZ6374 .R44   2000
341.5'84—dc21   99-059856

ISBN 0-472-08876-9 (pbk. : alk. paper)

Contents

Preface

The genesis of this book is rather odd. I received a phone call one day asking if I would talk to a community group about the conflict in Bosnia and the role of peacekeeping troops in maintaining stability. Because I knew next to nothing about Bosnia or peacekeeping operations, I initially declined the invitation. But as with any such response I hedged, offering to do my best if nobody else could be found more capable than I. As fate would have it I received a follow-up call suggesting that I was the local expert. I reluctantly agreed and began the process of learning what I could in the next week so that I would at least look respectable.

At the time I was working in New Zealand and the country had just been asked to contribute forces to a multinational effort. The local community group wanted to know what was going on in Bosnia, the prospects for a successful outcome, and the likelihood that some of its soldiers would not return alive—all questions for which I was devoid of coherent answers. The talk was organized around a "sing for your supper" format. I would give a talk; there would be a few questions that I could answer, defer, or avoid; and then supper would come, during which pleasantries would be exchanged, and afterward I could go home. Everything was going as planned, the talk went well, the questions were easy, and the food was coming out of the kitchen. Then, oh no, one more question from the back. And from a dentist.

Part of my analysis concluded that the response by the global community was probably not the most effective or efficient strategy that could have been organized, though I never really accounted for why. The question from the back called me to task. The exchange went something like this:

QUESTIONER: Dr. Regan, if the world's response to the Bosnian conflict is all wrong, could you please tell us what a good response would be, specifically what would work?

RESPONSE: Hmmm. Well, as I think about it. . . . Well, some of the policies, are, shall we say, um, ah . . . Well, for a moment let's think about what is trying to be maximized here. If you think in terms of costs and benefits, then what the world needs to do is make it too costly to continue fighting and very lucrative if they stop. . . .

In essence, I was stuck. I hadn't thought through just what would work under what types of conditions, and standing up there I could recall nothing in the literature that suggested strategies with a high probability of success. I waffled on the answer, ate dinner, and the next morning began a thorough literature review. Nothing systematic showed up, and the best that was offered as a way to think about when interventions should be successful relied on a very small sample of a few salient cases. The project had begun. I felt very strongly that as a social scientist I should have been able to answer that man's question, and I was slightly dismayed that as a discipline we had done little to inform the policy community on these types of issues. The key questions were (1) how do civil conflicts end? and (2) what is the role of outside actors in stopping the fighting between groups in conflict? The answer to the second question is of course part of the answer to the first question, a full explanation of which is far beyond what this book tries to address. I set out to attempt to develop an answer to the second question.

Building a conceptual foundation for the project posed some serious problems. My intellectual interests revolved around understanding how outside actors can influence the course of civil conflicts; I also think that this is at the heart of questions posed by the decision-making community. Focusing on the issues faced by the decision makers seemed to be a fruitful avenue to approach the study, and addressing questions in a manner that would appear intuitive to them would be important. First, adopting a decision-oriented frame of reference would allow concrete answers to the types of questions asked by the dentist. We need to know what works and when, and we need to speak in a language that allows for meaningful inferences and coherent policy advice. Second, I have become convinced that the gulf between social scientists and policymakers is much more a function of style and form than substance and/or disdain. So I set out to frame questions in a manner as I expected them to be asked by a decision maker. I tried to conceptually put myself in the meeting when the president, prime minister, or leader of the junta asked for opinions on what would work. My attempt was to develop policy-relevant generalizations from a rigorous social science method.

My mental games of being the "fly on the wall" during the decision-making process continually had me observing the decision maker pounding the desk demanding an estimate of the likelihood that a certain outcome would result. She never wanted to know about the effect of unit changes in an explanatory variable on unit (or percentage) changes in the outcome variable; she demanded information in a metric that was familiar to her. I had to think in terms of probabilistic outcomes, and these generally (though not universally) require dichotomous options—success or failure, right or wrong, acceptable or unacceptable. I settled on the notion of success, largely because success plays out over two arenas of importance to the decision maker. First, success or failure refers to the outcome of the policy itself. If it achieves the desired outcome—or some reasonable proximity thereof—then it could be considered successful. But the success or failure of the policy also has political ramifications. Political fortunes may be tied to the outcome of a given foreign policy, where a failed intervention may come with high political costs and from a successful intervention a leader reaps considerable political rewards. Success for these specific types of foreign policies, I determined, could be thought of in terms of stopping the fighting.

Many—probably most—political leaders contemplating interventions have agendas that are considerably more complex than simply stopping the fighting between groups in a civil conflict. These complex goals cover a wide range of political outcomes. But being that little fly on the wall exposed me to the notion that the overriding goal—and the one common thread among the potential range of alternative goals—was to stop the conflict and ensure region stability. An important follow-up question can then focus on just what we buy with an understanding of the role of interventions in stopping conflicts, and how this contributes to our understanding of the potential for other outcomes to result. Stopping the fighting between groups in conflict is not inconsequential by any means; in fact it may be the most commonly sought outcome from interventions. For policymakers this provides a yardstick from which to judge the prospects for achieving other goals. If you have reasonably solid expectations that you can get the sides to hold their fire for a considerable period of time, then you can probably extract trapped expatriates, resettle refugees, negotiate deals to ensure the viability of economic investments, begin to negotiate terms of a settlement, or deliver on a host of other desired outcomes. Stopping the fighting is very often the first step, and the one that the decision-making community needs to know something about.

Scholars and practitioners of conflict resolution have long argued that the management of conflict requires a unique set of circumstances to achieve a resolution. Some have argued that a precipice or a plateau is necessary, that a conflict needs to be ripe, or that there are phases and certain policies have to be coordinated with the particular phase of the conflict. This work contributes to much of the fine literature in this field, a considerable part of which also generates a wider audience within the policy community. The precipice or plateau, the ripe conditions, or the right phase may all be tied to the cessation of hostilities. If we know what helps to end the violent phases of civil conflicts, then we can begin to push further and explore the prospects for resolution once we have halted the combat. So there are strong theoretical implications to go along with the policy orientation.

Contemporary examples of where this intervention logic may apply are legion, unfortunately. Nigeria recently intervened to stop the internal strife in Sierra Leone; a collection of European and North American countries considered intervening in the civil war that swept Mr. Mobutu from power in Zaire; the United States intervened in Somalia, Haiti, and Panama in recent years; and a group of countries under the NATO umbrella intervened to stop the fighting in the Republic of Bosnia-Herzegovina. And more recently a number of NATO countries chose to militarily intervene in Kosovo. Much of the public debate about this intervention revolved around whether it could stop the fighting between the Serbs and Albanians. On the other hand, nobody intervened in the cataclysmic slaughter in Rwandan during the early part of 1994 until the French finally mustered the will to send in troops at the final stages of the conflict, and there has not been any observable outside interventions into the Algerian conflict that has taken tens of thousands of lives. Furthermore, the number of interventions that have been successful at stopping the fighting is rather low, while a cursory reading of history might suggest that most have not been terribly effective at achieving a range of alternative goals—unless of course you consider the intervention a goal in itself. Part of the problem, I argue in the chapters to follow, is that decision makers have only a meager grasp of just what will work under a given set of conditions. If they indeed are trying to take steps toward managing conflicts in the global village, then they seem to be operating on a fairly ad hoc basis. The social science community can help on this score, and this is but one attempt. I personally would not advocate making policy *solely* on the basis of the results presented in this research, but I would factor these results into any deliberations over whether and how to intervene.

Many unanswered questions arise out of this work, and I would hope that most become the subject of future research—both by me and others. Understanding how to calibrate the "carrot and the stick" would be useful information, how to effectively time an intervention, whether to intervene gradually or to descend in one swoop, and the effect of short-term management on long-term resolution are all important questions calling for answers. Unfortunately, any one volume cannot do justice to an entire topic. I hope others take up the challenge.

As with any project such as this, I have incurred debts, at least debts of gratitude. There is a dentist in Christchurch, New Zealand, to whom I owe a beer. Allan Stam, Patrick James, Herb Tillema, Gilbert Loushcer, Roy Licklider, Jacob

Bercovitch, Siddartha Chib, and Robert Johansen have all commented on various portions of the work. Marc Howard Ross not only read part of the manuscript, he also gave me some good advice, advice for which I think he owes me a beer. He challenged me to make the book accessible and pointed me toward an approach for doing so. I hope I was at least marginally successful, and if so, the shape of the book looks different because of him. The cost, however, was an increased work-load, an altered project, and a slightly more difficult life. All of that is worth the beer that he owes me. Will Moore read the manuscript at least twice, and his exten-sive comments have forced me back to the manuscript more times than he can imagine. His insightful comments have helped me reshape my arguments, clarify my discussions, and more clearly focus my analysis. When Marc Ross gives me that beer, I'll have to turn it over to Will.

There are institutional thanks to be distributed. The Department of Political Science at Penn State University interviewed me for a job, at which my job talk consisted of an early version of chapter 3. As it turns out, it was a much too early version. Probably half of the audience picked up a flaw that went unnoticed by me. I have since corrected the erroneous procedures, and I acknowledge their col-lective attention. They also did not offer me the job. Much of the research was car-ried out with funding from the University of Canterbury, Christchurch, New Zealand. The university provided not only a good environment but also funding for research assistants and a six-month sabbatical leave. I spent my leave as a guest of the Joan Kroc Institute for Peace Studies at the University of Notre Dame, which provided a healthy climate and enough resources to make my time productive. I was able to finish much of the central part of the book while in residence at the Peace Institute. Each of these institutions deserves my warm thanks.

In the end I hope that at least two things happen as a result of this work. First, that we begin to expand the boundaries of research into the causes and correlates of conflict and conflict resolution, paying as much systematic attention to how we stop conflicts as we do to how they start. And, second, that this helps to build one little piece of the bridge that can span the gulf between that part of the academic community that applies quantitative techniques to develop an understanding of the conditions for conflict and its resolution, and the policy-making community trying to formulate strategies and alternatives, all while flying somewhat by the seat of their pants. Alexander George was correct in suggesting that there was space that needed to be bridged, but it is more like a gulf than the "gap" to which he alludes.

ONE

Unilateral Interventions
and the Settlement of Conflicts

In 1967 the United States sent military transport planes to Zaire to help ferry Zairean troops to the front lines to put down an antigovernment insurrection. A reading of government documents from that period suggests that U.S. decision makers were uncertain about the appropriate actions and the particular strategy that might work if they chose to intervene (U.S. Department of State 1994). McGeorge Bundy likewise is attributed with assigning an estimate of the likely success of a U.S. intervention into the Vietnam conflict at somewhere between 25 percent and 75 percent. With some regularity decision makers around the globe are contemplating an intervention into a civil conflict. Their motives for intervening are varied, as are most historical interpretations of the outcomes of these interventions. A common thread across most such decisions is the lack of understanding about the conditions for successful interventions into civil conflicts. This book aims to reduce the uncertainty faced by decision makers contemplating an intervention by increasing our understanding of the types of interventions that work best under a given set of conditions.

The settlement of civil conflicts can be a function of each side's ability to manipulate the costs of continued combat. Outside interventions—either military or economic—provide one mechanism for the manipulation of both the costs of continued conflict and the benefits of achieving a settlement. One way to think about this is that if one side can increase the costs to an opponent from continued fighting, they at the same time increase their opponent's incentives to settle the conflict (Pillar 1983). Third parties can and do contribute to this manipulation of the costs and benefits, but there is little systematic knowledge describing the most effective way to do so. Framing the logic from the perspective of the decision maker deliberating over a prospective intervention and using evidence compiled from all civil conflicts in the period from 1945 to 1994, I will demonstrate that there are systematic patterns between intervention strategies and outcomes. The results of the analysis will increase our theoretical understanding of the role of outside actors in internal conflicts, as well as point to policy-relevant prescriptions.

My argument works from the premise that stopping the fighting between combatants is the main goal of third-party interventions, and although not a goal subscribed to by all intervenors, it appears to be a common objective in the history of international interventions. Identifying the conditions that lead to such an outcome has a range of potential benefits. First and foremost, identifying the strategies for intervening that have a high probability of stopping the fighting serves as a useful yardstick from which to evaluate policies. Second, much of the literature on conflict resolution asserts that military stalemates or an impending victory makes the conditions ripe for diplomatic efforts. A first step to diplomacy, however, may be the cessation of hostilities. And finally, if we develop an understanding of how to stop the fighting in internal conflicts, we open up avenues for research into the steps that can be taken to push beyond the mere settlement of conflicts toward their long-term resolution. In short, we can ask what a short-term respite in the fighting buys us in terms of long-term resolution, the equitable distribution of political and economic resources, and global or regional stability.

Of critical importance to the policy community is an answer to the questions of "when to intervene" and "under what conditions will which type of intervention strategy be most successful." If policymakers are going to commit the resources of their country in some distant land, they have an abiding interest in picking the right conflict and the correct strategy for intervening. The use of systematic, comprehensive, and rigorous analysis should inform policymakers grappling with the dicey questions of when, where, and how. Currently we lack coherent explanations that can account for the conditions conducive to interventions and the strategies likely to be successful. Without such explanations future policy is likely to remain ad hoc.

This book does not discuss issues of whether intervening is an ethical alternative open to members of the world community; others have addressed those issues much more cogently than I could (e.g., Damrosch and Scheffer 1991; Reed and Kaysen 1993). For example, there is considerable debate about the moral implications of outside interventions in internal conflicts and the conditions under which the goals of the intervenor meet such moral criteria. I take this as a completely separate line of inquiry and proceed from the premise that once the ethical concerns have been addressed practical considerations about what works, when, where, and how come to the fore. These two considerations are, of course, related. By almost any normative standard, interventions that exacerbate an existing conflict are bad for the intervenee, the intervenor, and the global community. Even an intervention undertaken with the most humane of intentions can create a rapidly deteriorating situation when the policy is either ill-conceived or poorly implemented. The U.S.-directed intervention in Somalia is a case in point. The intervention was initially designed to keep the warring clans at bay long enough to avert the famine taking root in the countryside. As the Somalian clans became more emboldened the U.S. forces became more hostile, leading eventually to the complete withdrawal of outside forces under somewhat incriminating circumstances. If this work has a contribution to make, it will be in increasing the likelihood that interventionary policies adopted by members of the global village will be successful at stopping the fighting between internal opposition groups. Hopefully the conditions for success will converge with the conditions that make interventions ethically acceptable and contribute to efforts to achieve a long-term solution to the conflict.

One might ask why this issue is so important to the foreign policy community, or more generally to the body politic. The United States, for instance, has undertaken a number of recent efforts to intervene in ongoing intrastate conflicts; some of those attempts are quite visible to the American public, some are seemingly quite effective, and for others the jury is still out. Both the public and the political leadership want desperately to avoid the debacles, such as in Somalia, while the leadership, at least, strives to minimize the political costs of intervening. If internal conflicts pose a threat to the wider community—not to mention imposing immense burdens on the health and well-being of civilian populations—then the world at large has an interest in the resolution of these conflicts. Outside interventions happen to be one mechanism available with which to contribute to the resolution process. When acting intelligently, the world community has a role to play in trying to stop the fighting in civil conflicts. The conflict in Bosnia makes this clear.

At the time this book was begun, the United States was debating the merits of sending in a military force to act as peacekeepers in the Bosnian conflict. Other interventions—Britain's and France's the most prominent—under the auspices of the United Nations had not proven very effective, nor had either the economic sanctions placed on Serbia and Bosnia, or the U.S. airdrops of food and medical supplies to the "protected enclaves." Given the brief history of the current phase of the conflict—the rape, plunder, pillage, and mass murder carried out by the warring sides—and the long-running historical enmity between the Serbs (largely Orthodox Christian), Croats (largely Catholics), and the Muslims, one must wonder whether outside actors can bring a halt to the carnage. Reflecting the American public's concern with bearing the human costs, the Congress resisted pressures to support the administration. What were the chances that outside actors could play an effective role in this conflict? Is a "big stick" the best way to intervene, or should a "big carrot" be offered instead—or in conjunction with the "stick"? Are these types of conflicts resolvable through outside interventions, or will they reach quicker, more-lasting resolutions without third parties taking an active role? As the book neared completion the jury was still out in Bosnia. The United States, along with other countries, sent in 20,000 troops, and the global community pledged hundreds of millions of dollars in redevelopment assistance. By early 1998 the fighting remained largely in abeyance, and efforts were being made to resolve the conflict. Time will tell whether the respite from the fighting can be translated into long-standing peaceful coexistence, if not cooperation. As this book now goes to press the military intervention in Kosovo has just ended and discussions about whether or not to intervene in East Timor have begun. The outcome of the Kosovo intervention is still not clear. And the anticipated effect of economic sanctions or a military force in East Timor are uncertain.

Whether or not the characteristics of the conflict or the strategy for intervening is in any way related to the outcome of the policy is the crux of the issue under scrutiny here. This book proposes that interventions should best be thought of in terms of decisions to intervene, for which the subsequent success or failure is a function of the context of the conflict and the strategy adopted by the intervenor. When the expectations are such that the rewards are slight and the costs prohibitive, then we should not expect to see many interventions. And as I will discuss shortly, the decision to intervene is laden with political costs that go far beyond the resources expended. The structure of a particular cost function for a decision to intervene will help determine if an interventionary policy will be adopted, and if so, what the strategy for intervening will look like.

Making the Decision to Intervene

Why states decide to unilaterally intervene in civil conflicts remains an elusive question. Although most would agree that a set of conditions compels interventions—or at least makes them increasingly likely—what those conditions are is a matter of debate. Some scholars see international politics and the superpower rivalry as the main explanation for interventions (Bull 1984; Feste 1992; Morganthau 1967); others look for explanations rooted in domestic and organizational politics (Yarmolinsky 1968), cultural affinities between the people in the target and intervening countries (Carment and James 1995a; Davis and Moore 1997), or the moral commitments of an intervening state (Blechman 1995).

The question of whether it is international or domestic politics that drives the decision to intervene is, as I see it, somewhat diversionary. Surely the decision involves many factors, encompassing a range of domestic and international considerations. But more important, interventions are undertaken when there is a reasonable expectation that the goals are achievable given the strategy for intervening and the conditions of the conflict. Rarely would one expect political leaders to choose to intervene under circumstances where they expected the intervention to fail. An intervention may be unsuccessful for domestic or international reasons, just as it may be undertaken for either reason.

If we accept the notion that decision making forms the basis for understanding interventions into intrastate conflicts, and that structural characteristics and attributes of the conflict contribute to the decisional calculus, then decision-theoretic approaches can be particularly useful in formulating hypotheses about when and if we might expect interventions, at least those undertaken unilaterally. Decision-theoretic analyses rely on the notion that the costs and benefits of alternatives and outcomes are evaluated, that they are judged in relation to expectations that a given alternative will achieve the desired outcome, and that the decision rule dictates that the strategy with the highest expected net benefit will be adopted (Bueno de Mesquita 1985). Although at times these assumptions might strain intuitive conceptions of decision making within the context of civil conflicts, they can offer a benchmark from which to judge empirical results. My use of a rational choice framework is not designed to allow me to present a formalized mathematical depiction of the decision process from which an equilibrium outcome can be deduced, but rather to set up a conceptual blueprint that will allow us to think coherently about the decision process and the inputs that shape the outcomes. To some degree this sets up the conceptual straw person who makes decisions based on certain well-defined criteria. The results of the analysis can be judged relative to the efficacy of our hypothetical decision maker. Inferences can then be drawn intelligently and accordingly.

Decision makers contemplating interventions must ask three basic questions: (1) how likely is it that the intervention will alter the course of the conflict? (2) will there be support from their international and domestic constituencies? and (3) what strategy for intervention is best suited to the particular conflict? Answers to these questions will determine if, when, and how a leader will choose to intervene. I posit at the outset that interventions will take place when (a) there is a reasonable expectation for success, (b) the projected time horizon for achieving the outcome is short, and (c) domestic opposition is minimal (see Blechman 1995; Daalder 1996). One of the main problems decision makers face is that they simply have little *ex ante* knowledge about the most successful strategies for intervening. In effect, answers to questions 1 and 2 are incomplete and ad hoc, leading to considerable uncertainty regarding the evaluation of point a. The chapters to follow outline the theoretical logic that guides the decision process and then use data on 138 intrastate conflicts in the post–World War II era to test ideas about the conditions under which states intervene, and the conditions under which those interventions are likely to be successful.

The data for this analysis will be culled only from *intra*state, or civil, conflicts. This is a departure in many ways from the broader body of research into the causes or correlates of third-party interventions in that it excludes cases of *inter*state conflict. It is a quite common occurrence for one state to intervene in an ongoing conflict between two sovereign countries, or between a sovereign country and an irredentist group across an international border (see Pearson and Baumann 1993; Tillema 1989). Interventionary behavior, furthermore, is often taken to form the basis for understanding the expansion or diffusion of war, and to some extent the willingness to intervene in an international conflict is implicit in alliance membership (Levy 1981; Siverson and King 1979; Siverson and Starr 1991; Smith 1996). The emphasis here, however, is on strictly internal conflicts, those that originate within the borders of a country and largely remain isolated as such. The reasons for this are fairly straightforward: (1) there is to date very little systematic work on third-party interventions into intrastate conflicts, (2) these types of conflicts appear to be increasing in number and geographic diversity, and (3) the decision to intervene seems to pose particularly thorny issues for the political leadership. International law—if not norms—proscribes interference in the internal affairs of sovereign states, except under a narrow range of circumstances, so interventions are almost always shrouded in some form of official rationale or normative justifications. The relative paucity of systematic research into interventions in civil conflicts can be tied largely to the overarching emphasis on and threat of international conflict. With the end of the cold war, ideas about threats to security and international stability have shifted somewhat, and civil conflicts are much more central to foreign policy making communities.

Conceptual Issues and Definitions

Forms of Intervention

Third-party interventions can take on many forms. The focus of this work is on two specific instruments of interventions that are used with some regularity: military and economic. This emphasis comes at the exclusion of diplomatic instruments that can be brought to bear on conflicting parties, such as the use of good offices, mediation, arbitration, and international forums. Conceptual differences exist that warrant the exclusion of diplomacy—at least at this juncture—and a brief word seems in order. Diplomatic interventions generally have lower costs than more-intrusive forms of interventions, they pose lower levels of risk, and the decisional calculus required to commit to a diplomatic intervention is different from that required when military or economic instruments are considered. Diplomatic interventions are generally targeted at solidifying the status quo, whereas other forms of intervention often attempt to alter the status quo on the ground. U.S.

deliberations over policies toward the Bosnian civil war reflect this difference between diplomatic and other forms of intervention. For example, the United States organized a forum for the warring parties of the former Yugoslavia to attempt to reach a peace accord, with the United States playing an active role in brokering an acceptable outcome. In this effort there was little political risk from failure, though much to be gained from a successful outcome. Under such circumstances, if it was successful, a major foreign policy achievement would be proclaimed; if the forum broke up without a resolution, it would have been portrayed as a noble attempt in spite of the recalcitrance of the implacable participants. In any event the public did not debate the merits or costs of hosting the peace negotiations. At the same time, however, the U.S. Congress seriously debated the prospects of sending 20,000 U.S. troops to Bosnia in an attempt to enforce any peace agreement reached at the bargaining table. Needless to say, some of the characteristics of a conflict associated with successful military and/or economic interventions are probably similar to those associated with success at the diplomatic table, though this will remain an empirical question to be addressed through further research.

The three questions and criteria mentioned earlier are not as central to the decision to engage in diplomatic efforts, largely because the decision maker incurs lower costs and can walk away from unsuccessful efforts without being unduly scarred by the process. Military or economic interventions pose an entirely different problem, primarily because they are an attempt to change the balance of power within the civil conflict itself (Freedman 1994, 9). By interjecting military equipment or troops in support of one side in the conflict, the relative capabilities of the combatants are altered—this is generally the intention of the intervenor. Economic instruments—either sanctions or rewards—can serve a similar purpose. Witness the military sanctions against the Bosnian government throughout 1993 to 1995, and the economic sanctions placed on Serbia in an effort to curtail their support of the Bosnian Serb forces. U.S. policy in Iraq, under the auspices of the United Nations (UN), are another clear example of an intervention shifting the balance of capabilities between combatants. The Kurdish opposition groups are able to organize largely because of the "no fly zones" imposed on Iraq. The cruise missile attack by the United States in 1996, and the widening of the no fly zone, in response to Iraqi attempts to move into Kurdish regions drastically constrains Iraq's ability to prosecute the struggle against the Kurds. Implicit in any effort to alter the balance of power between combatants is the notion that by creating an equality of capabilities (or a disparity) the supported side has the ability to either fight to a stalemate or compel the other side to acquiesce.

Any type of intervention comes with risks, costs, and potential benefits to the political leadership in the intervening country. The tangible costs are generally a function of the human and material resources expended in pursuit of the foreign policy goal, but these costs translate into political costs as a function of the success or failure of the policy. It is these political costs that are most salient to the policy community, and they are a product of (1) the interest of a domestic constituency in a particular conflict and (2) the outcome of an intervention.

For instance, Carment et al. (1997) argue that a strong ethnic affinity between the people in the warring country and those in a potential intervening country is a necessary condition for intervention. This suggests that there are not only costs to intervening but also costs to *not* intervening under some circumstances. On the other hand, the evening news showing pictures of the bodies of soldiers being dragged through the streets makes the policy look like a failure and incurs a large cost in terms of public support. Somalia in 1994 epitomized this situation, and it was shortly thereafter that the United States withdrew its forces. Not all intervening countries, however, are subject to the political scrutiny so prevalent in liberal democratic states, though to some extent all political leaders face questions of legitimacy based on the character of their domestic and international policies.[1] According to Carment and James (1995a; Carment et al. 1997), the institutional framework within which decisions are made can also influence the costs of intervening, with low institutional constraints and high ethnic affinities leading to greater pressures to intervene. The key to minimizing the costs to the political leadership is to advance a policy that (1) has a high probability of success, (2) adopts the appropriate instruments for the task at hand, and (3) requires a minimum of exposure to both opposing forces and domestic pressure. Adopting a policy with regard to the civil conflict that has a high probability of being "successful" minimizes the political costs to the leadership. Conversely, in some instances the policy choice that affords the greatest expected net benefit is to not intervene.

Knowing when to select alternatives other than intervention may be just as important to the decision maker as it is to know how to intervene successfully once the decision to intervene has been made. Since unsuccessful policies will generally incur greater political costs than successful ones, the basis for forming expectations is crucial. According to Neustadt and May (1986), generalizations made from history should play a central role in current deliberations, but although analogies to "most similar cases" can form a useful guide, history points to the need for a more systematic foundation for drawing expectations. Regardless of the form of the evidence we use to draw inferences about behavior, clear conceptual and operational definitions are required.

---

[1] The former Soviet Union, for example, came under increasing pressure from the general public as the conflict in Afghanistan waged on. Peace groups formed, composed of mothers of soldiers, former soldiers, and members of the sympathetic public. One of President Gorbachev's first substantial foreign policy initiatives was to pull the Soviet Union out of Afghanistan.

Defining Interventions

The place to start is with a conceptual and operational definition of an *intervention*. Conceptually an intervention involves the use of one state's resources in an attempt to influence the internal conflict of another state. From a military perspective this can include military troops, supplies, intelligence, or aid. Each of these can serve to buttress the existing forces of either the government or the opposition. Economic interventions can include sanctions or embargoes, or the granting or withdrawal of aid that helps to alleviate (increase) some of the costs of engaging the enemy. But operationally this leaves us far short of a workable definition, the area to which I now turn.

Operationally an intervention must be distinguishable from the notion of influence (Rosenau 1968). The problem in many respects comes from the entanglement of policies seeking to influence behavior from those attempting to intervene in a conflict, but as Rosenau (1968, 1969) and others (e.g., Wriggins 1968) have made clear, from a very broad perspective intervention is the business of international relations.

An operational definition of interventions should be built on two criteria: (1) that interventions are convention breaking, and (2) that they are authority targeted (Rosenau 1968, 167). The notion of convention breaking allows us to discriminate between the normal course of international influence and those relatively few forms of influence peddling we label interventions. If we cannot do this, then intervention and influence become synonyms in the language of international politics. Although in principle this delineation between conventional and nonconventional should be clearly recognizable, in practice it is not always straightforward, particularly when the focus is on intrastate conflicts. For example, economic assistance *can* be one form of intervention, yet it *can* also be just another form of influence (see Feste 1992; Wriggins 1968). In a country like El Salvador where U.S. economic aid has been the norm, any economic intervention on behalf of the government or the opposition must demonstrate that (1) changes in the aid program be tied directly to changes in the domestic political conflict, and (2) the changes in aid be sufficient—in terms of either quantity or quality—to conform to the conception of convention breaking. This would most often be easier to observe when the intervention involved military troops or support, while the use of economic forms of intervention may not be as clear-cut as one would hope.

The need to have the intervention be targeted at the authority structure is also an integral part of the definition of an intervention. By authority targeted I am referring implicitly to the goals of the intervenor, in that the intervention "is directed at changing or preserving the structure of political authority in the target society" (Rosenau 1968, 167). Manipulating the relative capabilities of the combatants is essentially attempting to do just that. For example, supporting an opposition group—either militarily or economically—can change the structure of the relationship between the state and members of society; supporting the government would tend to reinforce existing structures.

Although any given definition will rarely satisfy everybody, researchers must eventually come down on some side of the fence and make clear the operational criteria by which they will judge behavior. I will be no exception. The interpretation of the results must therefore be attentive to just where that fence is placed and on which side of it the researcher has landed. For purposes of this analysis I define third-party interventions in intrastate conflicts as convention-breaking military and/or economic activities in the internal affairs of a foreign country targeted at the authority structures of the government with the aim of affecting the balance of power between the government and opposition forces. This definition is quite convergent with that proposed by Feste (1992) and Rosenau (1968), though it has a much narrower application in terms of affecting the ability of the antagonists to wage war. This definition imputes a goal to the intervention, which I argue is necessary if the policy is to be systematically evaluated. There are undoubtedly multiple goals associated with any given intervention, though as will be discussed more fully, I assume that there is one overarching goal of trying to bring an end to the fighting between groups in the civil conflict by manipulating the relative capabilities of the combatants to wage war.

Defining Success

To evaluate the effectiveness of any intervention attempt we must first have a clear idea of what we mean by success and failure. My point of departure for outlining the goals of the intervenor works from the assumption that states intervene to stop the fighting between groups in conflict. Paul Diehl (1993) uses a two-dimensional indicator of success, incorporating the limiting of armed conflict and the facilitation of conflict resolution. His focus is on multinational peacekeepers, which are generally used under different circumstances than unilateral interventions, though the primary goal of halting the fighting is critical to either type of intervention and an essential first step in the resolution process (Damrosch 1993; Hampson 1996; Smith 1994). In some instances stopping the fighting is the explicit goal of an intervention, as the post–Dayton Peace Accords interventions in Bosnia seem to make clear. However, in many other instances stopping the fighting is more of an implicit goal—or a means to achieve an explicit goal—as the U.S. effort in Somalia suggests.

One way to view this is to consider that the intervenor tries to sufficiently bolster one side in the conflict in order to compel the opposing side to quit fighting. Continued fighting is rarely, if ever, the goal of a contending group. Ending hostilities can come in many forms, including, but not limited to, a negotiated or unilaterally declared cease-fire, the acquiescence of one side in the conflict, or the defeat of one side (Pillar 1983). Each in its own way would have the effect of stopping the fighting between antagonists, though each may or may not resolve any issues at stake. It is assumed that third parties do not intervene to exacerbate or prolong the fighting. The key issue here is the desire by the intervenor to bring stability to a specific region; one approach for achieving this—and the one that is under consideration—is the active intervention by a third party into the ongoing conflict.

Examples of recent interventions make the imputation of this goal quite reasonable. In Bosnia much of the effort of the intervening countries—both pre- and post-Dayton—was directed at bringing a halt to the fighting. Sanctions on Serbia were designed to get them to rein in the Bosnian Serbs; the safe haven concept had the expressed goal of stopping the fighting; and even the discussion of rearming the Bosnian government was predicated on changing the balance of forces so that the Bosnian Serbs would be compelled to negotiate. The recent intervention in Kosovo had the explicit goal of stopping the Serbian carnage against the Albanians so that the refugee crisis could be alleviated. Policies toward Rwanda and Somalia had similar objectives. The French efforts in Rwanda were targeted at stopping the slaughter, while in Somalia efforts were initially designed to ensure stability long enough to avert a famine. The U.S. intervention in the Dominican Republic in 1965 reflects this objective quite clearly (Lowenthal 1972), as does the more recent intervention by Nigeria in Sierra Leone in 1997.

In none of these instances were the interventions targeted at resolving the underlying issues in dispute, nor could one reasonably expect military or economic interventions to do so. The ends are simply inconsistent with the means. Even an intervention like the one carried out by the Soviets in Afghanistan had a distinctive flavor of trying to stop the civil unrest by using massive military force to impose the Soviet will on the people. While the effect was to flame the fires of unrest in Afghanistan, the Soviet policy was designed to stabilize the Afghan political environment and prevent the ascendancy of Islamic fundamentalism so close to the Soviet border. From a Soviet policy perspective, the least-preferred outcome was the one the Soviets ended up with. It would be difficult to imagine that the Afghan conflict is what the Soviets were out to achieve. Instead, the Soviets probably thought that they could readily put down opposition to the Afghan government closely aligned with them, and thereby stabilize one of their southern borders. Conversely, the response by the United States to the Soviet intervention was to support the Mujahideen from bases in Pakistan. To some this was an effort by the United States to impose a burden on the Soviets, but there was a significant political faction within U.S. decision-making circles who saw U.S. policy as a mechanism to force the Soviets to negotiate their way out of Afghanistan (Scott 1996). Increasing the probability of a stalemate was the avenue to a negotiated withdrawal.

Imputing this goal to the intervention process consciously excludes the role of trying to resolve the underlying issues involved in the dispute from the motivations behind the decision to intervene. Solving the often deep-seated issues associated with ethnic, religious, or ideological conflicts will require a much more concerted effort than the type of interventions addressed here (see Burton 1990; Carment 1993; Gurr 1993; Horowitz 1985). However, stopping the carnage associated with these conflicts is quite often the necessary first step before diplomatic initiatives can begin. Burton (1990) articulates a needs-based theory of conflict resolution, arguing that to resolve the underlying issues in the conflict, emphasis must be placed on addressing concerns such as identity and security. Kriesberg, furthermore, posits that outside interventions may be required when trying to move a conflict toward resolution. If a conflict is in a violent phase, outside intervenors may facilitate the stopping of the fighting, thereby allowing the resolution process to proceed (Kriesberg 1994). Zartman's (1989) hurting stalemate can also be a product of the kinds of interventions referred to here. If such a precipice or plateau is necessary for negotiations to succeed (Touval and Zartman 1989), then military or economic instruments may contribute to the development of precipice or plateau conditions.

Others have articulated a broader range of motivations behind interventions. For example, territorial acquisition; regional stability; protection of the intervenor's diplomatic, economic, or military interests; ideology; and the upholding of human rights have all been identified as goals of intervention (Cooper and Berdal 1993; Pearson 1974). To a large degree each of these is consistent with, and often a consequence of, stopping the actual military conflict between parties. One might argue further that the goal of intervention is to destabilize, not stabilize, the local environment. If that is a goal, then (1) there can only be a few such cases, because most states would prefer stability to instability, and (2) the effect would be to continually bleed everybody involved, including the intervening countries. The goal in these types of instances, I posit, is to stop the fighting on terms favorable to the intervenor and, in doing so, bring stability to the region. I do not deny that there are multiple goals behind any intervention but argue that very often the first step in achieving these other goals is the cessation of hostilities.

Taking a narrow view of success defined in terms of stopping the fighting might lead one to be critical of anything that flows from such a definition. The effectiveness of any military or economic intervention must be judged in terms of a multidimensional outcome, one might argue. But if the definition has a reasonable—albeit imperfect—fit with our referent world, then we can ask where such a definition, and the results that flow from it, might take us. Two areas seem to be worth briefly illuminating, one in terms of how the goals of interventions contribute to the formulation of policy, the other in terms of how they contribute to our understanding of conflict resolution and the general field of peace studies.

One of the difficulties faced by the policy-making community is that they do not have a good *ex ante* grasp of the strategies for intervening that will be increasingly likely to work, nor has the social science community done much to contribute to the necessary *ex ante* knowledge. What decision makers need to know when contemplating whether and how to intervene is what works under which types of conditions. Furthermore, the policy community needs to be informed in a language with which policymakers are familiar. In short, they need a combination of policy relevance and analytical rigor. Defining the outcome of interventions in terms of multidimensional goals generally removes one critical element from the policy community: a dialogue in a language with which policymakers are familiar. That language, I argue, is one of probabilistic estimates of potential outcomes. Multidimensional outcomes generally require scales, and scales lead to results expressed in terms of "units of change." A unit of change on a nominal ordering of outcomes means little statistically and even less to a policymaker. So we abbreviate the observed outcome by dichotomizing it, and in doing so we throw away information, though not necessarily forever. What we gain from the dichotomization is the ability to give policymakers probabilistic estimates of what works to stop the fighting under a given set of conditions. They can then evaluate how likely it is that stopping the fighting will allow them to achieve their other goals.

Another direction to push this analysis if one feels dissatisfied with a narrow conception of success is in terms of what stopping the fighting buys the world community. If we can effectively stop the fighting in the short term, what are the prospects for the longer-term resolution of the conflict? Those interested in the distribution of resources, issues of identity and security rights, or the curtailment of human rights violations might expand on this analysis to ask how short-term settlements affect long-term resolution, and ultimately our global community. A long-term comparative analysis across those successful and unsuccessful interventions—as well as the cases of nonintervention—may shed light on the broader issues associated with military or economic interventions. This will remain a task for future research, but it is consistent with much of the literature on conflict resolution and diplomatic interventions (e.g., Kriesberg 1992; Zartman 1995).

Under these conditions, operationalizing success is a particularly thorny topic. What is meant by success is crucial to evaluating the alternative strategies available to decision makers. Singer's (1963) concept of a preferred future behavior is useful, as is Licklider's (1993) definition of the end of civil wars. He considers a civil war to have ended when either multiple sovereignty ends or the violence is terminated for five years. This definition, however, is overly restrictive given the political expediencies associated with intervening in ongoing civil strife.

When we consider that intervening in civil conflicts involves decisions made by political leaders, the concept of success must be understood accordingly. Political leaders generally cannot make policies regarding interventions with a five-year time horizon, as would be consistent with Licklider's definition. Political forces dictate otherwise. The short-term time frame, moreover, is a function of expectations at the time of the intervention, even though the actual policy may play out over multiple years (e.g., Vietnam and Afghanistan). Obviously miscalculations are sometimes made. When we talk about third-party interventions into intrastate military contests, success must be conceived of in terms of either stopping the fighting or resolving the underlying dispute. The latter would make the barriers to success impossibly high relative to the tools employed, while political imperatives dictate that policies have a short-term horizon. Success in this analysis will be operationalized as the cessation of military hostilities for a period lasting at least six months. This definition adopts the same frame of reference for the end of militarized dispute identified in the Correlates of War data (Jones, Bremer, and Singer 1996) and fits with the first half of Diehl's (1993) two-part definition of successful peacekeeping interventions. Although stopping the fighting for this relatively short period of time would rarely even approach a resolution of the underlying issues at stake, six months without military hostilities can (a) give policymakers cause to claim success with their policy and (b) give a sufficient break in the fighting to initiate meaningful dialogue in an effort to resolve the underlying causes of the conflict. The post-Dayton interventions in Bosnia had a clearly defined short-term idea of a successful outcome: stopping the violence. What seemed equally clear is that the fighting had to stop before political and social changes could occur. The failed record of the UN and European Union mediation attempts while the fighting was under way attests to the usefulness of stopping the fighting. As we saw earlier, most decisions over when, where, how, or whether to intervene involve some calculation of potential costs and benefits (whether formally or informally); the political aspects of these costs shape the terms of the engagement. Since it is likely that costs will increase with time while benefits under the very best of circumstances (at least to the political leadership) remain constant, optimal strategies for intervention will have short time horizons. It is more likely, however, that this short time frame is exacerbated by declining benefits over time relative to the costs, adding even greater impetus to design intervention strategies that have a reasonable expectation of being successful in the short term.

The Value of This Project to the Policy Community

Given the increased interest in containing and resolving civil conflicts around the globe, as well as the increasing numbers of such conflicts in the post–cold war era (Gurr 1993, 1994), policymakers could be well served by access to systematically generated guidelines to help focus the decision process. Although any research like this will never be the panacea and cannot replace sound, logical reasoning during the decision-making process, systematic research can guide the deliberative process. Think of the number of times that blunders were made when, at minimum, anecdotal evidence was available to point toward the impending policy debacle (Neustadt and May 1986).

Policymakers face two conflicting hurdles when trying to formulate strategies for advancing national security by intervening in civil conflicts. On the one hand, they confront domestic constituencies that have an interest in the cessation of hostilities in their homeland. Ignoring ethnic homogeneities may come with political perils. The tacit support by the United States of the Catholic faction in the Northern Ireland struggle may attest to the political ramifications of ignoring constituencies with ties to their mother country. On the other hand, the general public is rather loath to commit resources in some distant land—particularly if the potential for human casualties is high—when there are problems on the home front that deserve attention. These competing pressures from the domestic community on decision makers trying to formulate policy can result in a tenuous balancing act. But domestic forces are only one part of the equation. The security elite charged with formulating foreign policy must put issues of national security at the forefront of their deliberative processes, and in doing so give short attention to the domestic considerations. The ministry or department of foreign affairs is not charged with catering to domestic constituencies (Kennan 1993). The role of weighing the relative influence of domestic and international concerns falls on the shoulders of the chief executive, who harbors an abiding interest in being both effective in the foreign policy realm and responsive at home. The results of the analysis outlined in this book contribute to the ability to juggle these factors effectively.

In this juggling of national security and domestic concerns the most costly outcome is to intervene and have that intervention fail. For the most part, the decision as to when, where, and how to intervene is one in which decision makers try to make well-informed speculations based on analogies to past policies. Analogical reasoning, however useful, is prone to faulty perceptions or the reliance on inappropriate cases. If policymakers had a blueprint in which the characteristics of the conflict, the strategy for intervening, and the likely outcome were considered in a way that suggested the probability of successful outcomes given certain conditions, then this would constitute a significant advance in the policy-making process. Alexander George (1995) argues that answers to these types of questions are at the forefront of the needs of foreign policy managers, and that social science needs to forge closer links with the policy community. Equally important is a clearer understanding of when and when not to intervene. Appropriately used, this research should provide policymakers with just such a set of guidelines. Although no social science research—whether based on qualitative or quantitative evidence—results in deterministic policy prescriptions (i.e., identifying a policy option that will always be successful under a given set of conditions), as a result of this project we can give prescriptive advice based on a probabilistic understanding of what worked and what did not in the recent past. At minimum, the following chapters make evident those conditions under which an intervention strategy is unlikely to be effective. This should facilitate decision makers' ability to at least avoid the blunders, if not tailor successful strategies. By informing the decisional calculus, this work can influence the way that decision makers think about interventions into civil conflicts. Their need to juggle domestic and international considerations will not change, but their ability to do so in an informed manner should.

Organization of the Book

The outline of the book follows what seems like a logical ordering of events in the decision process, moving from the decision over whether to intervene to the most effective strategy under a given set of conditions once that choice has been made in the affirmative. The bulk of these chapters adopts the perspective of a decision over a unilateral intervention with a very narrow goal. The analysis starts with chapter 2 describing the data to be used and the distribution of cases across regions, intervention strategies, and types of conflicts. One way to view these historical descriptions is as a snapshot of the conditions faced by policymakers, their strategies for intervening, and the degree to which they have been successful in their efforts. Chapter 3 poses the question of when states choose to intervene. It is clear that not all civil conflicts suffer the fate (or virtue) of outside interventions, and that states self-select themselves into or out of interventions for a variety of identifiable reasons. To fully evaluate the effectiveness of intervention strategies we first have to know when states choose to do otherwise. Chapter 4 then examines the conditions under which various forms of intervention are likely to achieve a successful outcome. This is the central focus of the book. Currently there is remarkably little systematic information with which to understand the outcome of interventions, or to guide the policy community. The advances here are significant over what our current state of knowledge has to offer. In combination, chapters 3 and 4 identify the conditions under which interventions are likely to be chosen and the strategies and circumstances that result in the greatest probability of successful outcomes.

Chapter 5 takes a different tack and examines the role played by multilateral interventions and the accompanying multifaceted strategies that can unfold under their auspices. Many would argue that stopping the fighting is far too narrow a goal for intervening countries, and to some degree the evidence supports this argument. The most clearly visible instances where stopping the fighting is a goal with very little relevance to the decision process can be seen in peacebuilding efforts carried out under the auspices of the UN, nongovernmental organizations (NGOs), or multilateral organizations (European Union, Organization of African Unity, etc.). In such cases the objectives usually entail putting a country back on its feet after the cessation of hostilities, rather than putting an end to the fighting, and therefore involve minesweeping operations, organizing elections, rebuilding roads, and outfitting hospitals. This chapter poses the questions of who intervenes and why when the goals and implements for intervening are more broadly conceived. The final chapter wraps things up by summarizing what we have learned, points toward future research, and draws out implications for conflict studies and policymakers.

TWO

Descriptive Evidence
on Conflicts and Interventions

This chapter serves two purposes. First it introduces the data that are used to examine some of the questions posed in the introductory chapter. Valid and reliable data are critical if we are to draw useful inferences about when interventions are likely and the conditions under which they will tend to be successful. And, second, we need a benchmark from which to judge our results. The data are of course central to the testing of hypotheses, without which the theoretical arguments will remain hunches. A common benchmark, on the other hand, gives us some way to judge the usefulness of the reported results. The benchmark can be thought of as a set of descriptive statistics that provides information about the characteristics of the conflicts, the strategies used for intervening, and the relative effectiveness of different strategies in various types of conflicts. This descriptive exploration employs simple bivariate statistics to paint a broad-stroked portrait of how interventions have been carried out and under what conditions they tend to succeed. But such a rudimentary form of investigation can at best serve as a prelude to a more systematic treatment to follow in the succeeding chapters.

To put this into perspective, the objective of this book is to develop a better understanding of the effect of various strategies for intervening under different conditions of conflict. Empirically testing hypotheses relating specific interventions to characteristics of the conflict will require models with multiple variables that can "control" for various concurrent causal effects. But it is also useful to know whether, in general, military interventions are more successful than the economic variety, or whether ethnic conflicts are more tractable than ideological ones. These types of questions are the focus of this chapter. One might think of this as the quintessential "holding all things constant," which most people realize is an extreme oversimplification of our sociopolitical world. But by going through this exercise we learn about the data being used, which in turn facilitates our interpretation of a more complex modeling of the world.

What follows is a summary of the data used in this analysis, the sources consulted in the compilation of the data, and a discussion of the descriptive statistics that result from simple bivariate analysis. This chapter sets the stage for the next two chapters; it also serves as a space-saving device by obviating the need to engage in an in-depth description of data, coding procedures, and sources as each subsequent chapter unfolds.

Data Description

To test the ideas articulated throughout this book a comprehensive set of data on intrastate conflicts in the post–World War II period was generated. These data incorporate not only those internal conflicts in which there were outside intervenors but also those conflicts in which there were no interventions. The data record characteristics of the conflict, the combatants, and the intervention (if any), as well as the success or failure of the intervention. The completeness of the data in terms of the conflicts included can be checked against those intrastate conflicts identified by Licklider (1995), where, although generated completely independently and with no prior knowledge of each other's research efforts, one finds a near-total convergence on cases. In short, the data reflect the population of civil conflicts in the post–World War II period that meet the conditions outlined in the following section.

Case Selection

The data expand and refine some of the more comprehensive compilations of data on military interventions—in both inter- and intrastate conflicts (see Pearson and Baumann 1993; Small and Singer 1982; Tillema 1989). I draw on each of these data sets extensively. The Small and Singer data adopt the convention of 1,000 fatalities for inclusion as a civil war; this casualty rate was relaxed for the data used in this analysis. Although civil wars may be the more visible and long lasting of the intrastate conflicts, a considerable number of civil conflicts clearly do not look like what we generally conceive of as a civil war. For example, the Bougainville conflict in Papua New Guinea, the Chiapas uprising in Mexico, or the religious conflicts in the northern states of India do not have the flavor of a "civil war" like that of El Salvador or Angola throughout the 1980s. However, these less intense conflicts can be a cause for concern among members of a regional or global community, lest they simmer and expand, leading to either the diffusion of the conflict or the need to address the human consequences of a protracted social upheaval, or both. An important question for this work is whether there is a threshold in the number of fatalities above which third parties intervene and, if so, whether the number of casualties affects the success or failure of the intervention. These are empirical questions that can be answered with the data drawn from a less restrictive view of civil conflicts.

I define intrastate conflict as armed combat between groups within state boundaries in which there are at least 200 fatalities. This lower threshold allows me to capture the seriousness of the conflict, yet it is high enough to exclude events such as "bloodless" coups, riots, and demonstrations. Two hundred fatalities conveys a sense that the demands of the opposition are such that the potential for further escalation is reasonably high.

Sources for these data included the Correlates of War Civil War database (Small and Singer 1982), the annual *Yearbook* of the Stockholm International Peace Research Institute (SIPRI), *Keesings Contemporary Archives*, the *New York Times*, the *Minorities at Risk Project*, the Military Intervention data generated by Herbert Tillema (1991) and Pearson and Baumann (1993), and, where necessary, historical documents pertaining to a specific case. Temporally the cases span the period 1944 to 1994, starting with the Greek civil war. Pushing the analysis back to the first half of the twentieth century posed conceptual and methodological problems that were best resolved by abbreviating the period under study. Conceptually, so much of the civil conflict in the earlier part of the century could be tied to anticolonial struggles and therefore shifts the debate from intra- to internation conflict (or what Small and Singer have labeled extrasystemic conflicts). Some of this carried over into the anticolonial movements in the post–World War II period, though these conflicts were not included in the population of cases used in this analysis. Methodologically, going back to the pre-1944 period made the search for reliable and valid data increasingly problematic, leading to an arbitrary point where the data might be reliable, and with a cutoff point having no theoretical or intuitive justification. Neglecting these difficulties in the case selection process could ultimately pose problems with subsequent interpretation. The most logical cutoff point, therefore, was the end of World War II and the beginning of the cold war.

Characteristics of the Conflict

Characteristics of the conflicts and the combatants make up one set of explanatory variables that contribute to our understanding of when third-party interventions are more likely to be successful. A key ingredient in these outcomes is the identification of the orientation of the groups in conflict. For example, civil disputes fought over religious or ideological issues may be more tractable to outside interventions than those fought over ethnic divisions because of the ease with which identity can be assumed or discarded (Kaufmann 1996). This characteristic of the conflict has implications for the political costs of intervening as well. If cross-national ethnic affinity acts as a political factor in decisions over whether to intervene (Carment and James 1995b), then understanding the extent to which this operates in the decision process is important. Accordingly, the ethnic, religious, or ideological orientations of the groups in conflict were identified and the conflict classified based on the orientation of the primary groups in conflict. The identification of groups was determined through the use of the Minorities at Risk classification scheme and the Correlates of War Cultural Data Set.[1] The first two groups (ethnic and religious) roughly correspond to what Gurr (1993) refers to as ethnonationalists, and militant sects. Ethnically based conflicts involve groups that identify with a distinct ethnic or cultural heritage; religious conflicts involve groups that are organized in defense of their religious beliefs. Ideological conflicts, on the other hand, involve groups contesting the dominant political or economic ideology, which can, but need not, incorporate an ethnic or religious dimension. Williams and Kofman (1989) use similar criteria to identify community conflict.

The threefold typology used here cannot provide mutually exclusive categories that sufficiently describe the complexity of many conflicts. This is a limitation, though not a crippling one. In most instances the orientation of the groups in conflict was fairly transparent, allowing for a somewhat straightforward identification. As is probably true with many civil conflicts, however, people often identify with more than one group. This would be particularly true in religious and ethnic conflicts, less so when the conflict is organized around ideological issues. The Bosnian conflict makes this point quite clearly. The ruling government of the Bosnian state generally identifies with Muslim religious faith; the Croats and the Serbs likewise identify with their respective Christian beliefs. But in each case there is also an identification with an ethnic grouping. Determining which is the most dominant orientation is not always easy, nor is the problem restricted to ethnic and religious conflicts. Ideology can also separate ethnically homogeneous groups, as one could argue it did in Zaire or Angola, though this poses less of a problem in terms of concurrent affiliations, where in most instances an ideological struggle brings together people of different ethnic, religious, and social backgrounds.

Although there is overlap, Gurr (1993) lists minority groups based on primary and secondary affiliations, and it is his primary orientation that is used to make the distinction between ethnic and religious conflicts in this analysis. One of the distinctions between religious and ethnic conflicts that makes this coding scheme germane is that the demand of the groups will often be at crosscurrents. For example, minority ethnic groups often suffer at the hands of a majority group by being cut out of political access and/or economic opportunities. Religious groups in

---

[1] The Correlates of War (COW) Cultural Data Set records ethnic, religious, and linguistic groups within countries, identifying each group's population and their percentage makeup of the total population of the country.

conflict, on the other hand, are often demanding the freedom to openly practice or advocate their spiritual beliefs. These distinctions, though somewhat cloudy in operational terms, are an important empirical dimension in a study of whether and how to intervene, as well as in the likely success of any interventionary policy. Kaufmann (1996), furthermore, argues that the tractability of civil conflict is directly related to the identity of the combatants, whereby certain types of identity patterns can be assumed or discarded more easily than others. Ethnic identity, for instance, is more difficult to discard than a religious or ideological identity; according to Kaufmann's argument, this makes the resolution of ethnic conflicts more difficult. Since ideological and religious identities can span the more physically traceable aspects of ethnicity, the ability to wage conflict, persecute participants, or separate combatants should vary across group orientation.

Other characteristics of the conflict that are important for understanding when to intervene and when interventions have an increased probability of success are (1) the strategic environment in which the conflict is being waged, including both cold war dynamics and the number of shared borders, (2) the existence of a humanitarian crisis associated with the conflict, (3) the number of fatalities, and (4) the intensity of the conflict. Fatalities not only denote an operational point for inclusion of cases but also reflect the seriousness of the social conflict and the extent to which it is entrenched in the society and visible to the global community. Sources for the number of casualties are generally the same as those for the conflict itself, including but not limited to the Correlates of War data, Tillema's intervention data, the *New York Times, Keesings,* and the Pearson and Baumann data on military interventions. The intensity of the conflict is operationalized in terms of the number of fatalities per year averaged over the course of the conflict. As will be discussed in subsequent chapters, the intensity of the conflict should influence the decision over whether to intervene as well as affecting the likelihood that any intervention will be successful.

Conceptually, humanitarian issues involve concerns over famine, refugee flows, genocide, and ethnic expulsions, though some broaden this conception to include factors associated with poverty and underdevelopment (Väyrynen 1996). But linking mass social dislocations to a civil conflict is not always a simple task where, for instance, the humanitarian crisis could be the cause of the conflict rather than a consequence of it (Väyrynen 1996). Operationally I define a humanitarian crisis associated with a civil conflict in terms of the extent of refugee flows, either as internally displaced peoples or as international refugees. A conflict associated with the flow of at least 50,000 refugees is considered to be of a concern on humanitarian grounds and was coded 1; otherwise, zero. Data were derived from the annual report of the U.S. Committee for Refugees (USCR), the United Nations High Commission for Refugees (UNHCR), the *New York Times,* and specific case histories where necessary.

The cold war is considered to have ended as of January 1, 1989, for reasons that will be more fully outlined in the following chapter. Although it is risky to "peg" the date that the cold war ended, I do so at the beginning of 1989 with the change in the U.S. presidency from Ronald Reagan to George Bush. It is argued that the effect of the cold war was such that it influenced the incentives to be garnered from an intervention, and ultimately, one might argue, contributing to the shift in the pattern of interventions from unilateral to multilateral efforts. One effect of the cold war was to compel the decision-making community to view most conflicts in terms of zero-sum outcomes. The impact of moving away from zero-sum formulations of world events should serve to shift the calculations of expected payoffs from interventions. Finally, intervening in an ongoing civil conflict requires both an opportunity and a willingness to do so, and a direct route to the opportunity and willingness is through a shared border (Siverson and Starr 1991). A contiguous border is operationalized in terms of the Correlates of War definition of either a land border or less than 150 miles of water separating two otherwise contiguous countries. The number of countries contiguous to the country experiencing the civil strife is the indicator used in the analysis.

Characteristics of the Intervention

The other set of explanatory variables critical to our understanding of interventions and their outcomes is composed of the characteristics of the intervention, or in more policy-relevant terms, the strategy for intervening. The complex mix of factors that can comprise an intervention strategy ranges from punishments to rewards, incremental policies to massive onslaughts, supporting the government to supporting the opposition. For this analysis I simplify that range by focusing on two components of the strategy: the form of intervention and the intended target. What is left out in this simplification process deserves mention, so before moving on to a discussion of what is deemed most important, let me talk about those other components of an intervention strategy that will be deferred.

An intervention strategy can involve, for example, a mix of incentives and punishments, which might be used to induce or reinforce behavior, or to compel action. Whether one approach is more effective, and under what constellation of factors, is a question without many answers at this juncture. Furthermore, an intervention strategy can be implemented in an incremental fashion—slowly ratcheting up the incentives or punishments—or it can unfold in one massive swoop. The UN policy toward Iraq in 1991 is an example of the latter; the U.S. interventions in Nicaragua and El Salvador are examples of a more incremental process. At the end of the Gulf War when the Iraqi government began persecuting the Kurdish populations, the UN imposed swift and sweeping economic and military sanctions on Iraq while restricting the ability of the Iraqi military to advance against the Kurds by imposing a no fly zone. In Nicaragua and El Salvador the United States gradually increased and decreased the amount of assistance given to the contra in Nicaragua or the government in El Salvador, hoping, it would seem, that each incremental change would be sufficient to compel the desired action.

Whether the speed or sequence with which an intervention takes place or the emphasis on rewards versus punishments affects the outcome, is an interesting and vital question, but one for which we lack sufficient theoretical understanding from which to identify empirical generalizations. For example, to specify a statistical model reflecting the role of time or the sequential unfolding of an intervention we have to have a reasonable grasp of how these two factors interact and contribute to the observed outcome. Negative (or positive) empirical results derived from a poorly specified model mean very little, just as a linear test of an underlying curvilinear process may show no systematic relationship, yet a more valid exponential specification may identify a strong relationship. Unfortunately, the current state of our understanding about the relationships among time, sequencing, and rewards and punishments leaves us unequipped to tease out potential causal mechanisms. But this does not leave us totally impoverished with regard to our ability to capture the intricacies of the intervention dilemma. It simply means that we have to postpone some of the questions and continue to rely on intuition and analogous comparisons in the decision-making process, at least until somebody takes up this further challenge.

Given these limitations and my operational definition of an intervention outlined in chapter 1, I focus on three generic forms of intervention (military, economic, and mixed), and two targets of the interventions (government and opposition). Military interventions encompass the supply or transfer of troops, hardware, intelligence, air or naval support, and logistical support to the parties in conflict or, as may be the case, the cutoff of any such aid currently in place. Economic interventions involve various forms of economic aid, and economic sanctions or embargoes. Mixed strategies are those that incorporate some combination of military and economic instruments. The critical point in each instance is that the military or economic behavior conforms to the convention-breaking and authority-targeted criteria outlined in the first chapter. Sources for data on interventions include those previously mentioned but also include country-specific case histories when necessary.

Keeping in mind the criteria of convention-breaking and authority-targeted activities for interventions, determining when an intervention has been attempted and whether it was successful can present difficult coding problems; two particular difficulties stand out. The first, and generally the more tractable, is determining when a particular intervention is directly linked to the conflict at hand. Often this is a straightforward determination; at times it imposes quite difficult decisions. For example, arms transfers (to either the government or opposition) in the midst of armed conflict poses few difficulties. U.S. aid to UNITA or the Soviet actions in Afghanistan are cases in point. However, economic aid to a government fighting a guerrilla war presents a more difficult coding problem. El Salvador is a useful example. Would the United States have given economic aid in the absence of a serious challenge to the government? Maybe, but possibly in different amounts or combinations. My coding procedure looked for (1) any explicit linkages between aid decisions and the progression of the conflict and (2) any convention-breaking support that coincided with the initiation of or changes in the conflict.

The second coding problem is less tractable than the first and stems from an inherent difficulty in linking any particular intervention to the outcome of the fighting. Identifying successful interventions requires the linking of the intervention to at least a six-month respite from the fighting. Sometimes, again, this is relatively easy. In cases of military interventions it was often possible to make the necessary connection between the intervention and the outcome without much difficulty. The Dominican revolt stands out. Other forms of intervention at other points in time tend to have a more obscure relationship between cause and effect. In the coding process I tried to err on the side of caution, making it particularly difficult to achieve a successful intervention. The U.S. support for the Nicaraguan contra is useful here. Although large amounts of military and economic support were poured into the contra effort, it was difficult to directly link this support to the end of hostilities. The fighting eventually did end, but only after a Sandinista defeat at the ballot box. The U.S. intervention may have contributed to the electoral defeat of the Sandinista party, but it is difficult to make that determination from the data at hand.

A quite compelling argument can be made that who intervenes matters in the likely outcome of the intervention attempt. As will be made more explicit in chapter 4, major powers have far greater latitude over the potential range of intervention mechanisms than do minor powers; therefore, interventions by major powers should have a greater impact on the course of the conflict. In the realm of economic interventions major powers would have both more to offer and more to withhold than a minor power trying to influence the course of a conflict. Likewise militarily major powers would tend to have a greater range of alternatives and weigh in disproportionately on one side of the conflict. Major power status was operationalized in terms of the Correlates of War classification, with the indicator coded dichotomously identifying whether an intervenor was a major or minor power.

In spite of any shortcomings, the data described in the following present a remarkably comprehensive overview of those civil conflicts in the post–World War II period. We know who was fighting, how many casualties, whether there was a large number of refugees as a result of the fighting, who intervened and how, and which interventions contributed to an end to the fighting. Collectively these factors help to account for when and under what conditions policies with regard to interventions will be carried out. We will start this process with simple, but important, bivariate statistics.

Descriptive Analysis

Based on the preceding criteria and sources, 140 intrastate conflicts were identified, of which 90 had at least one third-party intervention. Within these 90 conflicts there were a total of 197 individual interventions—with each intervention in a conflict coded separately on each dimension of the intervention itself. The individual coding of each intervention allows for the examination of the effect of multiple interventions into the same conflict, including those conflicts with interventions supporting competing groups in contention. Furthermore, I have data on 49 civil conflicts in which there were no outside intervenors. This control group allows me to examine the conditions under which interventions are more likely and then press the analysis further to explore the conditions for success once the decision to intervene has been taken, allowing me to explore the characteristics that led to the different policy choices.

Of the 140 intrastate conflicts identified in the postwar period, 38 of them were still ongoing as of 1994, 10 of which began as recently as 1992. When broken down into the year that the conflict started, it becomes clear that the 1960s ushered in an era more prone to the initiation of intrastate strife (see table 2.1); this is consistent

TABLE 2.1. Number of Conflict Initiations per Year

1944	1	1950	2	1960	4	1970	4	1980	4	1990	4
1946	2	1953	1	1961	1	1971	4	1981	2	1991	7
1947	2	1954	2	1962	3	1972	5	1982	4	1992	10
1948	5	1956	3	1963	5	1973	1	1983	4	1993	2
1949	1	1958	2	1964	1	1974	3	1984	3	1994	3
		1959	1	1965	4	1975	6	1985	3		
				1966	2	1977	2	1986	3		
				1967	3	1978	6	1987	2		
				1968	2	1979	4	1988	3		
				1969	1			1989	3		
Totals	11		11		26		35		31		26

Note: *Missing years are without conflict initiations.*

with Gurr's findings (1994) and largely reflects the instability that came with the withering of the colonial system. The artificial borders created by the colonial powers—particularly across the African continent—and the ensuing power vacuums created when the colonial governments pulled out sparked an upsurge in internal conflicts. Furthermore, the apparent increased frequency of intrastate conflict in the 1990s does not yet constitute a clear change in the trend—at least as determined by comparing the difference in means between the 1980s and 1990s.[2] For example, if there were just two conflicts initiated each year for the subsequent five-year period of the 1990s, the total for this decade would be 36 conflicts, only three more than the total for the decade of the 1970s. However, events in the early part of the 1990s suggest that the cold war may have acted as a constraint on ethnopolitical strife, though it remains to be seen whether the trend toward increased civil conflict will continue. Africa and Asia are clearly the most conflict prone, accounting for approximately 34 percent and 25 percent of the conflicts, respectively; Europe accounted for only 9 percent of the conflicts, while figures for the Middle East and the Americas, respectively, are 18 percent and 14 percent.

In terms of intervenors, nearly 40 percent (76 cases) of all interventions were carried out by major powers, and the remainder were attributed to minor powers. The United States, with 35 interventions, accounts for by far the most instances of interventions, while the Soviet Union, or Russia, intervened 16 times. France and Britain were involved in ten and nine interventions, respectively (see table 2.2). Of the 190 cases of intervention only about 30 percent were coded as contributing to the stopping of the fighting. There were eight cases in which the UN intervened in civil conflicts, at times actively supporting one of the combatants, though these cases are excluded from the analysis. Examples where the UN intervened on behalf of one side in a civil conflict include the Congo crisis in 1963 and South Africa throughout the 1980s. Bosnia and Cyprus represent two instances where the UN intervened with a neutral orientation. A discussion of interventions that are neu-

TABLE 2.2. Most Frequent Intervening States, by Number of Interventions

United States	35
USSR/Russia	16
France	10
Britain	9
China	6
Cuba	5

[2] The difference in means between the 1980s and 1990s is 2.1 ± 2.2 at a 95% confidence interval.

tral and under the auspices of a multilateral organization will be taken up systematically in chapter 5.

When breaking down the success or failure of different intervention policies by the type of conflict and the target of the intervention attempt, we begin to get a sense of how past policies were implemented and how well they fared. These data suggest that interventions are about equally likely to be on behalf of the government as they are on the side of opposition forces, with 91 supporting opposition, 94 supporting government, and 9 coded as neutral. The neutral interventions are accounted for mainly by two conflicts, Cyprus and the Chadian civil war of 1978 to 1982. The data also demonstrate that a purely economic intervention strategy is rarely undertaken, while a strictly military strategy is the most common form of intervention (military, 73%; economic, 5%; mixed, 21%). The success of each type of intervention, regardless of the target, reflects an overall success rate of about 30 percent, with each individual type of intervention mirroring the overall success rate (see tables 2.3 and 2.4). The most successful intervention strategies have been either to support the government through military interventions (a success rate of just under 50%) or to intervene economically on behalf of the opposition, though only

TABLE 2.3.   Success of Intervention Strategy by Conflict Type
When Supporting Government

	TYPE OF INTERVENTION				
	Military	**Economic**	**Mixed**		
Religious	6[a]	0	2	8	
	3[b]	0	0		
	50%[c]	0%	0%		
Ethnic	33	0	7	40	**Row Totals**
	16	0	2		
	48%	0%	28%		
Ideological	24	2	20	46	
	11	0	7		
	46%	0%	35%		
	63	2	29	**94**	**Total Cases**
		Column Totals			

Note: *Overall Success Rate, 41%;* [a]*,* [b]*, and* [c] *apply to each group of figures.*
[a]*Total cases.*
[b]*Number successful.*
[c]*% Successful.*

when the parties to the conflict are organized along ethnic lines (60% successful). However, the small number of cases of purely economic interventions should breed caution in our inference. Interventions supporting the government were more than twice as likely to succeed as those supporting the opposition (41% vs. 17%).

Although I have assumed that interventions are undertaken to bring an end to the hostilities, it is conceivable that the interventions themselves prolong the conflict. A close look at the data suggests that this can be one consequence of interventions—and one with numerous examples—though not a necessary consequence as many alternative examples would make clear. The U.S. intervention in Vietnam and the Soviet intervention in Afghanistan are two examples of intervention policies gone wrong. It is unlikely that either country intervened in order to create the quagmire that ensued, even though one consequence of the interventions appeared to be a prolonging of the conflict. The U.S. intervention in support of the Mujahideen in Afghanistan may, however, fit this mold of an intervention designed to prolong a conflict. Although there was a debate within decision-making circles as to the goal of U.S. policy—bleeding the Soviets or compelling their departure and thereby settling the conflict—there can be little doubt that the U.S. efforts made the Soviet's role more difficult, possibly prolonged the

TABLE 2.4. Success of Intervention Strategy by Conflict Type
When Supporting Opposition

	TYPE OF INTERVENTION				
	Military	Economic	Mixed		
Religious	7[a]	0	2		
	0[b]	0	2	9	
	0%[c]	0%	100%		
Ethnic	31	5	2		
	4	3	0	38	**Row Totals**
	13%	60%	0%		
Ideological	35	3	6		
	6	0	1	44	
	17%	0%	17%		
	73	8	10	**91**	**Total Cases**
		Column Totals			

Note: *Overall Success Rate, 17%;* [a], [b], *and* [c] *apply to each group of figures.*
[a]*Total cases.*
[b]*Number successful.*
[c]*% Successful.*

conflict, and surely contributed to the Soviet decision to withdrawal (Scott 1996). One empirical question worth exploring is whether the interventions in the 70 percent of the cases that were not successful contributed to the prolonging of the conflict rather than its amelioration. Pearson (1974) gives some reason to suspect that this might be one consequence of military interventions, though the evidence is far from conclusive. Although always subject to potential liabilities associated with counterfactual inferences, some exploratory analysis can shed light on the question of whether interventions necessarily prolong a conflict.

Empirically, the mean duration of all ongoing conflicts is just over 16 years, regardless of whether there have been outside interventions. At the same time, the mean duration of all conflicts that have been settled, and had outside interventions, is seven years. Thirty-eight of these conflicts (20%) lasted one year or less, 62 percent of which had at least one intervention, with the intervention succeeding just over 60 percent of the time. Excluding those conflicts that lasted less than a year brings the mean duration up to nine years. In conflicts in which there were no interventions, the mean duration was only 1.5 years, with the longest conflict lasting only a decade. In general this supports the notion that outside interventions contribute to the prolonging of the conflict. However, two questions would need to be addressed before one can infer anything approaching a casual relationship: (1) do multiple interventions make resolution more intractable? and (2) do third parties generally intervene in conflicts of long duration rather than contributing to the length of the conflict? An affirmative answer to the first question suggests a causal process between interventions and the extension of the conflict; an affirmative answer to the second question points to a spurious inference from the data.

Addressing the first question is fairly straightforward, and although somewhat tempered by the response to the second question, it also helps to answer it. For all resolved conflicts that had outside interventions, if there were multiple intervenors, the mean duration was just under nine years. For those conflicts with only one intervention, the mean duration was just over three years. Not only are interventions associated with longer running conflicts, but also it seems that the more intervenors involved, the more likely that the conflict will be a long one. In fact, almost all the conflicts with one or two interventions were less than the nine-year mean duration (92%), and better than four out of five of those conflicts with three interventions lasted less than nine years (83%). However, when there are four intervenors, only two out of five (38%) conflicts end before the mean duration of nine years, whereas with five or six intervenors, only about 50 percent of the conflicts are shorter than nine years in length (see table 2.5).

The question of whether states tend to intervene in conflicts of long duration, rather than the interventions themselves prolonging the hostilities, cannot be answered definitively with the data at hand. The preceding data on single and multiple interventions suggests that some interventions may extend the length of the conflict by making resolution efforts more difficult, particularly when there are multiple intervenors. There also appears to be no systematic relationship between the number of intervenors and the number of casualties (table 2.6), contributing to the inference that, in general, interventions take place across a broad spectrum of intrastate conflicts, and that more outside actors do not necessarily result in a more violent conflict—at least in terms of overall casualties.

Those conflicts without interventions have their own distinctive patterns. Of the 49 conflicts, 31 (63%) have been resolved, while 18 remained ongoing as of 1994. The mean duration of those conflicts in which the fighting had ended was just short of 1.5 years; the mean duration of those ongoing conflicts without third parties intervening is nearly 18 years. Seventy-two percent of those that have been resolved lasted one year or less, while 44 percent (8 of 18) of the ongoing conflicts have been under way for at least 15 years. Those conflicts without interventions are distributed in much the same geographic patterns as those with interventions, with Asia and Africa accounting for 33 percent each, the Americas and the Middle

TABLE 2.5. Number of Intervenors and the Duration of the Conflict

Number of Intervenors	Longer Than Mean Duration (%)	Less Than Mean Duration (%)
1	24	76
2	27	73
3	28	72
4	63	37
5	52	48
6	50	50

Note: *Mean duration = 9 years.*

TABLE 2.6. Number of Intervenors and Number of Casualties

Number of Intervenors	NUMBER OF CASUALTIES		
	<4,000	4K through 27K	>27,000
1	19	11	8
2	10	8	19
3	6	17	20
4	11	11	8
5	5	5	19
6	6	0	6

East 13 percent and 15 percent, respectively, and Europe only 6 percent. The majority of the conflicts without outside intervenors took place along ethnic divisions (54%); ideological conflicts accounted for 31 percent of these cases, and religious conflicts, 15 percent. Furthermore, comparing the extent of the casualties across conflicts with and without interventions contributes to the inference that these are important differences that in part determine the outcome of an intervention. For example, the number of casualties falling into each of the quartiles reveals that conflicts with interventions tend to be bloodier than those without third-party interventions. Whether this is one piece of the selection criteria used by potential intervenors or is the result of the interventions themselves will be taken up in the next chapter (see table 2.7).

A clear understanding of whether or not an intervention prolongs a conflict requires certain a priori knowledge of how long the conflict would have lasted without the interventions—or with fewer intervenors. If one is to conclude that a conflict was prolonged because of an intervention, then it is necessary to demonstrate how long the conflict would have lasted without the intervention. The preceding descriptive evidence gives some basis for drawing such inferences, but the counterfactual argumentation poses a formidable challenge to overcome. Unfortunately this counterfactual argument is one that constrains much of social science research (Tetlock and Belkin 1996), and one for which conclusive systematic evidence will not be forthcoming in the short term. The alternative argument—that interventions take place in long-running conflicts and those with greater numbers of casualties—has some basis in the decision-making logic, as we will explore in the next chapter.

Conclusion

The preceding discussion of coding rules, sources, and the description of the data was intended simply to lay the groundwork for the chapters that follow. As a result

TABLE 2.7.   Distribution of Mean Number of Casualties by Quartile
and Intervention Status

	QUARTILE		
	25%	**50%**	**75%**
Intervention	3,000	20,000	122,000
Nonintervention	1,000	5,000	20,000

of the descriptive statistics, we know how the conflicts are distributed across geographic, ethnic, religious, and ideological dimensions; we know who is intervening and with what instruments; and we know the extent to which interventions are effective at contributing to a halt in the fighting. Although meaningful inferences are difficult to draw at this juncture, these descriptions are useful for setting the stage for the chapters that follow.

The following three chapters address questions of (1) when do states intervene? (2) what conditions contribute to successful interventions? and (3) how do multilateral interventions differ from unilateral ones? Each chapter starts by presenting the theoretical framework that can guide our understanding. I then articulate hypotheses from those arguments and subsequently test those hypotheses against the data discussed in this chapter. The next chapter focuses on tackling the selection bias problem that is inherent in attempts to evaluate the outcome of policy. We can only evaluate those instances in which the policy of interest (in this case interventions) was chosen, yet to do this effectively we need to know when or under what conditions the decision will be made not to intervene. I will begin to address this issue by developing a decision-theoretic model that we can use to think about the conditions under which the intervention option will be chosen or rejected. This essentially posits that decision makers go through a cost-benefit maximizing procedure; we can then consider the various factors that influence the expected net benefits from policy choices. I will not go through an extensive formalization of this decision logic but simply use it to make more explicit the criteria by which alternatives are judged. This chapter is necessary less for its intrinsic policy relevance than for its usefulness in setting up the discussion in the chapter that follows it. It is difficult to judge the results of the fourth chapter—the main focus of this study—without first having some sense of the criteria and outcomes spelled out in the third chapter.

I argue in chapter 3 that costs are a function of both the international and domestic environments, as are potential benefits. The decision-theoretic framework also makes clear that subjective estimates—by the potential intervenor—of the probability of achieving a successful outcome are critical to understanding when an intervention will be undertaken. Tests that capture some of the main components of the model give us insights into the selection criteria and allow us to more systematically evaluate the conditions associated with successful interventions, the topic taken up chapter 4.

If one of the critical factors in deciding to intervene is an a priori estimation of when an intervention policy is likely to be successful, then decision makers currently seem to rely more on ad hoc criteria than a systematic evaluation. In the fourth chapter I propose a model that suggests that intervenors are trying to manipulate both the net costs from continued fighting, and the expectations that each side holds regarding the effect of the intervention on their adversary. In essence, an intervention is trying to make it too costly to one side and convince everybody that this is so. The results of the multivariate analysis will then point to more effective strategies for intervening under given sets of conditions. Combining the results of chapters 3 and 4 should point to a set of conditions that increase the probability of effective interventions.

THREE

The Decision to Intervene

The decision to intervene—whether unilaterally or as part of a multilateral effort—is usually fraught with difficult questions about the political viability of any such policy and the likely outcome of each proposed strategy. Addressing the issues of what works and when will be the subject of the following chapter, but I first need to confront the issue of when interventions are likely. This chapter proposes a framework that will guide our understanding of the decision to intervene, derives hypotheses about when we would expect interventions, and then tests them against data on internal conflicts with and without third-party interventions.

Intervening in civil conflicts is always a risky business, even though the frequency with which outside actors do so may mask the extent of the risk. Understanding the conditions under which outside actors will intervene in intrastate conflicts not only is central to our ability to evaluate the effectiveness of past interventions but also contributes to our understanding of the diffusion of war or lesser forms of international conflict. Furthermore, the relatively recent cascade of prescriptive advice suggests that a pressing need exists for a systematic analysis of the conditions that lead to interventions and the subsequent effectiveness of any intervention policy (e.g., Dorman and Otte 1995; Kanter and Brooks 1994; Smith 1994; Solarz 1986). The puzzle that we face is one with numerous examples and analogies.

France's decision to intervene in Rwanda at the later stages of the genocidal slaughter of the Tutsi in 1994 epitomizes the difficult and risky nature of unilat-

Chapter 3 is a revised version of my article "Choosing to Intervene: Outside Interventions in Internal Conflicts as a Policy Choice," *Journal of Politics* 60, no. 3 (1998): 754–79. I thank the University of Texas Press for permission to reprint it here.

eral intervention decisions. The extent of the carnage was quite dramatic and by far dwarfed the capabilities of the small UN force sent there as observers a couple of years earlier. France, furthermore, had been caught supplying arms to the Hutu in the lead-up to the cataclysmic events of April, though they vehemently denied any official involvement in the arms transfers. There was considerable pressure at the global level to intervene, but in the aftermath of the perceived debacle in Somalia no country was willing to take the gamble. To some degree the short straw fell to France, which felt a need to recoup international credibility (Adelman and Suhrke 1996). The U.S. intervention against the Sandinista government of Nicaragua was also a risky undertaking. At the international level the United States had to endure condemnation and a legal defeat at the World Court, while domestic opposition led to congressional curtailment of funding and ultimately the basement operations of Oliver North at the National Security Council. By the time the Reagan policies came fully to light they involved the selling of arms to Iran in order to fund the contras in Nicaragua, and a special prosecutor appointed to investigate breaches of the law.

Probably the most vexing example is that of the former Yugoslavia. As the country of Yugoslavia began to disintegrate, the level of internal violence escalated proportionately. One view of this disintegration has the republic of Serbia—which dominated both the political and military machinery of the state—attempting to maintain some semblance of unity by brute force. Without exception, no other states unilaterally intervened militarily or economically to stop the carnage. Most efforts by outside parties involved diplomatic initiatives, and those for the most part took the form of diplomatic recognition of the breakaway republics. On the other hand, when the newly independent state of Bosnia-Herzegovina erupted in civil war, a number of interventions attempted to bring a halt to the fighting. These efforts culminated in NATO intervening with 60,000 troops and commitments for hundreds of millions of dollars in reconstruction assistance.

Why did one phase of the conflict result in a number of interventions by outside actors while the other did not? Both conflicts involved members of the same communities (the Bosnian conflict represents a subset of the larger Yugoslavian unrest), with Muslims, Serbs, and Croats on various sides of each divide; both took place in the same geographical location; and both appeared to pose a similar threat to the stability of the central European region. But interventions only took place in the latter conflict. To evaluate the effectiveness of interventions in civil conflicts—for example, how likely it is that the NATO intervention in Bosnia resulting from the Dayton Peace Accords will contain the violence long enough for civil relations to take root—we first must understand the conditions under which interventions are likely to take place. This need for an understanding of the decision to intervene is driven by two factors: (1) knowing the conditions under which states will intervene will inform us about certain aspects of the conflict and conflict resolution process and (2) evaluating policy without first addressing the issue of when we should expect to see an observable behavior can lead to a selection bias in the evidence used to make judgments about the policy.

The list of intrastate conflicts with and without interventions is relatively long, and there does not appear to be any intuitive criteria by which one can determine when an intervention is most likely to take place. The United States intervened in Colombia in the 1950s but not in the failed revolution of 1948; neither did it intervene in Paraguay in 1947 but did in Guatemala seven years later. Rwanda has experienced a number of internal conflicts since the 1960s, but only the most recent one led to a unilateral intervention. The United States essentially intervened twice in the Somalian conflict prior to 1991, once in support of the opposition forces, and then switching sides to support the government. Chad seemed to attract outside interventions to its civil wars, yet nobody intervened in the Nigerian conflicts throughout the 60s, 70s, and 80s. More recently, a U.S.-led NATO force intervened in Kosovo after much debate in the various capitals of Europe and North America.

The concern at this juncture is with unilateral decisions to intervene; I will address multilateral interventions in chapter 5. The unilateral decision is a special case, and it is much more common than collective efforts. Until the end of the cold war it was difficult to get the world body to agree on a specific policy with regard to internal conflicts. Even if a conflict was not being waged over ideological issues, ideologically opposed foes at the UN would view an intervention in zero-sum terms. A few collective interventions in internal conflicts occurred during this period, but they were more the exception than the rule. States may self-select out of potential interventions for numerous reasons related to both domestic and international considerations. For instance, we would not expect a political leader to intervene in a conflict in which she or he expected the policy to fail, but rather in such cases we would anticipate that the decision maker would adopt some alternative policy. To fully understand this decision process I need to articulate a conceptual framework that will point to testable predictions.

When and Why States Choose to Intervene

The key to making sense of rigorous empirical analysis is the articulation of a sound theoretical argument. In developing the logic behind the decision to intervene I will assume the following: (1) interventions result from conscious state policy and (2) the choice of policy is the result of a rational, utility-maximizing decision-making process. At its simplest form this means that decision makers weigh the cost and benefits of alternative actions along with their estimation of the probability that any action will achieve the desired outcome. These assumptions do not deny that the decision process is complex (Scott 1996) or that it is oftentimes shrouded in moral dilemmas (Blechman 1995). Rather, the assumptions are meant to define the decision rules by which we can begin to understand the choice of policy. Solarz (1986), for instance, tells us when an intervention policy should be chosen, but he does not articulate the criteria by which such decisions are made; Scott (1996) informs us that the process of deciding involves many factors but not how the specific outcome of the debate is derived.

I assume that three conditions must be met before the political leadership would undertake an intervention policy: (1) there is a reasonable expectation for success, (2) the projected time horizon for achieving the outcome is short, and (3) domestic opposition is minimal (see Daalder 1996; Kanter and Brooks 1994). These conditions essentially describe some of the most salient aspects of the cost and benefits decision makers face as they consider specific policies. The practical implications of these assumptions can be seen in the public discourse during the U.S. deliberations over intervening in Haiti, Zaire, Rwanda, and Bosnia, to name a few cases. In each instance the effect of the policy in Somalia (1991–1993) can be readily felt. In Haiti and Bosnia clear deadlines for exiting were established before the intervention went forward, and in each case the deadline was short relative to the magnitude of the problems the interventions sought to resolve. In the debates over whether to participate in a Canadian-led effort to assist refugees in the Zairean conflict in late 1996, one of the key criterion guiding U.S. decision makers was a short-term duration of the planned intervention. Even though the intervention policy was never fully implemented, the United States did agree to contribute troops. The role played by subjective estimates of success is also evident in these cases. Rwanda appeared to pose insurmountable problems and in spite of the magnitude of the slaughter, the U.S. leadership overcame its humanitarian impulse and decided against intervention. The recent tragedy in Somalia loomed large. In Haiti and Bosnia the need to have a high probability of success translated into the design of intervention policies that employed massive uses of force. The role of time, the likelihood of success, and public support are not confined to military interventions, though they do weigh more heavily when troops are involved. The increased vulnerability to human losses drives this process. However, economically supporting one side in the conflict has to be seen as a viable strategy by the policy community, and one used with some regularity. Either economic sanctions or economic inducements can be a form of intervention that can sway the fortunes of war.

Successful interventions will generally maximize political benefits while minimizing political costs; failure would tend to do the opposite. Benefits that result from an intervention can be found in numerous quarters, including both domestic and international factors. The political and the material and human costs and benefits of an intervention are intertwined, with the link tied to the political arena in which the decisions are made. The broad parameters of these factors, further-more, are such that decision makers must be cognizant of them while grappling with the conflicting advice, divided allegiances, and bureaucratic inertia charac-teristic of any complex decision. Equally important is that the extent of costs and benefits associated with any particular policy regarding intervention would be inti-mately linked to the success or failure of that intervention policy. For example, if there were two identical interventions—in terms of human and material costs—and one succeeded and the other failed, we would expect the political costs of the failed intervention to surpass those associated with the successful policy. The dif-ficulty of determining the likelihood of success, *ex ante,* of any given intervention strategy is the crux of the problem faced by decision makers. If they knew at the time of the decision the likelihood that their policy would succeed or fail, their ability to make coherent policy would be increased. I take up this question in the following chapter, but it is magnified by our lack of understanding of the condi-tions under which we would expect interventions to take place.

With this background of how the political environment surrounding an inter-vention structures the costs and benefits of an intervention policy, we can move on to develop a model of the conditions under which a political leader will choose to intervene. It is unlikely—both practically and conceptually—that a decision maker confronted with a choice over whether or how to intervene in the internal conflict in another country will choose to intervene when (1) they have no rea-sonable expectation of a successful outcome or (2) the costs of intervening far out-weigh any potential benefits from doing so. In the following section I articulate a model of the conditions that have to be met before an intervention option will be chosen.

As I develop my decision-theoretic model a conceptual issue about the appli-cation and the effectiveness of my approach should be kept in mind. I am going to articulate an expected utility framework from which we can think about the decision process. This framework essentially offers a heuristic device that allows us to focus on the tradeoffs, the estimations, and the expectations that a decision maker contemplating an intervention must face. By emphasizing the costs and rewards associated with the various potential tradeoffs we can then look to our understanding of politics in the international and domestic environments to develop ideas about those factors that are most salient in determining the costs, benefits, and estimations of the likely outcomes. Although hypotheses will not be formally deduced from the decision-theoretic model, the model will be useful in helping us think about the causal impact of various arguments extant in the liter-ature. I believe that the hypotheses articulated probably could be derived from a more formal treatment of the proposed model, but that it is neither necessary nor particularly useful at this juncture.

Satisfying the Conditions for Intervention

For analytical purposes I will make the assumption that the decision to intervene is not strategic, by which I mean that the decision is not a function of the moves or countermoves of the target country but rather a result of internal processes in the intervening country. Events in the target country affect an intervention decision through the impact on expected outcomes, and the costs and benefits, but the decision over whether or not to intervene results from the internal dynamics in the potential intervenor.[1] From a formal perspective I am assuming that the subjective estimate of the likelihood of a given outcome is exogenous to the relationship between intervenor and target (Tsebelis 1990). If this assumption is incorrect, then the inferences from the model may also be incorrect. The assumption, I think, is reasonable. When France intervened in Rwanda in 1994, it is unlikely that the potential response of the Hutu or Tutsi leadership greatly influenced their decision. More likely, they considered the situation on the ground and their capabilities before deciding to intervene. France's estimate of the probability of success would not have been determined by the moves and countermoves of the Hutu or Tutsi to France's intervention.[2]

In determining the strategy to be taken, the potential intervening country estimates the probability of success and weighs the costs in terms of international reputation, national interests, and domestic constraints against potential benefits that accrue in these realms. As discussed in the opening chapter, I assume that a successful outcome is one in which the intervention contributes to the cessation of hostilities. Clearly not all interventions have the explicit goal of stopping the hostilities, but other conceptions of success considered by potential intervenors can often be achieved by stopping the fighting, or at some level require this as a necessary first step. It is equally clear that military or economic interventions in civil conflicts cannot be effective at conflict resolution. Decision makers seeking regional or global security would generally prefer that an internal conflict end without them having to expend resources to achieve that outcome. But they would

---

[1] Smith (1996) explicitly models the decision to intervene on behalf of an ally as a strategic interaction. His recursive model suggests that perceptions regarding the likelihood of an outside intervention affects the dynamics of the conflict between the challenger and defender. The thrust of his model works from the premise that a challenge has not yet been made, and that the beliefs about the behavior of the third party will influence the course of the conflict. This chapter differs in the sense that I work from the premise that a conflict is under way and a third party—for a host of reasons—is deciding whether or not to intervene in this ongoing conflict. My focus is on the decision of the intervenor; Smith's is on how that decision affects the conflict.

[2] On the other hand the *effect* of an intervention on the course of the conflict would be a result of strategic calculations on the part of the belligerents. From that perspective, perceptions about the outcome of an intervention are endogenous to the relationship between the belligerents (see Smith 1996). This, however, is a different question than the one posed here but will be taken up in the following chapter.

also prefer to expend some resources if they thought that their efforts could ensure stability. If we assume that they get no utility from the act of intervening, then they would not intervene if they had a low expectation about the role of an intervention in ensuring stability.

By intervening to stop the fighting a state incurs costs, and any state would have a greater utility for a halt to the fighting if they did not have to incur those costs. Issues of national interest revolve around security and stability, and an internal conflict that threatens these interests poses a problem for national decision makers. If the expectation is that an intervention will succeed, then, ceteris paribus, a decision maker would have greater utility for intervening than not intervening and having the conflict continue without a short-term end point. If successful, a state can gain more from a halt to the fighting than they expend in the intervention. If there is little hope of successfully bringing the conflict to a halt, then a potential intervenor would generally prefer not to intervene. In other words, continued fighting is preferred to continued fighting after the costs of a failed intervention.

The cost of an intervention policy is comprised of material and human resources and audience costs. Human and material costs are in part a function of the strategy of the intervention. For instance, economic sanctions forego access to the markets in the sanctioned country, imposing substantial burdens on some sectors of society. The cost of a resource may rise—such as oil—or the price of a commodity that cannot be sold may decline because of a glut in the market. Similarly a military intervention involving troops and/or equipment incurs, at minimum, the cost of the supply and transport of the hardware, while at the extreme a military intervention can result in the loss of life. These human and material components get translated into political costs, and these costs are to some degree a function of the success of the intervention. A successful intervention that results in a number of deaths is less costly than a similar intervention that fails; although material costs are the same, the political costs are higher in the failed intervention. This "cost of failure" is exacerbated by the relative lack of gains associated with the failed policy.

The political nature of intervention decisions also implies audience costs for a decision maker that come from interested constituency groups—either domestic or international. When contemplating interventions, decision makers have to weigh the competing demands of these various groups, who will often be at odds over the preferred policy. The U.S. policy toward the conflict in Bosnia is a case in point. On the one hand, vocal and powerful groups were arguing for a minimal involvement, while at the same time groups were protesting in front of the White House about the lack of a forceful U.S. response to the carnage in Bosnia and calling on the president to send in troops. In this type of environment the decision maker incurs audience costs, costs for being too timid, too indecisive, or too aggressive. Some of these costs are incurred even when the decision is made not to intervene, though they could generally be considered to be minimal relative to the cost of intervention. As with human and material costs, audience costs can also be a function of the success of the outcome. The cost function associated with intervention decisions can therefore be expressed as: $C_i = \Sigma material + \Sigma audience$, where C_i reflects the costs of intervening.

The decision to intervene is also a function of the decision makers' subjective estimate of the likely outcome of the conflict and the effect of the intervention on that outcome. Because costs and benefits attributable to the intervention are related, in part, to the success or failure of the intervention policy, the greater the subjective probability of success, the greater the expected utility for intervention. The type of intervention strategy affects the costs of intervention, but also the likelihood that a specific policy will be successful. For example, a full-scale military intervention might have a greater chance of success than simply the supply of military hardware or information, or to take it further, economic aid, even though such an intervention is not politically expedient. I assume that beliefs about the effect of specific strategies for intervention on the likely outcome of the effort are incorporated into the subjective estimates of the potential success of the intervention, such that the evaluation of the likely outcome of an intervention takes into account the decision makers' beliefs about what works and when. In general, then, the greater the subjective probability that an intervention will lead to a successful outcome, the greater the expected utility to be derived from that intervention.

Conceptually we can think of an intervention decision comprising two separate utility functions, such that the process of determining a policy requires two distinct evaluations. First, the question is posed as to the likely outcome of the conflict without an outside intervention. If the subjective estimate of the probability of a successful settlement is high without an intervention, then the expected utility for not intervening is high and the decision process stops there, without setting in motion the discussion of an intervention policy. The second stage poses the question of the likely outcome of the conflict after an intervention, but decision makers only address this issue if the expected utility of not intervening is sufficiently low. If the estimated probability of a successful outcome with an intervention is low—when p is small—then the state is unlikely to intervene; when p is high we are more likely to observe interventions, ceteris paribus. These two conditions can be expressed as:

$$EU_{ni} = q(U_s) + (1-q)(U_c) - \Sigma C_{ni}$$
$$\text{and}$$
$$EU_i = p(U_{sw}) + (1-p)(U_f) - \Sigma C_i$$

where EU_{ni} is the expected utility of not intervening, q is the probability that the conflict will be settled without outside influence, and ΣC_{ni} are the costs associated with not intervening. The costs, of course, do not reflect material costs, but rather any audience costs associated with not intervening in a conflict for which there is a constituency advocating intervention. EU_i reflects the expected utility from an intervention, with p representing the decision maker's estimate of the probability that the intervention will result in a successful outcome; ΣC_i are the costs associated with the intervention, reflecting human, material, and audience costs. U_s reflects the utility to the potential intervenor from a successful settlement without an intervention, U_{sw} is the utility of success with an intervention, U_c is the utility of continued fighting without an intervention, and U_{fi} is the utility of a continuation of the fighting after an unsuccessful intervention.[3]

One way to think about the preferences over the range of outcomes is that $U_s > U_{sw} > U_c > U_{fi}$. Any potential intervenor would generally prefer the conflict to be settled without incurring the costs of an intervention. Similarly, they would prefer to bear the costs of an intervention, if it were to be successful, over having the conflict continue because of the lack of an intervention effort. Any outcome, however, is preferable to intervening in a conflict and having the conflict continue. In this case a state would incur the costs of the intervention without the benefit of the end of hostilities.

Given this approach to thinking about the decision, three factors can influence the expected utility of intervening: costs, utilities over outcomes, and estimates of the likelihood of achieving a successful outcome; all are intertwined. As the costs increase—either human, material, or audience—the expected utility for intervention decreases. For example, the greater the domestic opposition to an intervention policy, the lower the expected payoffs from that policy; the lower the payoff, the less likely would be an intervention. In a similar vein, the larger the scale of the operation, the greater the costs and subsequently the lower the net payoff, all else being equal. When the utility for a successful settlement of a civil conflict increases, the higher will be the net payoff from intervening, and the more likely the intervention. The utility for success would generally be a function of national interest and domestic concerns tied to ethnic affinities and humanitarian issues (Blechman 1995; Carment and James 1995b; Feste 1992; Morganthau 1967). So, for instance, if the civil conflict was being fought in a border country with strong ethnic ties across that border, then presumably the potential for contagion

---

[3] Empirically these two steps in the decision process may be evaluated simultaneously, though this does not change the usefulness of the conceptual framework developed here. If in actual fact this is a simultaneous process, the effect on the preference ordering over the outcomes or the relationship between the subjective estimates of p and q would be nil. Expressing the decision as a simultaneous process would yield:

$$EU_{ni} - EU_i = [q(U_s) + (1 - q)(U_c) - \Sigma C_{ni}] - [p(U_{sw}) + (1 - p)(U_f) - \Sigma C_i]$$

when $EU_{ni} - EU_i > 0$, then there would be no intervention. In terms of conceptual clarity, however, it seems that the two-step process gives greater purchase.

would be high and the utility for a successful settlement large. The high utility would be a function of the demands for action on the part of the public with ethnic ties in the disputing country, and the benefits derived from increased security. This, again, appears to closely reflect the situation faced by the Soviet Union before they intervened in Afghanistan and is consistent with interventions by neighboring countries throughout Africa, such as South Africa's interventions in Angola, Zimbabwe, and Mozambique.

Subjective estimates of the likely outcome of the conflict with and without an intervention would also be a critical variable in the intervention calculus. In the preceding inequalities, if q is high and p is low, then it would be unlikely that we would observe an intervention because a potential intervenor would expect a settlement without an intervention; conversely, if q is low and p is high, then intervening is more likely the policy of choice. There are some aspects of the relationship between p and q that need to be relegated to a gray area of understanding. First, when q is high, it is not clear that p would also be high; that is, when a conflict is expected to settle by itself, an intervention would not necessarily have a high probability of being successful. If nationalistic sentiments play a key role in the conflict, then an outside intervention may exacerbate the tensions, turning a resolvable conflict into one that becomes increasingly drawn out. But to conceive of an intervention under those conditions—when q is high—one would have to consider that an actor derives utility from the intervention itself, something that I assume does not happen. A violation of this condition might have a consequence in which a failed interventions leads to a deepening conflict. Empirically there are many such examples. The second gray area is when either p or q are in the middle range, where the policy outcome is uncertain. Here we might expect a potential intervenor to attempt to test the waters by threatening intervention. The threat will reveal additional information with which to judge p and q. A potential intervenor would threaten the challenger[4] with intervention if they do not take steps toward the settlement of the dispute. Specifying the theoretical conditions for threats as an intermediary policy of choice should be a topic for further research. But we might expect, for instance, to observe verbal threats to intervene when the likely outcome from an intervention is difficult to determine. Threats would allow the decision maker to judge both the effect of a potential intervention in the target country, and the shakeout of the constellation of domestic forces for and against such a policy.[5] The key to understanding when or under what conditions an intervention will be undertaken lies in articulating the circumstances in which (a) the potential benefits from intervening outweigh costs and (b) the probability of a settlement with and without an inter-

---

[4] The notation of a challenger in this instance refers to the parties being opposed by a potential intervenor. This of course could be either the government or the opposition.

[5] The implications of prior threats for the outcome of a study such as this are quite profound, even though the practical difficulties seem insurmountable. For instance, if there were a population of cases that

vention (p and q) are low and high, respectively. From this we can proceed to ask questions about the types of factors that would influence a decision maker trying to maximize expected utility over a decision about intervening.

Two competing paradigms suggest different costs and benefits associated with various characteristics of the conflict and/or the intervention. A realist understanding of world politics, for instance, would point to global and regional geopolitics as the explanation for interventions. When security is threatened, or when geostrategic interests are at stake, interventions would be increasingly likely. The benefits that accrue from ensuring national security outweigh any costs that would be incurred. By the same token, domestic political considerations—driven largely by humanitarian concerns or ethnic affinities—would have little influence over the decision of whether and when to intervene. The costs of an intervention, therefore, would largely reflect the material and human costs of the policy, with few costs imposed for not intervening. National security drives the decision (e.g., Feste 1992).

From a nonrealist perspective, factors other than geopolitics will contribute to the expected payoff from an intervention policy. Responding to a humanitarian crisis may bring international and domestic praise, as could stopping the carnage inflicted on a particular group of people. Domestic opposition to a proposed intervention may also sufficiently affect the expectations about prospective payoffs. These domestic and ethical motivations behind foreign policy are not of immediate concern to those who adopt a realpolitik view of the world, but they can offer considerable explanatory power when considering the decision to intervene in civil conflicts (Vertzberger 1993).

The world, however, is not so black and white. Both domestic and international factors contribute to foreign policy decisions. In the modern world, humanitarian crises affect the entire global community to some extent, and at times states act in pursuit of alleviating the humanitarian consequences of civil conflicts. Domestic constituencies may press strongly for such active policies, particularly when the conflicts and the resulting carnage may play out through local news media. At the same time geostrategic interests have considerable influence over the formation and implementation of foreign policy. Any policy to undertake an intervention probably reflects both domestic and international pressures. Others, such as Stam (1996), have also demonstrated the critical role played by domestic and international politics in the formation of national security policy.

If we think about evaluating empirically the conditions under which we would expect outside interventions, at least four specific hypotheses can be derived. Two would reflect expectations consistent with a realpolitik understanding of world

included an expressed threat to intervene—some of which were carried out and some not—then the counterfactual argument about who might have considered but rejected an intervention policy would be severely weakened. Unfortunately, finding a population of threats is a monumental task far beyond the immediate scope of this project.

politics, one consistent with a liberal view of the world, and the fourth consistent with conditions that influence the subjective estimates of the likely outcome of an intervention. There is a close interplay here between the expected utility model, which is used to illuminate the tradeoffs of the decision process, and our prior theoretical understanding of the forces that influence the making of foreign policy. My description of those factors that influence the cost and benefit calculations will be drawn from prior empirical regularities, intuitive hunches, and logical deductions. Generally speaking, from a realpolitik perspective, specific characteristics of the international system structure will determine the outcome of foreign policy debates. Shared borders and the climate of the cold war would be two structural conditions that could impinge on state security. From a liberal perspective, however, we would expect domestic politics to play a more central role in the making of foreign policy. For example, humanitarian crises associated with civil conflicts could lead to a sense of moral outrage on the part of a domestic audience, which would then exert pressure on their government to take action (Blechman 1995; Kohut and Toth 1994). When conflicts result in large numbers of casualties or lead to large social dislocations, we would expect third parties to face increased pressure from domestic constituencies to take some form of remedial action, even if there is no apparent geopolitical interest. The intensity of a conflict straddles the fence between the two forces acting on the decision process. On the one hand, highly intense conflicts tend to be associated with the humanitarian concerns of a liberal perspective; on the other, highly intense conflicts may pose severe threats to regional stability, of paramount importance to the realist. But regardless of the usefulness of either of the two paradigms as a mechanism for understanding the decision process, the role of the intensity of the conflict reflects to a large degree the effect of certainty or uncertainty on the decision to intervene. It is quite likely that in intense conflicts both q and p will be low (low expectation that the conflict will be resolved without outside interventions, and low expectation about the efficacy of an intervention). One result of this should be a decreased likelihood of observing outside interventions, even though political leaders may see an intervention as necessary to stop the fighting.

Specific Hypotheses

From the preceding discussion four specific hypotheses will be explored, which will give us some indication about the conditions under which we are likely to see outside interventions in intrastate conflicts.[6] In my empirical testing I do not

---

[6] This is obviously not an exhaustive list of hypotheses; others could certainly be articulated. The thrust of the theoretical argument can, however, be adequately evaluated on the basis of these four hypothe-

attempt to estimate the utility, the costs, or the subjective estimates of the probability of different outcomes for specific intervenors. Rather than develop indicators of these components of the model I take them as latent—or unobserved—variables and instead develop indicators of those factors that should influence each component of the model. The variables in the empirical model generally reflect contextual conditions and characteristics of the conflict, as will be discussed in the following. I use these factors to identify the types of conflicts that are most likely to attract outside intervenors. From this we can intuit the role of those conditions in leading to the decision to intervene or not.

HYPOTHESIS 1

The greater the number of countries bordering an internal conflict, the more likely will be outside interventions into the conflict.

Close proximity to a country in conflict increases the expected utility from a successful settlement of the dispute from a number of perspectives. First, when a country shares a border with a country in conflict, the potential for contagion is high. National security is threatened to the extent that instability on a border decreases political control in that region, increasing the benefits from settling the conflict. Additionally, ethnic affinities in cross-border communities will generally be higher than in those environments where large distances separate ethnic groups, generating domestic constituencies that influence the decision process, and therefore imposing high audience costs for not intervening. The opportunity and willingness to intervene increases with proximity and has been shown to be related to the increased propensity for wars to expand across territorial boundaries (Siverson and Starr 1991). Finally, proximity affects both the cost of intervening and the ability to correctly estimate the probability of being successful (e.g., Boulding 1962). The more countries that are in the direct vicinity of the conflict, the more likely it is that one or more of them will choose to intervene.

HYPOTHESIS 2

Given an ongoing conflict, the greater its intensity, the less likely will be outside interventions.

The ferocity with which the conflict is waged contributes to the calculations of expected utility. A very intense conflict will generally take a substantial interven-

---

ses. The availability of data make other potential hypotheses difficult to test at this juncture. For instance, the timing and role of verbal threats to intervene are clear examples.

tion to bring a halt to the fighting; the larger the intervention, the greater the costs of adopting such a policy. But also the more intense the conflict, the less likely it is that an intervention will be successful, in effect p will be small, making the expected utility from intervening low. As mentioned earlier, the "sunk costs" of the combatants is already very high and the emotional climate likely to be feverish. Under these types of conditions anything but a large military force will appear to have a dim chance of success. A reasonable chance of success is critical to a decision to initiate an intervention, both in terms of its intuitive necessity and the logic of the decision-theoretic model. For example, if p is sufficiently low, any net benefit from an intervention will be weighted down by the low expectation of achieving the desired outcome. It would take an intervention with a very high payoff relative to the costs to overcome the dampening effect of a low estimate of the likelihood of success. Very intense conflicts are more likely to be those where the subjective estimate of the prospects for success are low. In Rwanda, April 1994, where tens of thousands of people were being killed per week, the response to the emerging crisis by the small Belgian and UN missions was to pull out rather than be reinforced. It was not until the killing had gone on for three months that the French sent in a military force, by which time the bulk of the slaughter was over, reducing the necessary magnitude of an intervention and increasing the probability that it would be successful.

There are, of course, benefits to intervening in intense conflicts that result from humanitarian aspects of the mission (Dowty and Loescher 1996), but with a low probability of success the intervenor is too likely to end up with the least preferred outcome—a failed intervention. Large countries with global interests might generally have the capability to intervene with the necessary force, but they often lack sufficient national interest in doing so. The smaller countries that stand to gain most from local stability generally lack the capability to intervene in a manner that has a high probability of success.

HYPOTHESIS 3

When there are large social dislocations or concerns about an impending humanitarian crisis, the probability of an outside intervention increases.

Massive social dislocations pose moral, logistical, and resource dilemmas for the global community, such that containing the violence that leads to humanitarian crises becomes a prime concern to policymakers. Although potential intervenors might have less to gain from a national interest perspective, the domestic costs of not intervening come to the fore when humanitarian issues are at stake. Kohut and Toth (1994) show that one of the few conditions under which the American public will sanction the use of force in an internal conflict is when humanitarian concerns are most salient. There are two ways to think about social dislocations and humanitarian crises in civil conflicts, in terms of refugee flows or casualties. These two consequences are linked but clearly not identical factors. A large numbers of casualties generally implies that the local society has been fractured by the conflict. In civil conflicts, casualties are spread across the civilian and military spheres, leading to disruptions in the economic, agricultural, and social sectors of society. Many people under these conditions flee their homes, and at times even their country. Conflicts with a large number of casualties or refugee flows also tend to attract the attention of the world community. For instance, a cursory look through the appendix, which lists the cases of civil conflicts, would point out the general familiarity of those conflicts in which a lot of people were killed or forced to flee, and the relative obscurity of the many low-level conflicts. Intervening when such humanitarian issues are prevalent will increase the benefits and decrease the audience costs for not acting.

The intensity of a conflict and the potential for a humanitarian crisis may, but need not, be linked. Intense conflicts probably lead to large social dislocations more often than not, but the flow of refugees or widespread famine can result from less intense conflicts just as readily. The first Shaba crisis in Zaire in 1977 resulted in a relatively small number of fatalities from the conflict but created a relatively large number of refugees and internally displaced persons. On the one hand an intense conflict makes the decision to intervene trickier and less likely, while on the other the humanitarian concerns generally associated with such conflicts makes an intervention alternative more compelling. This poses a conundrum for the decision makers because there may be two competing indicators suggesting diametrically opposed policies.

HYPOTHESIS 4

Interventions in intrastate conflicts were more likely during the cold war than in the post–cold war period.

During the cold war any internal dispute could easily be cast in terms of the ideological contest waged between the East and West. From a realpolitik perspective internal conflicts that are in areas with strategically important resources, involving regional allies, or in global powers' sphere of influence will provide incentives for intervention. With East-West issues being less salient, however, fewer conflicts generate a sufficient benefit from concerns over the national interest to outweigh potential costs. The caution instilled by the East-West tension during the cold war contributed to the utility to be gained from confronting the adversary in a third country by minimizing the potential for a direct confrontation. Interventions and counterinterventions were a means to advance strategic interests. With the end of the cold war much less can be justified in terms of the dominant ideological objectives, resulting in a decline in benefits to be derived from intervening. Without this need to counter an intervention by an ideological foe we should see a decrease in the propensity to intervene, at least unilaterally.

This argument generally runs counter to much of the conventional wisdom and some of the scholarly debate regarding the role of the cold war as a constraining force in international politics (e.g., Mersheimer 1990). Internal conflicts, however, have been the fertile ground upon which the cold war was fought, with war by proxy being the outlet for East-West aggression. Rather than acting as a constraining force, the zero-sum environment of the cold war increased the expected payoff from confronting the adversary on the territory of a third party. Supporting one side of an internal conflict (or not supporting) during the cold war could have a perceived influence on the strategic balance between cold war adversaries, resulting in an unacceptable decline in national security. This strategic calculation would be much less pronounced in the cold war's aftermath. During the cold war, victory and defeat of "allies" or "opponents" was often a dichotomous outcome, regardless of how extensive the carnage. In the post–cold war era, where ideological and bloc politics matter less, strategic considerations will be given less weight in the decision over intervention. With the end of these ideological hostilities, unilateral interventions are increasingly constrained by domestic considerations and ultimately give way to collective interventions (Vertzberger 1993).

Research Design and Testing

The hypotheses outlined in the last section were tested against the data on intrastate conflicts in the post–World War II era described in chapter 2. The unit of analysis used in this part of the study is the conflict. Although the data are disaggregated into cases of intervention, the central question here is whether characteristics of the conflict or the context in which it is waged affect the likelihood that outside parties will choose to intervene. There are conceptual problems in using the conflict as the unit of analysis because the emphasis of the empirical model shifts from the perspective of the individual decision maker to the aggregate case, asking in essence whether certain structural and contextual conditions increase the probability of an intervention. This shift in emphasis is a result of the difficulty of identifying a population of potential intervenors—some of which do intervene and some that do not—in a way that does not unduly bias the analysis. The potential for selection bias—either over- or undersampling—is large. The usefulness of the results to follow will turn in part on the validity of the inferences that we can draw from the evidence relating conditions of the conflict to an intervention, and then to the decision-making process itself. In trying to arrive at the dyad as the unit of analysis, a difficult question revolves around just what dyads to use. If you use all possible dyads, then there is an obvious bias toward the nonintervention decision. If only cases of conflicts with interventions are chosen, then there is a strong bias toward the intervention decision, and we would never know which countries considered but rejected that option. Lemke (1995) argues that relevant dyads are defined in terms of regional—or geographic—criteria, though such criteria come in to question when the issues involve intervention in civil conflicts. Each conceivable method has its own conceptual and empirical liabilities.

One of the key elements of a dyadic analysis would be to pick up instances where intervention was considered but rejected, on grounds consistent with the model. But a dyadic analysis would not necessarily bring us any closer to this ideal unless we had the ideal way of determining the population of potential intervenors in each conflict. To pick up the "nonintervention, though considered it" cases, there would have to be some visible trace consistently left behind from the deliberative process. In most instances identifying the existence of these deliberations in the public domain would be a monumental task, and any resulting population most likely would result in a serious challenge to the reliability and validity of the data. One way to attempt to identify conditions of relevancy in defining dyads is to look for an indication of threats to intervene that were ultimately not carried out. If there were common characteristics to these threatening states, then a condition for dyadic relevancy could be established. A random sample of the conflicts used in this analysis was surveyed in search of visible traces of threats to intervene. Presumably cases of interventions would generally be preceded by threats to do so, though clear threats were not always evident. But more important in instances of nonintervention, threats might betray elements of an evaluation of an intervention option that was never exercised. Just over 50 percent of the cases of nonintervention were included in the sample (27) and of those 27 nonintervention cases, in six instances there were indications of threats to intervene. Unfortunately those six cases did not reveal any common characteristic from which to draw inferences about relevant dyads; moreover, their numbers might not have been sufficient to do so even had a common theme developed. The further implication is that no outside actor considered intervening in the other 22 cases, though this is a difficult argument to sustain.

Ultimately it is the decision process that is key to understanding the choices made, but each decision is predicated on a number of domestic and international conditions that constrain choices and influence the decision process. We can advance our understanding of the decision-making process by closely examining the conditions under which certain types of decisions are made. Strong evidence relating structural or contextual conditions to certain types of decisions can allow us to draw inferences about how those conditions affect the decision calculus.

Since the counterfactual question of which states considered intervening, but chose not to, is difficult to disentangle conceptually and empirically, I will postpone that task until it becomes more manageable. For the empirical analysis, then, I use the conflict as the unit of analysis, control the multivariate model for the number of shared borders, and skirt the issue of the counterfactual claim that all states are potential intervenors. Although not the ideal, focusing on the conflict does allow us to draw meaningful inferences about the decision criteria of potential intervenors by evaluating the hypotheses derived from the theoretical model; we can then infer from the structural and contextual constraints to the decision criteria used by a decision maker. A critique of this research design, furthermore, needs to be tempered by the goals of the exercise, which are twofold. First, we need to get a handle on the conditions under which outside parties will intervene in internal conflicts so that we can intelligently evaluate the effectiveness of those policies. On this score the limitations of the research design are not terribly debilitating. As we will see, there are systematic conditions under which third parties choose or reject an intervention option, and these systematic patterns will help us understand what happens when states do choose to intervene. Second, the social science community as a whole needs to develop ways to address selection bias problems. Here I am less successful, though the effort should lead to strategies that increase the effectiveness of future research designs.

For instance, the implications of this research design can be felt in a number of areas, where possibly other designs might provide additional useful information. The two main problems revolve around potential endogeneity of explanatory variables and the selection bias question. Future research may be able to solve these difficult issues, but they remain intractable at this juncture. The endogeneity problem can be seen with the use of casualties as an indicator of the likelihood of intervening. In the referent world the cumulative number of casualties in a conflict is monotonically increasing over time, and decisions are made based on an understanding of the number of casualties at the time of the decision. At various points along a trajectory in casualties, decisions over interventions are evaluated. This would suggest that a survival analysis would yield information about the timing of actual interventions. Two difficulties arise. First, data on casualties are generally reported in aggregate terms and are rarely dynamic enough to permit survival-type analyses—particularly in civil conflicts where there is a blur between military and civilian casualties and oftentimes concerted efforts to hide the magnitude of the latter. Second, this would take us back to the need to adopt a dyadic research design for which the problems are illuminated by the selection bias issues.

For example, capturing the effect of shared borders (hypothesis 1) becomes particularly problematic, largely because of the counterfactual issues associated with knowing when a state considered intervening. Theoretically all states contemplate intervening in each internal conflict, with the vast majority of them simply rejecting the alternative as too costly with no appreciable payoff and a relatively low probability of affecting the outcome. To capture this potential relationship the dyad would have to be the unit of analysis. Examining the decision from a dyadic perspective might allow a fuller examination of the role of shared borders in the intervention calculus, but it would virtually swamp the statistical effect of those interventions by bordering countries. We know that there were at least 190 interventions in 89 conflicts, yet the number of dyads would be somewhere between 5,000 and 18,000, depending on the year and/or number of countries in the system at the time.[7] Since the overwhelming majority of countries will not have intervened during this period, any statistical result would be driven by the noninterventions. More important, however, it is somewhat nonsensical to think that all states consider intervening in all civil conflicts regardless of geographical location, the climate of the international system, or their material capability to implement any intervention policy. Bolivia surely did not consider intervening in Russia's struggle against the breakaway republic of Chechnia. If I were to use the intervention as the unit of analysis (as in the next chapter), the cases of conflicts without interventions would be excluded, and there would be no variation on the dependent variable.

The theoretical framework that structures this part of the research suggests a set of conditions under which interventions will or will not be undertaken. The yes/no nature of the question requires an analytical tool that can incorporate dichotomous outcomes. A logit procedure satisfies this requirement and is becoming an increasingly common tool in data analysis in the social sciences (for a discussion see Bennett and Stam 1996; Hensel and Diehl 1994; Regan 1996). The logit estimator is much like ordinary least squares (OLS) but it makes a very different assumption about the distribution of the outcome variable. OLS assumes that data on the outcome variable can range from positive to negative infinity and that the errors are distributed normally. A dichotomous choice variable violates these assumptions and can therefore lead to biased and inconsistent estimates of the effect of the explanatory variables. The estimated coefficients associated with the logit are not interpretable in the same way that an OLS-generated coefficient is; a further transformation is required to determine marginal effects (to be explained shortly). The signs associated with the logit coefficients do reflect the direction of the marginal impact. The specification of the logit model that will predict the likelihood that a third party will intervene in an ongoing civil conflict is as follows:

---

[7] The number of dyads can be found by identifying possible pairs of states, where the number of distinct pairs is equal to $N(N-1)/2$. Using a system of 100 countries we get approximately 5,000 dyads; 190 countries results in approximately 15,000 dyads.

$$\text{Intervention} = \beta_1 \times \text{casualties} + \beta_2 \times \text{intensity} + \beta_3 \times \text{humanitarian issues}$$
$$+ \beta_4 \times \text{cold war} + \beta_5 \times \text{number of borders} + \varepsilon$$

Operational Criteria

The operational definitions for each of the variables have been outlined in chapter 2, but I will briefly reiterate them here for expositional clarity. Five variables are used to account for the likelihood of interventions in internal conflicts:

1 *Contiguity* is operationalized in terms of either a shared border or less than 150 miles of water separating two otherwise contiguous land masses. The indicator used is the number of contiguous countries to the one involved in the conflict.

2 *Conflict intensity* is operationalized in terms of the number of casualties per year.

3 Data on *casualties* reflect commonly reported figures and were derived from various historical sources including the *New York Times*, *Keesings*, *Facts on File*, and the *Times of London*.

4 A *refugee crisis* was operationalized in terms of refugee flows, with 50,000 internally displaced persons or external refugees used as the cutoff between a crisis and a noncrisis. The variable was coded 1 if there was a crisis; otherwise, zero. Data were taken from the annual report of the U.S. Committee for Refugees (USCR) and the United Nations High Commission for Refugees (UNHCR). Unfortunately there is no systematic reporting on refugee flows prior to 1960, and there is no reasonably comprehensive alternative. For conflicts prior to 1960 I relied primarily on the *New York Times*, but also on specific historical narratives to try to minimize the amount of missing data. The number of missing cases is eight; four of which had interventions, four that did not.

5 The *cold war* is considered to be over as of January 1, 1989. Although any date that ends the cold war is somewhat arbitrary, January 1989 marks the transition from Ronald Reagan to George Bush in the American presidency and only predates the complete destruction of the Berlin Wall and the political unification of East and West Germany by a relatively short period of time. By 1989 Mikhail Gorbachev's revolution was sufficiently entrenched to allow the United States and the USSR to increasingly find areas of issue convergence rather than divergence. Conflicts such as Nicaragua, Afghanistan, and Angola were beginning to wind down, and by 1990 the United States and the USSR were cooperating in the struggle to oust Iraq from Kuwait. Pre– and post–cold war conflicts were coded dichotomously.

Empirical Results

The results of the logit analysis can be interpreted through two approaches. The first focuses on the coefficients associated with the logit procedure, which give some indication of the *direction* of the empirical relationship between the outcome to be explained and the explanatory variables. The second approach involves transforming these coefficients into estimates of the *probability* of an intervention given a specific set of conditions. The second component has considerably better interpretive appeal and will form the basis for the bulk of the discussion to follow. In general, the results of the analysis confirm the central arguments already presented, with one exception. The role of borders, it appears, has the opposite effect on the likelihood that an outside actor will intervene than was argued theoretically. For the other variables in the model, the signs of the coefficients are in the direction predicted by the theoretical argument, and for all but one we have a high degree of confidence that they are not the result of chance.

Table 3.1 presents the results of the logit analysis in terms of the coefficients associated with each of the explanatory variables. In broad terms we can see that an increase in the intensity of the conflict and the number of shared borders decrease the probability of an outside intervention (table 3.1), while all the other factors increased the likelihood of an intervention. The model itself is robust—as evidenced by the log likelihood function—and the marginal effects of the explanatory variables are strong.

TABLE 3.1.   Logit Model for Interventions in Intrastate Conflicts, $N = 130$

Variable	Coefficient	S.E.	Significance
Intensity	−1.8E-05	8.02 E-06	.04*
Refugees	.43	.40	.28
Cold war	1.13	.37	.00**
Casualties	1.5E-05	6.43E-06	.01**
No. borders	−.16	.08	.04*

Note:−2 Log likelihood, 144.1; Chi square test, 36.1 with 5 degrees of freedom; p < .000.
*p < .05; **p < .01.

| | PREDICTED OUTCOMES | | |
	No Intervention	Intervention	Percentage Correct (%)
Observed Outcomes			
No Intervention	17	28	37.7%
Intervention	11	74	87.0%
Percentage Correct	60%	72.5%	

Overall correct predictions: 70%

When we look at the substantive effect of the individual variables on the probability that we would observe an intervention, the results demonstrate a strong substantive impact (table 3.2). For example, to judge the marginal effects of each variable we can use a hypothetical conflict as a base.[8] For our purposes this hypothetical conflict is one in which (1) the intensity was low, (2) the conflict took place after the end of the cold war, (3) there were less than 50,000 refugees, (4) there is only one bordering country, and (5) the number of casualties was low. In this hypothetical environment the model suggests that there would be a 50 percent chance of observing an intervention. This hypothetical case, moreover, is not without close analogies in the referent world. Lebanon in 1988–1990, Moldova in 1992, and the Bougainville conflict in Papua New Guinea starting in 1988 meet these "hypothetical" conditions, with the exception that Moldova and Lebanon have more than one shared border. In the first two conflicts there were outside interventions; in Papua New Guinea there was not.

When holding each variable at the base value and varying the intensity of the conflict, we can see that when the intensity is high, the probability of observing an intervention drops to only 15 percent, a 35 percent reduction in the likelihood of observing an intervention. The effect is also graduated, as can be seen by the substantive effect of a more modest increase in the intensity level. This is consistent with theoretical expectations and would appear to reflect the increasing difficulty of conceiving of a successful outcome as the level of conflict intensity rises. The role of the intensity of the conflict in the decision to intervene can be quite dramatic in very brutal conflicts, as table 3.2 makes clear. The intensity of the conflict influences the ability of the decision maker to adequately judge p and q. This uncertainty over the outcome of the conflict after an intervention probably breeds caution on the part of the decision makers. Combined with the increased size of any intervention required to overcome the sunk costs of the combatants, we can anticipate that the uncertainty results in a decrease in expected utility from an intervention as the intensity increases. The cold war increased the probability of an intervention by 25 percent, such that a low-intensity conflict with a relatively small number of casualties had a 75 percent chance of having an outside intervention if it was during the cold war. The existence of a humanitarian crisis increases the probability of an intervention by 10 to 60 percent, and conflicts with casualties approaching 200,000 have a near certainty of attracting an outside intervenor. This could, in part, reflect the effect of the intervenor on the conflict itself, though direct evidence is difficult to ascertain (Pearson 1974; Regan 1996). Fur-

---

[8] This transformation is carried out by the following operation: $\text{Log}\,(P/1 - P) = (X1 \times b1) + (X2 \times b2) + \ldots (X3 \times b3)$, varying each value of $X1 \ldots Xn$. Exponentiating the equation gives $(P/1 - P) = e^{\Sigma equation1}$. Solving for P gives the probability of success (see Roncek 1991).

thermore, a high-casualty conflict is not synonymous with a humanitarian crisis, though such a conflict would be highly visible to a domestic audience and generate public support for an intervention on humanitarian grounds.[9]

The number of shared borders, on the other hand, tends to reduce the probability of an outside intervention. This is a puzzling result and runs directly counter

TABLE 3.2.   Marginal Effects on Changes in Probability of Intervention

Base Hypothetical Conflict	Probability of Intervention	Change in Probability (%)
Low intensity (1,000)		
Post–cold war		
One bordering country		
No refugee crisis		
Low casualties (1,000)	.50	
From: Base		
To: High intensity		
(Int = 120K; Casualty = 30K)	.15	−35
(Int = 20K; Casualty = 5K)	.43	−7
From: Base		
To: Cold war	.75	25
From: Base		
To: Refugee crisis	.60	10
From: Base		
To: High casualty	.94	44
(Casualty = 200K; Intense = 2,000)		
From: Base		
To: No. shared borders		
2	.46	−4
3	.42	−8
5	.31	−19
9	.19	−31

[9] In fact, the two variables are not very highly correlated. The Pearson's R between the existence of a humanitarian crisis and the number of casualties is only .35; it is .53 when using a Spearman's rho.

to the hypothesized relationship. From table 3.2 we can see that shifting the loci of a conflict from one with a single bordering country to one with five contiguous neighbors decreases the probability of an intervention by 19 percent. There are three plausible explanations, though no one seems sufficiently compelling to account for the counterintuitive result: (1) as the region in which the conflict rages gets more congested, the potential volatility in that region breeds caution; functionally, neighboring states worry that their involvement may lead to them becoming involved in the fray as a combatant. In essence bordering states have an interest in intervening, but the more of them there are, the less likely that any one figures that it can be successful; (2) the collective action problem comes to the forefront, leading all states to deny responsibility for action; and (3) it is an artifact of the data, and really there are many more interventions that were not picked up in the coding process. This would suggest that as the number of bordering states increases, the effort to ensure plausible deniability also increases. Interventions become deeply covert, and traces in the public domain are difficult to find. Of the three potential explanations, the last one is the most difficult to defend and the first one most intuitively appealing. If it were a data problem, the results would probably not be so systematic and robust, which they are, and time would tend to reveal even the most covert of interventions. The collective action explanation assumes that there is a perceived "responsibility" to settle the conflict, when in the pull and haul of international politics it is more likely allies, enemies, and resources than responsibility that guide the decision, particularly if the conflict is in a bordering country and has the potential to spread. It is that fear of a contagious conflict that may compel states to avoid intervention when the number or size of a potential coalition increases. The lack of a clear explanation for the finding suggests that the notion of "opportunity and willingness" needs to be reexamined (Siverson and Starr 1991).

Overall, the results of the analyses lend support for the general framework of the model, suggesting that the decision to intervene results from a mixture of constraints imposed from domestic and international quarters. Feste (1992) and Bull (1984), for example, focus too narrowly on the role of geopolitics as the condition for intervention, and Blechman (1995) is on firm ground when he argues that domestic politics can drive the decision to intervene when humanitarian issues come to the fore. We can infer from these results that strategic interests are important in the intervention calculus, but so too are domestic political considerations, as evidenced by the high probability of interventions when humanitarian issues come to the fore.

Discussion

In terms of specific inferences and implications, a few important points are evident in this analysis. First, the cold war was clearly a major factor in the decision to intervene. Although the majority of the conflicts used in this analysis were not ideologically based, the polarized structure associated with the cold war apparently weighed heavily in the decision-making process. Two things probably happen as the system becomes less polarized: (1) there is a decrease in pressure to intervene on geostrategic grounds, and (2) interventions begin to take on a multilateral character under the auspices of the UN or some other supranational organization. The first response is consistent with both the logic and the evidence presented earlier. The outcome of civil conflicts is no longer viewed in rigid zero-sum terms, and therefore there is less to gain from offsetting the potential advances of an adversary. Furthermore, without the pressure to compete ideologically, collective efforts are easier to organize and implement. This is also consistent with what we see in our referent world, and some evidence supports this conclusion.

Second, the centrality of subjective estimates of the likely outcome of an intervention cannot be overstated. If the intensity of a conflict is a valid indicator of subjective estimates of successful intervention policies, then these estimates appear to play a critical role in determining the outcome of policy debates. This result is convergent with a casual understanding of recent history—at least as it pertains to the United States. The need for a high degree of certainty about short time frames and successful outcomes has tended to drive recent debates about U.S. interventions into Haiti (1994), Bosnia (1995), and Zaire (1996), and, more recently, Kosovo (1999). One way to turn a short-term policy into a long-term intervention is to have a low estimate of the probability of success at the time the decision was made, and to make the decision to intervene anyway. Uncertainty over likely outcomes, therefore, shows up as a declining probability of interventions.

Third, humanitarian issues do seem to matter in decisions about how to respond to civil conflicts. Survey research has made clear—again, at least in the United States—that people do see a legitimate role of government to be relieving some of the social stresses caused by civil conflicts (Blechman 1995; Kohut and Toth 1994). The evidence here supports this notion and suggests that governments respond to these humanitarian pressures. In some instances the response to massive refugee flows may be couched in terms of national security (Dowty and Loescher 1996), but this cannot be the dominant case, and regardless of the grounds for justification, domestic constituencies do seem to matter in these types of decisions.

And finally, the role of geographic contiguity needs to be addressed. As discussed earlier, none of the explanations for the counterintuitive result that the greater the number of shared borders, the less likely an intervention makes much sense. The role of geographic contiguity in the diffusion of interstate conflict seems well established (see Siverson and Starr 1991), yet that established pattern runs diametrically opposed to the results of this study. A realist view that states act in pursuit of power or stability would point toward decisive action in a neighboring conflict, and there may be a way in which this is consistent with the evidence presented here. Since an intervention would deplete resources, as the number of potential adversaries increase (i.e., a greater number of shared borders) the intervening state would increase its vulnerability through the process of intervening itself. In a hostile strategic environment this depletion of resources in a neighbor's conflict might have grave consequences for domestic security, possibly leading to constraints in the decision process. In any event, the lack of a clear and logical explanation calls for further investigation, particularly in an attempt to rectify the discrepancy in the relationship across inter- and intrastate conflicts.

In the referent world, moreover, these results look quite compelling. The example of Rwanda is useful. During the Rwandan upheaval of 1994 most states were clearly reluctant to take decisive and unilateral action. The killing was so intense that smaller neighboring states were probably incapable of bringing the slaughter to an end; the capable states were unwilling to try. Essentially, estimates of p—the probability that an intervention would succeed—were too low. The magnitude of the killing and the impending refugee crisis, however, meant that ethical issues surfaced within the global community. France eventually did take unilateral action, largely motivated by political and humanitarian considerations (Adelman and Suhrke 1996). Zaire has also suffered the fate of numerous internal conflicts since independence from Belgium in 1960. In 1962 and 1967 Western allies intervened decisively in Zairean conflicts, there were some hints of Soviet interventions as well (U.S. Department of State 1994). The civil war of 1996 generated a serious discussion about intervening, but no country chose to take unilateral action, and the appropriate conditions for a multilateral intervention could not be reached. The cold war was over.

India's intervention into the Sri Lankan conflict is also quite predictable given the preceding analysis. The conflict in Sri Lanka has resulted in a relatively large number of casualties, and more than a couple of presidents and prime ministers have been assassinated as a direct result of action by participants in the conflict. But the conflict in Sri Lanka had not been very intense—in terms of casualties per year. The fighting was steady and prolonged, but there were not periods of spasmodic slaughter such as took place in Rwanda, Burundi, or Cambodia. The intervention took place during the later phase of the cold war, though neither India, Sri Lanka, nor the conflict was overly caught up in cold war politics. Some, however, argue to the contrary that cold war politics did play a role in India's involvement in Sri Lanka (de Silva 1991). And from India's perspective there was a refugee problem building in its southern state of Tamil Nedu that put pressure on the Indian government to take decisive action (de Silva 1991). Each of these factors would predict an increased probability of India intervening.

Given the potential impact of intervention policies on regional or global stability, we have very little systematic understanding of their effect, and even less about the conditions under which they are undertaken. This void of knowledge has become much more glaring as the world's collective gaze has shifted from cold war politics to regional conflicts. This chapter moves us forward in the search for clarity surrounding the conditions under which we might expect third parties to intervene unilaterally. And although the results do not represent the definitive answer to when interventions should be undertaken, the results do represent a systematic and coherent first step at developing a way to answer some pressing questions faced by foreign policy communities.

The results of this analysis lead us to the following chapter. In attempting to evaluate the conditions under which interventions contribute to the cessation of hostilities, we must first be cognizant of the selection bias problem. We need to know when states self-select themselves out of interventions because they do not expect to be successful or they see very little potential payoff worth the risk. Although this analysis cannot tell us definitively who will intervene in specific conflicts, it does give us a reasonable indication of which types of conflicts will attract unilateral interventions. The evidence presented in this chapter suggests that there are identifiable conditions that influence the likelihood that an outside actor will intervene in an internal conflict. From this foundation we can go on to examine the conditions under which any interventions have an increased likelihood of being successful.

FOUR

The Conditions for
Successful Interventions

The central focus of this book is on understanding the outcome of interventions, the topic that I take up in this chapter. From a policy perspective this is the critical piece of information, for it is the understanding of what has and has not worked in the past that helps shape future policies. This chapter evaluates past intervention efforts along a number of dimensions to identify those conditions that have a greater probability of leading to a successful outcome. Based on the previous chapter we have a sense of when interventions are likely, and as I argued in that chapter the political nature of intervention decisions ties the likelihood of intervention to the perceived probability that a given intervention policy will ultimately succeed.

There are two ways to think about determining the likelihood of the success of an intervention strategy: (1) in terms of a general policy of intervention, regardless of any selection criteria as to the type of conflict, and (2) in terms of particularly difficult cases faced by the policy community. This second category would be those intense conflicts in which large numbers of people are being killed in a relatively short period of time. We know that as the intensity of the conflict increases the probability of an outside intervention decreases. This is an understandable response given the reluctance with which policymakers would choose to undertake a "nonwinnable" policy. In fact, as the intensity of the conflict reaches rather extreme levels the probability of an intervention becomes quite low. But we also know that the greater the level of social dislocations associated with the conflict, the more likely is an outside intervention. To some degree this sets up a

Chapter 4 is a substantially revised version of my article "Conditions of Successful Third-Party Intervention in Intra-State Conflicts," *Journal of Conflict Resolution* 40, no. 1 (1996): 336–59. I am grateful to acknowledge Sage Publications, Inc., for this earlier work.

policy conundrum with the intensity of the conflict—epitomized by the extreme slaughter—weighing in against an intervention, and public anxiety over humanitarian issues and concerns over national security auguring for an intervention. The dilemma among the policy community over what might work in these types of situations calls for greater attention by the academic community. In short, cases of intense civil conflicts give us a useful analytical comparison to the broader population of third-party interventions and gives policymakers additional information from which to make choices.

Examples of Cases and Decisions

To frame the issues at hand, I begin with a brief—and somewhat anecdotal—history of two civil conflicts in which third parties intervened. The first case is that of Zaire (then—and now—called the Congo) in 1967 and the Belgian and U.S. interventions; the second will be the Sri Lankan conflict starting in 1982 between the Tamil separatists and the government, with India intervening militarily. These cases are two of many potential examples, but they are rather interesting cases that should illuminate some of the issues to be discussed.

The 1967 Zairean conflict is often referred to as the Katanga mutiny because it was led by a group of largely European mercenaries and a mutinous group of soldiers from the Congolese army. After a postindependence civil war lasting the better part of five years, the Congolese government achieved a reasonable level of normalcy. This relative quiet was a welcome relief to the United States and Western Europe, who considered the civil war to be an integral part of the East-West struggle and suspected the Soviet Union of funneling arms to the opposition. Little direct evidence of Soviet involvement was found, though the Soviets did make offers of arms and advisers to the fledgling government. Many of the former Belgian colonists who decided to remain after independence were from the Katanga region and were the proprietors of the large mining and banking concerns. The civil war from 1960 to 1965 was largely fought over attempts to secede the Katanga region from the Congo and declare an independent state. Despite numerous attempts by the UN, the United States, and to some degree the Belgians to reintegrate Katanga and the primary opposition leader, Mr. Tshombe, into the Congolese government, these attempts ultimately failed and led to his exile, trial, and conviction (U.S. Department of State 1994).

On July 5, 1967, the mutineers, led by Jean Schramme, a Belgian businessman turned mercenary, attacked the town of Kisangani, killing and wounding hundreds of government troops and civilians. What started as a band of about 100 opposition troops grew to a force of more than 1,000 and presented a serious challenge to the government in Kinshasa. Not only would the cessation of the Katanga region pose a serious threat to the stability of the Congolese government of Mobutu, but it would eliminate the resources produced in this region from the coffers of the central government. To prevent the defeat of his government forces in the Katanga region, President Mobutu requested assistance from the United States and Belgium. For its part the United States provided military transport planes that moved Zairean troops and equipment up to the front lines. Most seem to agree that the support of the United States contributed considerably to the morale of the Zairean troops and the ultimate settlement of the conflict. Contrary to the requests by Mobutu, Belgium's role tended to favor the opposition forces—aligned largely with business interests with ties to Belgium—by punishing the government economically. Their intervention turned out to be largely unsuccessful.

Some points about the conflict and the intervention deserve mention. The number of casualties was low, and the conflict itself played out over a relatively short time. The combatants split over essentially ideological lines, with ethnicity or religious orientation playing little or no role. To the United States, the East-West issue loomed large (U.S. Department of State 1994). The U.S. intervention involved the supply of military logistic support to the Zairean government, which proved instrumental in stemming the tide of the opposition initiatives. According to published accounts and declassified U.S. documents, Zaire's troops were proving woefully inadequate at taking the fight to the mercenaries, and in the process morale was rapidly fading. The U.S. logistical assistance apparently did two things: (1) helped organize and focus the government's offensive, and (2) demonstrated to the opposition that there would be an overwhelming force arrayed against them. The mutiny was relatively short-lived with the mercenaries commandeering planes or boats or finding a way out of the country on foot. From the U.S. perspective, the intervention was highly successful and relatively cost free; the outcome for the Belgians was markedly less desirable.

The Tamil rebellion in Sri Lanka is quite a different conflict from the Katanga mutiny in Zaire. First, the conflict is organized along ethnic lines, with the minority Tamilese demanding autonomy from the majority Singalese. Second, the conflict has been raging for an extended time, having roots that go back decades and with the main thrust of the conflict starting in 1982. The number of casualties, both combatants and noncombatants, has been high. Furthermore, a few presidents and prime ministers in both Sri Lanka and India have been assassinated by people with direct links to the conflict. The Tamil separatists have ethnic affinities to the Tamilese people in the state of Tamil Nadu in India, resulting in domestic pressures on the Indian government to defend the Tamilese in Sri Lanka. There is reason to believe that the prime minister, Rajiv Ghandi, wanted to maintain the support of the government in Tamil Nadu and helping the Tamils in Sri Lanka was one mechanism to do so (Brogan 1989). The Indians ultimately sent in a military force of upwards of 60,000 troops in an attempt to bring a halt to the fighting (Diehl 1993).

The Indian intervention resulted from a negotiated agreement with the Sri Lankan government identifying principles of a resolution to the conflict. One aspect of this conflict resolution process was the Indian intervention. To many of the Singalese majority this was a violation of their sovereignty and a "sell-out" by their government to the demands of the Indians. To most observers the intervention was initially seen as an attempt to assist the Tamils by constraining the government's ability to suppress their movement. This was consistent with Indian relief drops to the Tamilese strongholds, in violation of Sri Lankan sovereignty in June of 1987, and with the pressure from ethnically homogeneous groups in the state of Tamil Nadu. Even though the Indian intervention was designed to produce conditions conducive to a cease-fire, factions within the Tamilese movement increased the tempo of their military efforts, leading to the Indian military suppressing the Tamilese. By the time the Indian troops withdrew in 1990 they had achieved a level of brutality barely matched by the Tamilese or the Singalese and never came close to bringing a halt to the fighting. The conflict still rages on today.

Two interventions into two different types of conflicts result in two quite different outcomes. The following argument suggests that the conditions for success or failure of the intervention can be tied to the characteristics of the conflict and the strategy used to intervene. If decision makers had a reasonably good grasp of the types of interventions that worked under various conditions, then efforts to control the violent aspects of civil conflicts might have a greater impact on the ultimate steps toward the resolution of the issues at stake. It is considerably more difficult to negotiate resolutions when the combatants are in the midst of armed conflict. What follows will contribute to the development of a framework with which civil conflicts can be managed, possibly facilitating diplomatic efforts targeted at resolution.

Classifying Interventions

Although our theoretical and empirical understanding of the conditions that effect the success or failure of third-party interventions are rather meager, the need for greater attention has already been made clear. Alexander George (1995), for instance, makes the case that for coherent conflict management policy to be articulated and implemented, policymakers need systematic information on (1) strategies for conflict resolution, (2) specific knowledge of the conditions under which such strategies tend to succeed or fail, and (3) the role played by the various actors in determining the outcome of the conflict. This chapter contributes to the generation of that systematic knowledge in a manner that should increase the coherence of the policy process. However, there are limitations to what will be derived from this analysis, with certain types of conflicts and some forms of intervention being left out. Not all conflicts are created equal, and unfortunately neither do they all fit nicely into one analytical package.

Of importance in decisions over where and how to intervene in civil conflicts are two general categories of information: (1) characteristics of the conflict and (2) characteristics of the intervention. Aspects of the domestic and international political arena would have already played their hands in the decision over whether or not to intervene. Once that decision has been made, it is the characteristics of the conflict and the strategy for intervening that will have the greatest impact on the effectiveness of the policy.

The decision to intervene in an intrastate conflict reflects, inter alia, concerns over who is fighting and why; as such, one critical aspect of the decision calculus will involve the cultural characteristics of the disputants. Likewise, the makeup of the participants to the conflict affects the strategy for and likelihood of successful third-party interventions. For example, a conflict rooted in ethnic or religious grievances may be more amenable to outside interventions than ideological conflicts, even though the latter may be just as likely to attract intervenors. Intergroup grievances are often tied to discriminations and disadvantages between the conflicting parties, as well as their distinct cultural identities (Gurr 1993). The specific character of these opposition groups, therefore, should influence the intervention strategy used to bring about a cessation of hostilities. Not only will some types of conflicts be more susceptible than others to outside interventions, but also the knowledge of the differing effect of the root causes of the conflict on the likely success of an intervention would be useful to policymakers grappling with the decision over how to intervene. Kaufmann (1996) argues that the nature of identify patterns influences the effectiveness of outside military interventions in resolving conflicts. According to his theoretical reasoning, the ability to assume or discard a particular identity will affect the veracity with which the combatants adhere to their positions. Ethnic identity is more difficult to shed than either religious or ideological orientations, on the one hand making it easier to design solutions to the conflict, but on the other increasing the polarization of the groups in conflict.

Three contrasting examples will help illuminate the influence of the orientation of the groups in conflict on the likelihood of a successful third-party intervention. The now familiar Jihad, or Holy War, where religious fundamentalist groups are fighting to oust the infidels has taken center stage in some parts of the world. Islamic groups in Afghanistan, for instance, have taken the struggle to such a feverish pitch that the war to expel the Soviets appeared somewhat tame by comparison. When the Mujahideen successfully defeated the Soviet-backed government in 1990, many thought the troubles in Afghanistan were over. But when the victorious Mujahideen broke into factions, religious differences became the most salient operative variable in the renewed conflict. Certainly other factors such as power struggles and historical animosities contribute to the vigor with which the conflict is waged, but it is the religious orientation that dominates the divisions between the warring parties. The civil war in Nicaragua that overthrew the Somoza regime in 1979 had a different character. The opposition groups, led by the Sandinista party, were composed of various segments of the Nicaraguan society. Leading members of the ruling party—most notably members of the Chamoro family—sided with peasants and Marxists to challenge the legitimacy of the Somoza government. Although working under a common banner to overthrow the government, the Sandinista opposition did not all share common values as to the form that a new government would take; the subsequent reinitiation of the conflict under the banner of the "contra" movement reflected, in part, the nebulous makeup of the Sandinista coalition. The Eritreans in Ethiopia waged a decades-long struggle for independence, and throughout ebbs and flows in their fortunes in battle they maintained sufficient organizational support to eventually prevail in the struggle. The roots of the civil war can be linked back to the process of colonization and decolonization, with the ethnic Eritreans being denied the right to their own nation through the vagaries of the colonial system.

Each of the conflicts has similarities with the other two, but the differences are of most importance to us. If we think about these conflicts from the perspective of identity—which Kaufmann uses as the key determinant of the success or failure of military interventions—then the Eritrean and the Afghan conflicts reflect situations in which the geographic entity, the country, is occupied by separate nations; to a large degree members of one nation control the state apparatus. So there is one country with two or more nations fighting over issues of self-determination, or identity. In the Nicaraguan conflict, with its ideological orientation, you have one country, one nation, but a disagreement over the economic, political, and social direction that the current ruling coalition is taking. Burton (1990) raises these issues of identity to the level of a "Rosetta stone" for the understanding and resolution of conflict. Although he acknowledges that addressing questions of identity can require long-term strategies, short-term steps at conflict settlement must also be attended to—and are affected by—the makeup of the groups in conflict. If issues of identity play such a key role in the initiation of civil conflicts and their ultimate resolution, then those same issues of identity will affect the relative effectiveness of third-party interventions. Conflicts that have no easy lines of demarcation, and where the calculations of the combatants are determined more by emotions and history than by gains and loses, may require intervention strategies that differ from those conflicts with a different set of identity patterns.

The mechanisms for intervening in intrastate conflicts are also varied. For example, the UN identifies three goals in terms of resolving ongoing conflicts: preventative diplomacy, peacemaking, and peacekeeping (Boutros-Ghali 1992). Each goal requires a different strategy of intervention. Although advocated under the banner of multilateral interventions (which I deal with in chapter 5), the first of these relies primarily on the acumen of the available diplomatic corps; the other two initiatives generally entail the use of military and/or economic instruments. For a number of reasons diplomacy is a distinct category of intervention from either the military or economic variety, and it is the latter two that are the focus of this analysis. Even though these two forms of intervention are often undertaken jointly—as they were, for instance, in Bosnia—for analytical purposes the isolation of the more intrusive forms of intervention can help to clarify some of the policy issues that decision makers regularly confront. Furthermore, many acknowledge that stopping the fighting is a prerequisite for diplomatic initiatives to take root (Diehl 1993; Hampson 1996; Mitchell and Banks 1997; Smith 1995).

An effective strategy for intervening incorporates a mix of the appropriate instruments with the right target. Outside interventions, for example, involve military, economic, or a mix of the two instruments, *and* they can take place on behalf of the government or opposition forces. Much of the prescriptive advice that has been forthcoming in the policy journals has tended to follow an implicit formula of assuming that the intervention would be on behalf of the government in power (e.g., Connaughton 1992; Haass 1994; Howe 1995; Kanter and Brooks 1994). But as the evidence in chapter 2, and much of the cold war policy from the United States and the Soviet Union has made clear, support for the opposition is often the policy choice. The effectiveness of the intervention attempt is influenced by whether a state supports the opposition or the government. Reasons of efficiency, legitimacy, and logistics all support this notion, yet the impact of these factors may differ across intervention instruments. For example, economic coercion—generally thought of as sanctions—may be more effective when targeted at the government than the opposition, because it is conceptually and practically difficult to embargo an organized rebel movement. At the same time, imposing sanctions on a government is considerably easier. However, military aid, in terms of hardware, may have a greater relative impact when in support of the opposition rather than the government. The government may already have a preponderance of capabilities over the opposition, so each additional unit of military equipment would only change the balance of capabilities by a small amount. On the other hand, a relatively modest supply of military hardware may increase substantially the capabilities of the opposition vis-à-vis the government. An intervention with military force, likewise, may be more effective when in support of the government, because the international community would hardly consider the deployment of troops against a recognized government as a legitimate action (although it has been done on a number of occasions), thereby limiting the ability of the intervenor to make the most effective use of its forces.

Although military interventions may be the most visible, they are not the only form of third-party intervention into intrastate conflicts. Economic instruments can be, and have been, a forceful tool with which to intervene in ongoing domestic disputes, both through positive inducements and punitive sanctions. The debate over whether or not sanctions will achieve a desired outcome echoes in both academic and policy circles. During the buildup to the Gulf War against Iraq, many in the U.S. Congress and in the various European parliaments were arguing over the track record of economic sanctions, with one group suggesting that they would work given enough time and the other claiming that they just never work. A similar debate resonates through the halls of academe (Baldwin 1985; Cortright and Lopez 1995).

In many intervention attempts, moreover, we are likely to see a mix of strategies, with economic inducements or punishments used alongside their military counterparts. Combining military and economic instruments increases the range of areas from which an intervention can manipulate the calculations of the combatants as they try to determine the utility from continued fighting. In effect, what I have outlined is a classificatory scheme by which we can think about third-party interventions. We have three general types of intrastate conflict: ethnic, religious, and ideological; three basic strategies for intervening in these conflicts: military, economic, and mixed strategies; and the target of the intervention identified as either the government or the opposition. What is critical at this juncture is to outline the goals of the intervenor and a theoretical framework from which we can understand any particular choice of strategy and its effectiveness.

The Logic Behind Interventions and the Mechanisms for Success

Earlier I discussed why certain characteristics of the conflict or aspects of the intervention itself would contribute to the success or failure of the policy, but I didn't address the question of just what interventions attempt to do and how they do so. If we go back to our assumption of decision makers as rational actors, we can get a sense of the logic behind an intervention and its effect on the course of a conflict. Even in the thick of a civil conflict, the leadership in both the opposition and the government need to calculate the costs and benefits of the various options available for carrying forward the struggle. An outside intervention is an attempt to alter those calculations in a manner that leads to the outcome preferred by the intervening party. As Freedman (1994) argues, military interventions are a method of altering the constellation of forces within the conflict to the extent that it influences the relative balance of power. To many adherents of the realist model of world politics it is the relative balance of capabilities that determines when states go to war, and conversely, when they sue for peace (Morganthau 1967; Wagner 1993; Waltz 1979).

Given this understanding of the mechanisms that drive decisions regarding the initiation and termination of hostilities, the key to any intervention strategy is to alter the calculations by which the antagonists arrive at particular outcomes. Focusing on the outcome of the end of the violence, an intervention strategy needs to make it too costly for the combatants to continue fighting. This can be achieved by either making the actual costs of fighting prohibitively high or by making the benefits of not fighting particularly attractive. A successful intervention strategy, then, will result in a cost-benefit calculation by the antagonists that leads to not fighting providing the highest expected outcome. The overwhelming force used by the outside parties in the Bosnian conflict was designed to make it clear that continued fighting would come at an unacceptably high cost. This was evident in the NATO bombings of the Bosnian-Serb positions overlooking Sarajevo prior to the Dayton agreements, where explicit warnings were made that linked continued shelling of the city to the near certain destruction of the weapons and positions used in the attacks. The Bosnian-Serbs, it appeared, learned the lesson rather quickly, as did the Belgian mercenaries in the Katanga province of Zaire in 1967 after the United States intervened with military support for the government. The same logic influenced the scale of the intervention by NATO troops in the post-Dayton period. It seems clear that the massive use of force altered not only the balance of forces but also the calculations in the various ruling coalitions. Equally important to increasing the cost of continued fighting, however, was the promise of rewards if all parties abided by the terms of the cease-fire.

In chapter 3 I articulated the decision-making logic from the perspective of the potential intervenor and argued that the decision was not strategic in the sense of the actions of the target influencing the calculations of the intervenor. However, the effect of the intervention—and the actions that it contributes to—is such that an intervention leads to a strategic calculation on the part of the combatants. In this sense the response to the intervention is a function of the antagonists' expectations about the effect of the intervention on the opposing side in the conflict. In other words, A's decision of whether and how to intervene in a conflict between B and C will reflect A's expected payoff from the intervention. As discussed earlier, this expected payoff incorporates information about domestic and international constraints, the expected benefits from a successful policy, and the subjective probability of the outcome of the conflict with and without an intervention. The objective of the resultant policy, however, is to influence calculations by the combatants about the relative costs and benefits of continued fighting and the prospects for achieving their desired outcome if they do continue the struggle militarily. The combatants' decision in this regard reflects a strategic calculation by the opposition (B) and the government (C) about the effect of the intervention on the other's willingness to press on with the military aspects of the conflict. So, for instance, B's calculations will reflect in part B's expectations about the effect of the intervention on C, and vice versa.

The choice of the decision maker in the intervening state is to determine this optimal strategy given the context of the conflict, the decision rules of the antagonists, and the expected probability of any one strategy securing the cessation of hostilities. This is where the characteristics of the conflict and the strategy for intervening come to the fore. Since the effect of an intervention plays out through the strategic calculations between the combatants, getting both sides to the conflict to determine that ending the fighting is in their best interest may be a difficult task. The task, moreover, is complicated by the differing characteristics of the conflict. For instance, a military intervention into an ideological conflict may alter the balance of capabilities to the extent that one side opts to negotiate rather than fight, but it seems just as likely that the intervention may send the opposing side out in search of additional weapons from *its* ideological patrons. Furthermore, simply ratcheting up the level of hostility might not lead to the strategic calculation by either side that negotiating is in its interest. Depending on the scale of the sunk costs—which we can think of in terms of the number of casualties—it may take an economic incentive to contribute to the calculation that a "ripe" environment is presenting itself.

The strategic calculation that an outside intervention must influence can be expressed as: $EU_i = (\text{Costs}_{cf} + \text{Benefits}_{nf}) \times j^*$; where EU_i reflects the expected utility to actor i from an intervention, Costs_{cf} reflect the costs of continued fighting, Benefits_{nf} reflect the benefits from terminating the hostilities, and j^* reflects actor i's perception of actor j's estimated expected utility from the intervention. If j^* is low (or conversely, i^*) then the expected payoff from an intervention to actor i is going to be low and the likelihood that the intervention will be successful correspondingly low. The mechanisms for intervening under these conditions that have the greatest probability of a successful outcome would be those that increase the costs to both sides from continued fighting, increase the benefits to both from agreeing to put down the guns, and does so in a manner that both sides come to a similar conclusion.

Given this framework, the strategy for intervening should influence the likely success of any intervention attempt. The strategy can be conceived of in terms of both the type and the target of the intervention. Either military or economic interventions can be used to influence both the costs and the benefits of the combatants' decision about whether or how to continue the conflict. Each approach to intervening potentially taps into separate mechanisms to affect the decision calculus. Economic incentives, for example, might offer rewards for a quick settlement, whereas military support might increase the battlefield constraints on one of the parties (affecting both the costs of continued fighting and the benefits from stopping). The offer of redevelopment assistance, for instance, may sufficiently increase the costs of fighting and the potential benefits from restraint to influence the perceptions by both antagonists that a cease-fire proposal is serious. Military support for either side could have a similar sobering impact on the likelihood of a halt to the fighting. The combined effect of economic and military instruments should be able to influence the course of the conflict well beyond the ability of either individual strategy. In a sense, then, the combined effect may be greater than the sum of the parts. We might expect, therefore, that under normal conditions a mixed intervention will have the best chance of achieving a successful outcome. From the perspective of the combatants, the ability to sustain a united front against an opponent will involve both the degree of support within the constituent base and the relative alignment of military forces; each of these can be manipulated by outside parties.

From a political vantage point economic constraints or inducements can partially contribute to the allegiances of the constituents behind either of the centers of sovereignty. Using sanctions or rewards to move this center of support toward a more compromising approach to the conflict should be effective in altering the calculus of the opposing leaderships. But an economic intervention probably is not sufficient, under normal circumstances, to bring an end to the fighting. The balance of military forces will also contribute to the expected outcome of the combatants, and military interventions are used to alter the relative capability of the opposing forces. Equally matched forces, for example, may lead to the perception of an impending stalemate, while a preponderance of military capabilities may give reason to push for further gains. But neither would military intervention by itself be the most effective strategy, in the norm, to move the parties far enough toward a compromise that an end to the fighting would be a likely outcome. Intuitively at least, military interventions often seem to exacerbate a bad situation leading to increased conflict rather than its diminution. As we recently saw in Somalia, a vastly superior military force simply became a target for the antagonists previously pitted against each other; the Soviet intervention in Afghanistan also serves as a poignant example. This need to sway both the cost-benefit calculations and the perception of the likely effect of the intervention on the opponent would suggest that a mixed strategy should be more likely to succeed than either a military or economic intervention alone. Furthermore, given the logic of how the intervention purports to influence decision making, there is little reason to expect, inter alia, that a military or an economic intervention independently will be more successful than the other. The context under which a nonmixed strategy will give the upper hand to a military or economic initiative is critically important, though those specific conditions under which one is more effective than the other deserves more concerted attention than is possible here.

The strategy for intervening, moreover, is also a function of the target chosen by the intervenor. Political imperatives often dictate who will be supported and who opposed by the outside party, but targeting the government or the opposition should not have the same probability of a successful outcome of the intervention, all else being equal. For reasons associated with the disparity in resources between the central government and the opposition forces, in general we would expect the existing balance of power to side with the ruling coalition. At the same time the efficiency of any third-party intervention should be greater when the intervention attempt supports the sitting government. Military interventions supporting opposition forces usually violate the spirit and the letter of international law and the charter of the UN. As such they would tend to be more clandestine, more difficult to organize logistically, and less likely to have a smooth flow from the donor through the leadership in exile (or in a "secure" enclave within the disputed territory), and out to the soldiers in the field. By contrast, military aid in support of the government is official, aboveboard, and distributed through an existing network for supply and integration. But simply because the government is the conduit for third-party interventions does not imply that governments are usually the recipients of third-party support. For instance, support for one side in the conflict can result from positive inducements to the supported side or negative sanctions to the opposing side. If we think about Singer's (1963) model of internation influence, threatening or punishing the opposition can be interpreted as intervening on behalf of the government, as can the rewards or promises made directly to the government. However, for reasons of efficiency, legitimacy, and stability, support for the government should lead to more successful outcomes.

And, finally, who intervenes is important. For example, the role of the status of the intervenor should be a critical factor in the likely outcome of any intervention attempt. This, again, can be seen most clearly in the effect of the large European countries and the United States in the post-Dayton intervention in Bosnia. Larger countries have a greater degree of latitude when it comes to organizing an intervention strategy. Major powers not only have larger and more projectable military forces but also a wider range of economic resources that can be brought to bear in a foreign policy role. A small country offering economic incentives or imposing sanctions should have a different effect on the calculations of the combatants than a similar intervention by the United States. Regardless of the side on which a major power intervenes, the effectiveness of that intervention strategy should be greater than that of a similar strategy by a nonmajor power. The ability to affect the cost-benefit calculations of combatants in an intrastate conflict must be a function, inter alia, of the resources that any potential intervenor can bring to bear.

From the preceding argument a number of hypotheses can be derived:

HYPOTHESIS 1

Interventions into civil conflicts will have a higher probability of success when they involve mixed strategies rather than single focused strategies.

When trying to influence the expected payoffs from continuing versus stopping the fighting, intervenors need to manipulate as many variables as possible. Furthermore the intervention must influence the subjective estimate of the likelihood of a positive expected payoff to both opposing groups in the conflict. Creating the expectation by the opposing sides of these positive payoffs should be advanced by pushing on both ends of the stick, so to speak. Mixed interventions can influence both the potential costs and benefits, and across a much broader spectrum, than either a military or economic intervention alone, and therefore should increase the probability that the intervention will be successful.

HYPOTHESIS 2

Interventions into civil conflicts will have a higher chance of success when targeted toward ethnic or religious, as opposed to ideological conflicts.

Even though ideological identity should be easier to shed than ethnicity, the prospects for counterinterventions by patrons for the opposing side increase the likelihood that an intervention will not contribute to a cessation of the fighting. The temporal aspects of a conflict should also influence the willingness of the combatants to agree to halt the fighting (either through defeat, capitulation, or cease-fire). Ideological conflicts generally do not have the option of postponing the fight until better conditions prevail, as do long-running ethnic or religious conflicts. The current strife in Bosnia, for instance, is often discussed in terms of repressed animosities successfully kept in check by the authority of the Tito regime. Religious conflicts, moreover, should be somewhat more amenable to outside interventions than ethnic conflicts because it is easier to shed religious identity than it is ethnic identity.

HYPOTHESIS 3

There will be a higher probability of success when the intervention supports the ruling coalition rather than opposition forces.

In general, efficiency is increased when the intervention supports the government, and even though a military intervention in support of the opposition may disproportionately increase the opposition's capabilities relative to the same policy in support of the government, this would probably not offset the effect of efficiency. Furthermore, a military intervention on behalf of opposition forces generally violates international laws and norms, restricting the scope of potential forms of support for the opposition. The government's subjective estimate of the likely effect of the intervention in support of the opposition will generally be low, decreasing the expected utility from stopping the violence.

HYPOTHESIS 4

The probability of a successful intervention decreases as the number of casualties increase.

When the sunk costs of a conflict are already high, an incremental increase in the cost of that conflict will have little effect on the veracity with which the groups contest. Likewise, benefits that might accrue from an intervention are marginalized when they have to overcome such extreme pressure to right the wrongs of the conflict by taking the struggle more aggressively to the opponent. Because both sides would have a similarly entrenched attitude, both of the antagonists' subjective estimate of the effect of an intervention on the adversary would be small.

As we have seen in the previous chapter, however, conflicts with a high number of casualties are more likely to attract outside parties, with the interventions driven largely by domestic political concerns. But the fact that countries are more likely to select themselves into these interventions does not make them more likely to succeed. What we have are situations where third parties are increasingly likely to intervene in conflicts in which they are increasingly likely to fail in their efforts, and strangely enough these conflicting preferences and outcomes make logical sense.

HYPOTHESIS 5

Interventions by major powers will tend to be more successful than the same intervention by a minor power.

This follows from the logic of trying to manipulate the costs and benefits of continued fighting. A major power not only has more resources (both military and economic) to bring to bear on the combatants, but also the combatants' subjective estimates of the effect on the opponent will also be higher than when a smaller country intervenes. Major powers generally have more political influence, greater projectable forces, and a larger array of economic incentives or punishments. Relative to a nonmajor power these added capabilities should influence the effectiveness of an intervention.

Research Design and Testing

The hypotheses just discussed have been subjected to empirical examination against the data described in chapter 2. While I will not reiterate the data concerns at this time, I will discuss the models used to test the hypotheses. I opened this chapter with a suggestion that not all interventions are created equal; as such, it may be useful—both theoretically and practically—to carry out this analysis in two steps. The first examines the conditions for successful interventions across the entire range of conflict intensity; the second separates out those cases that portend to pose particularly vexing problems for the decision-making community; namely, ones that rage at a rather high level of intensity. Intense civil conflicts differ from the more general case on a number of dimensions that suggest there is analytical and policy benefits to be gained from a more discriminating analysis. First, when the level of hostilities is high, the decision over intervention can take on the character of a crisis of a decision-making problem. The crisis can be a result of the domestic and international pressures to do something to stop the slaughter, but these pressures run counter to the perceived likelihood that any politically salient intervention will be effective. The time available for decisive action is short and policy advice is likely to be conflicting. Under these types of conditions policymakers need to know what works in this specific type of conflict, as opposed to a less violent variety. Second, because of the higher visibility of intense civil conflicts, the public is more concerned with the progression of the conflict and the outcome of any intervention policy (Blechman 1995; Kohut and Toth 1994). The media, accordingly, will follow these conflicts more closely, making the political costs associated with an intervention policy more immediately tangible. And, finally, because of the extreme conditions within intense civil conflicts, the risk associated with intervening are higher and the difficulty of tailoring an intervention to fit the conflict more difficult to implement. Obviously these factors are all interrelated and translate at some level into an increased risk of incurring unnecessarily high political costs for an attempted intervention. Under conditions of uncertainty, political leaders are more likely to do nothing when action is called for (Rwanda and Burundi are examples), or design a strategy for intervening that has a low probability of success because they do not have sufficient information from which to work. The ability to conceive of a successful policy *ex ante* appears to be somewhat limited, so when leaders do choose to intervene in these types of conflicts, knowing the best strategy would be highly beneficial.

Intense Civil Conflicts

Conceptually an intense intrastate conflict is one that results in a large number of casualties in a relatively short period of time (Small and Singer 1982), though there are other ways to think about the intensity of a conflict. For instance, a conflict within a geostrategically important country may be intense from a national security perspective, while one that threatens genocide against a particular ethnic group may be intense from a humanitarian orientation. For this analysis the intensity of the conflict was defined in terms of the number of casualties per year, with 10,000 casualties per year marking the operational cutoff between intense and nonintense conflicts. When people are dying in relatively large numbers, the conflict becomes increasingly visible outside the immediate geographic region and generates increasing pressure from nonstate interest groups. This has two immediate consequences. First, an intense conflict poses security concerns for geographically proximate countries. When the level of violence is high, neighboring countries must take note of the conflict and fear the potential threat to stability in their own country. Second, extreme levels of violence in intrastate conflicts tend to create widespread dislocations in the social infrastructure upon which large numbers of noncombatants depend. Movements of refugees, famines, and the proliferation of land mines are but just a few examples. This increased visibility puts pressure on other countries to do something. That "something" usually involves some form of intervention to help facilitate the end of hostilities.

Examples of some of the intrastate conflicts used in this analysis will illuminate the extent to which these cases capture public attention, threaten regional stability, and/or cause grave concern for issues of human rights and will set them apart analytically from the more general case of outside interventions in internal conflicts. In Somalia, between 1991 and 1994, deaths have averaged nearly 55,000 a year; over the five-year period this averages out to 4,500 deaths per month. Rwanda and Bosnia both top Somalia's monthly average by considerable amounts (Rwanda, 10,000/month; Bosnia, 7,500/month), with Rwanda averaging well over 100,000 deaths per year between 1990 and 1994, with a particularly spasmodic episode of interethnic slaughter in the early part of 1994. Zaire in the first half of the 1960s was also in the throes of an intense civil conflict, averaging more than 50,000 deaths per year. In each of these instances outside actors intervened in the conflict, though there are a number of intense conflicts in which no outside actors took part. The Rwandan conflict in 1965, Burundi 1988, and the original conflict over the breakup of Yugoslavia are examples of intense conflicts without outside interventions. While the 10,000 fatalities per year cutoff is somewhat arbitrary, it is relatively insensitive to changes in the threshold.[1]

Analytical Approach and Testing Procedures

In my empirical analysis I again employ a logistic regression estimator to evaluate the hypotheses articulated earlier. Then I use the results of that analysis to estimate the likelihood that a given strategy for intervening will be successful under a given set of conditions. The outlines of a logit regression and how it contributes to our understanding of the outcome of interventions deserves a brief reiteration. A logit regression allows the analyst to ask a question of the data that has a dichotomous answer, or outcome variable—in this case, whether an intervention was successful or not. Even though there are alternative ways to think about the outcome of interventions, by dichotomizing the outcome we reap the rewards of analytical parsimony and policy relevance. Let me explain why.

To adequately inform the decision-making community, social scientists have to pose questions in a manner consistent with that community. As I have argued, policymakers converse in a language more consistent with subjective estimates of the likely outcome of the proposed policy. A more traditional OLS regression procedure that would attempt to identify the effect of intervention policies over a range of potential outcomes is less efficient for a couple reasons. First, the outcomes from intervention policies that could be identified would be categorical and not placed on an interval scale as would be suggested by the notion of a spectrum of outcomes. Ordinary least squares estimations are not designed for these types of data. Furthermore, the interpretation of the results of the analysis are not only problematic methodologically but also confusing for the policy community. Interpreting OLS results involves some variation on the effect of a unit change in the explanatory variables on a unit change in the outcome variable. So, for instance, we might learn that moving from an ethnic to an ideological conflict (a one unit change in the explanatory variable) results in a .5 unit change along the range of outcomes. But a .5 unit change does not have a concrete meaning; there is no .5 outcome on a categorical scale. What is generally meant by such a statistical result is that varying the explanatory variables results in some movement along the string of artificially ordered nominal variables. How far along that spectrum? Well, that's the difficult part to interpret because the method is inconsistent with the data; therefore, scholars as well as policymakers lack a clear understanding of the

---

[1] For example, little changes in the makeup of the cases until the threshold is lowered to 6,000 fatalities per year. Lowering the threshold to 8,000/year picks up only three additional conflicts; 7,000 fatalities picks up three, two of which run concurrently in Nigeria. At 6,000 fatalities, a total of 13 new conflicts are added to the list.

marginal effects of certain policies, and the policy community has nothing concrete to grasp.

Equally important, however, is the inability of OLS estimations to speak in the language of the policy community. One of the reasons, I would contend, that the quantitative study of international relations has a relatively poor record vis-à-vis the economic discipline in their influence on policy is that the former group does not cultivate a policy audience. Economists, for example, can give an estimate of the effect of a rise in interest rates on the level of unemployment, and although they may be wrong as often as they are right, the policy community understands how to interpret their results (to a large degree economists work with data that permit a more intuitive interpretation). If the foreign policy community thinks and interacts in terms of subjective estimates of outcomes, then we increase our influence over this community by designing studies that convey information on terms similar to their deliberations. Dichotomizing the outcome of interventions allows us to carry out this task. What we lose in the initial analysis by the dichotomization can be recouped through more-nuanced discussions of specific incidents and a critical interpretation of the analysis. Given this background let me move to the results of the analysis.[2]

Results of the Analysis: The General Case

In this presentation of the results of the analysis I move from the general to the specific, reporting first on the success of third-party interventions in the entire sample of cases. This broad sample, you may recall, consists of 190 cases of interventions into 89 intrastate conflicts; the conflicts range from rather small events where fewer than 1,000 people were killed, to an upper bound where something approaching one million casualties resulted from the hostilities. Some of the less violent conflicts include the Sanyang coup in Gambia in 1981, the first Ogaden conflict in the early 1960s, and the Shaba crisis in Zaire in 1977. The more violent conflicts tend to roll off the tongue with greater clarity, such as the Congo crisis of 1960–1965, Uganda in the 1980s, Somalia in the early 1990s, and the Sudanese civil war begun in the early 1980s, all of which resulted in casualties counted in the hundreds of thousands. Following a discussion of the more general case, I disaggregate the sample along the lines of the intensity of the conflict.

Table 4.1 presents the results of two models linking the characteristics of the conflict and the strategy for intervening to the outcome of an intervention. Model 1 represents a simple additive model where the strategy for intervening consists of the independent effects of characteristics of the conflicts, the choice of target,

---

[2] For a technical discussion of logit regression, see Greene 1993, Hanushek and Jackson 1977, or Kennedy 1987.

and the instruments employed; Model 2 represents an interactive relationship between the two components of the intervenors' strategy, along with the characteristics of the conflict. Model 2 in this sense is a better representation of the implementation of an intervention strategy because it allows us to examine the effect of the instrument for intervening as it interacts with the chosen target, as opposed to two separate events. Decision makers often do not have the option of choosing the target—political imperatives determine who that will be—yet they need to know what works under the combination of alternatives presented to them. Initially what these coefficients tell us is the direction of the impact of each variable on the outcome of the intervention, where, for example, a negative coef-

TABLE 4.1. Results of Logit Regression on the Success or Failure of Intervention, General Category of Interventions, $N = 189$

Variable	Model 1	Model 2
Ethnic conflict	−.33	−.34
	(.67)	(.71)
Ideological conflict	−.47	−.37
	(.67)	(.70)
Mixed intervention	−.87*	
	(.50)	
Supporting government	1.35**	
	(.37)	
Casualties	-1.71×10^{-6}	-2.28×10^{-6}
	(1.67×10^{-6})	(1.78×10^{-6})
Major power	1.09**	1.31**
	(.41)	(.43)
Mixed support for government		.38
		(.57)
Mixed support for opposition		.94
		(.83)
Military support for government		1.96**
		(.45)
Economic support for opposition		.69
		(.93)
Constant	−1.51**	−1.96**
	(.69)	(.77)

Model 1:	Model 2:
Log likelihood = 100.52	Log likelihood = −96.21
Chi square = 25.11, 6 degrees of freedom, $p < .000$	Chi square = 33.72, 8 degrees of freedom, $p < .000$

*$p < .10$; **$p < .05$; numbers in ( ) are standard errors.

ficient means that that variable is associated with a decline in the probability of a successful outcome. Furthermore, each of the various indicators are captured with a series of dummy variables—with the exception of casualties—so that the intuitive interpretation is judged relative to the omitted variable in the model. For example, in both Models 1 and 2 ethnic and ideological conflicts are included in the model, but religious conflicts are left out. Therefore, the interpretation of the coefficient associated with the ethnic and ideological variables is judged relative to the likelihood of a successful intervention in a religious conflict. A negative coefficient suggests that interventions are less likely to be successful than in a religious conflict under similar conditions. In tables 4.2 and 4.3, I transform these coefficients into estimates of the probability of a successful outcome—a much easier metric to interpret.

Models 1 and 2 tell us something about the conditions or strategies for successful interventions in the general category of intrastate conflict. In Model 1, supporting the government appears to lead to a greater likelihood of success than support for the opposition, and we can reasonably expect that relationship to hold; likewise, there is support for the notion that major powers in general are more successful than nonmajor powers. The degree of statistical confidence in the remaining variables is weak, leading to caution regarding any inferences that might be drawn. Model 2—an interactive model capturing the strategy for intervention—is stronger than Model 1, though still not terribly robust. Major powers, again, are considerably more likely to be able to stop the fighting than nonmajor powers; military support for the government is considerably more likely to halt the fighting than military support for the opposition. In neither of these models, however, does there appear to be any evidence that the type of the conflict matters much in influencing the likely outcome of the intervention. Initially this would seem to run counter to the major premise of the work of Kaufmann (1996).

In general, what do we learn from these models and where can we take it? Tables 4.2 and 4.3 help in this regard, though we need to be cautious at this juncture in our interpretation because of our inability to confidently judge the "true" relationships as reflected in some of the weak support from tests of statistical robustness. Given these caveats, the transformation of the coefficients into probabilistic estimates of a successful outcome can point in some useful directions. One way to make use of the ability to transform logit coefficients into probability estimates is to judge the effect of the variables against some hypothetical case. We can then ask what the effect is of moving from the hypothetical conditions to some other condition, just as we did in chapter 3. In table 4.2, for instance, the probability of a change from failure to success is displayed for a given change in a specific explanatory variable from the base, using the results from Model 1. The hypothetical base used for comparative purposes is a conflict in which (1) the conflict is oriented around religious divisions, (2) the number of casualties were toward the low end of the spectrum, (3) the intervention is by a nonmajor power, and (4) the intervention was a military intervention in support of the opposition. This hypothetical conflict, furthermore, is not totally hypothetical in that it is consistent with the conflict in Northern Ireland and Libya's support for the IRA, as well as the conflict in Lebanon, 1988–1990, with Israel's support for the opposition. According to both models, the probability of observing a successful intervention under these "hypothetical" conditions is at best 18 percent. The results of the analysis in Model 1 suggest, therefore, that if you had the same intervention

TABLE 4.2. Individual Effects of Changing Conditions for Intervention on the Probability of Success, Model 1, General Category

Base	Probability of Success (%)	Change in Probability of Success (%)
Religious conflict		
Military intervention		
Support opposition		
1,000 casualties		
Nonmajor power	18	
From: Base		
To: Ethnic conflict	13	−5
From: Base		
To: Ideological conflict	12	−6
From: Base		
To: Mixed intervention	8*	−10
From: Base		
To: Economic intervention	18	nil
From: Base		
To: Support government	46**	+28
From: Base		
To: Major power intervention	39**	+21
From: Base		
To: 990,000 casualties	3	−15

*p < .10; **p < .05.

into a low-casualty ideological, rather than religious, conflict, the probability of a successful outcome would be just 12 percent, a decline of 6 percent in the likelihood of stopping the fighting. Likewise, moving from the base conditions to an intervention on behalf of the government increases the probability of stopping

TABLE 4.3. Individual Effects of Changing Conditions for Intervention on the Probability of Success, Model 2, General Category

Base	Probability of Success (%)	Change in Probability of Success (%)
Religious conflict		
Military intervention		
Support opposition		
1,000 casualties		
Nonmajor power	12	
From: Base		
To: Ethnic conflict	9	−3
From: Base		
To: Ideological conflict	8	−4
From: Base		
To: Mixed intervention, support opposition	26	+14
From: Base		
To: Mixed intervention, support government	17	+5
From: Base		
To: Military intervention, support government	49**	37
From: Base		
To: Economic intervention, support opposition	22	+10
From: Base		
To: Major power intervention	34**	+22
From: Base		
To: 990,000 casualties	1	−11

**$p < .05$.

the fighting by 28 percent (to 46%) over the same policy supporting the opposition. Major power interventions are also more likely to succeed under similar conditions.

Going back to the hypothetical case, one critique of the results might be that the real-life analogies did not have stopping the fighting as the goal of the interventions. In a sense, however, they did. Libya's preferred outcome was that the IRA would be successful at compelling British withdrawal from Northern Ireland. In part the results of my analysis would suggest that Libya could have increased the likelihood of their intervention succeeding by supporting the British government rather than the IRA. This is a nonsensical conclusion, because for political reasons Libya did not have such a choice. In other conflicts there does seem to be a choice of which side to support. France's reluctant intervention in the carnage of Rwanda in 1994 could have sided with either the Tutsi minority or the Hutu-led government at the time. To many observers it appeared that France was coming to the aid of its traditional ally, the Hutus, even though the Tutsi eventually prevailed in the conflict (Adelman and Suhrke 1996). As it stands. the French creation of a "save haven" for the fleeing Hutus did contribute to the end of the fighting, at least for the short term. What this highlights, however, is the need to examine the interactive effects of potential intervention strategies.

Using the interactive model, Model 2, we get a broader range of results with a more-nuanced interpretation of the effect of various strategies of intervention on the outcome of the effort. For example, from Model 1 (table 4.2) we know that supporting the government increases the probability of success over a similar policy in support of the opposition, as does an intervention by a major power over that of a nonmajor intervenor. All of the other variations in the model lead to reductions in the probability of success over that obtained from the base situation. However, from Model 2 (table 4.3) we see that a number of strategies for intervening are actually better than a military intervention in support of the opposition. As with Model 1, supporting the government is generally more successful than supporting the opposition. A mixed intervention is more likely to be successful than the base conditions (in support of the government, 17%), even if the mixed intervention is in support of the opposition (26%). Economic support for the opposition increases the likelihood of success by 10 percent over military support for the same group. Keeping in mind that economic support for the opposition can be a result of economic sanctions placed on the government, it suggests that sanctions might be an effective tool for conflict resolution.

A few interesting results come out of this component of the analysis, some reasonably intuitive, some not. First, regardless of which model is chosen, varying the type of the conflict seems to matter little in the change in the likelihood of a successful intervention. Moving from a religious to an ideological conflict has the largest swing in the probability of success, declining 6 percent in Model 1 and 4 percent in Model 2, but in neither case do we have sufficient statistical confidence in the strength of the identified relationship. Ethnic and religious conflicts seem to have about the same probability of success, all things being equal, and the level of statistical significance is such that we cannot tell these two types of conflicts apart anyway—at least in terms of the probability of an intervention stopping the fighting. Second, high-casualty conflicts are considerably more difficult to control than the low-casualty variety. In Model 1 the probability of success drops by 15 percent when moving from a conflict with 1,000 fatalities to one having nearly a million. In Model 2 the observed likelihood of success declines from 12 percent to 1 percent. Again, the caveat must be made at this juncture that our level of statistical confidence in some of these relationships is weak and inferences must be made accordingly, though this does not totally deflect our ability to draw inferences.

The low statistical confidence does not mean that the identified relationship is necessarily incorrect but suggests that as the level of confidence declines it becomes increasingly difficult to distinguish between the null model, of no systematic relationship, and the one identified in the analysis. For example, as the standard error (identified in tables 4.1 and 4.4) increases relative to the size of the coefficients, the probability that the coefficient is a result of a random process increases. Therefore, we have a difficult time determining whether the coefficient reflects a systematic relationship or a random event. The standard level of acceptance of the statistical significance of a coefficient is when the chance of the coefficient reflecting a random process is less than 1 in 20 (in general, the coefficient divided by the standard error is about 2.00—the T statistic). In Model 2, for example, the coefficient associated with the increase in the number of casualties is significant at the .20 level, meaning that there is a 1 in 5 chance that the identified coefficient is a result of chance alone. However, you can calculate the probability that the relationship operates in the direction identified by the sign of the coefficient *and* is different from zero by using a one-tailed test of significance. If we have enough confidence in this directional relationship, then we can be reasonably certain that the effect is in the direction identified, though the magnitude of that effect is in question. In the case of high-casualty conflicts, for instance, the degree of confidence that we have that the coefficient is negative and nonzero in Model 1 is about 85 percent and in Model 2, 90 percent. This suggests that with an 85 to 90 percent certainty, interventions into high-casualty conflicts are less likely to be successful than the same intervention into a low-casualty conflict. This may not meet conventional norms for judging the usefulness of identified empirical relationships, but it gives us considerably more information to operate under than simply arguing that the strength of the relationship is uncertain.[3] Furthermore, given the crosscurrents by which the role of casualties seem to operate—on the one hand

---

[3] The calculation for the one-tailed test is Prob $\beta > \beta_0 = Z = \beta - \beta_0 / \sigma\beta$.

increasing the pressures to intervene, and then subsequently decreasing the likelihood that the intervention will be successful—it suggests that policymakers face difficult choices in the more violent and visible conflicts.

The Intense Case

For the intense conflicts I apply the models used in the general case to the more narrowly defined group of conflicts already discussed. Table 4.4 displays the results of the statistical analysis. From the coefficients in both models, for instance, we can see that a religious conflict has a greater probability of success than either an

TABLE 4.4. Results of Logit Regression on the Success or Failure of Intervention, Intense Category of Interventions, $N = 57$

Variable	Model 1	Model 2
Ethnic conflict	−1.28	−1.27
	(1.15)	(1.17)
Ideological conflict	−2.06*	−2.08*
	(1.13)	(1.20)
Mixed intervention	1.03	
	(.82)	
Supporting government	.55	
	(.66)	
Casualties	-6.32×10^{-6}**	-6.37×10^{-6}**
	(2.82×10^{-6})	(2.82×10^{-6})
Major power	1.12	1.10
	(.76)	(.76)
Mixed support of government		1.71*
		(1.02)
Mixed support of opposition		1.07
		(1.05)
Military support of government		.45
		(.84)
Constant	.88	.93
	(1.24)	(1.38)

Model 1:	Model 2:
Log likelihood = −29.76	Log likelihood = −29.53
Chi square = 15.50, 6 degrees of freedom, $p < .01$	Chi square = 15.96, 7 degrees of freedom, $p < .02$

Note: *There were no instances of purely economic interventions in intense conflicts; economic instruments were therefore left out of the analysis.*
*$p < .10$; **$p < .05$; numbers in ( ) are standard errors.*

ethnic or an ideological conflict, though given a level of statistical significance that is below the convention of .05 for ethnic conflicts, we need to be cautious about the inferences we draw. The number of casualties also seems to make a considerable difference in the outcome of the intervention, where moving from a low- (relatively speaking) casualty conflict to a high-casualty conflict decreases the prospects for a successful intervention, and here we have a high degree of statistical confidence in this result. These results also suggest that supporting the government is better than supporting the opposition, and that as the type of intervention moves from a military to a mixed strategy, the likelihood of success increases. The presentations in tables 4.5 and 4.6 give a more intuitive view of the effects of these variables on the outcome of intervention attempts. In table 4.5,

TABLE 4.5. Individual Effects of Changing Conditions for Intervention on the Probability of Success, Model 1, Intense Category

Base	Probability of Success (%)	Change in Probability of Success (%)
Religious conflict		
Military intervention		
Support opposition		
10,000 casualties		
Nonmajor power	69	
From: Base		
To: Ethnic conflict	38	−31
From: Base		
To: Ideological conflict	22*	−47
From: Base		
To: Mixed intervention	86	+17
From: Base		
To: Support government	79	+10
From: Base		
To: Major power intervention	87	+18
From: Base		
To: 990,000 casualties	1**	−69

*p < .10; **p < .05.

for instance, the probability of a change from failure to success is displayed for a given change in a specific explanatory variable from the base. The hypothetical base used for comparative purposes is a conflict that is oriented around religious divisions, in which there have been 10,000 casualties, and that has had a military intervention by a nonmajor power in support of the opposition; the estimated probability of success of this intervention is 69 percent.

TABLE 4.6. Individual Effects of Changing Conditions for Intervention
on the Probability of Success, Model 2, Intense Category

Base	Probability of Success (%)	Change in Probability of Success (%)
Religious conflict		
Military intervention		
Support opposition		
10,000 casualties		
Nonmajor power	70	
From: Base		
To: Ethnic conflict	40	−30
From: Base		
To: Ideological conflict	22*	−48
From: Base		
To: Mixed intervention, support opposition	87	+17
From: Base		
To: Mixed intervention, support government	92	+22
From: Base		
To: Military intervention, support government	79	+9
From: Base		
To: Major power intervention	87	+17
From: Base		
To: 990,000 casualties	>1**	−70

*p < .10; **p < .05.

This hypothetical case, again, is not entirely hypothetical in that it is consistent with a number of actual interventions, such as Libya's support for the opposition in the Sudanese civil war in 1983 and Syrian intervention into the Lebanese civil war, 1975–1988. Table 4.5 suggests that given the same conditions but having the intervention take place in an ideological conflict, for example, there would be a decrease in the probability of a successful intervention of 47 percent. A military intervention in support of the opposition in an ideological conflict of this intensity has only a 22 percent chance of success, given historical patterns. So supporting an insurgency with the goal of bringing the government to the negotiating table—or overthrowing it—is a policy with a slim chance of success. On the other hand, moving away from a sole reliance on military instruments to include economic tools increases the probability of success under base conditions from 69 percent to 86 percent, a 17 percent increase in the likelihood of success. The practical interpretation is that if you are going to support the opposition in a religious struggle, perhaps coupling military support with economic sanctions on the government is a much better strategy than just the military component alone. Furthermore, going from a conflict with 10,000 casualties to one approaching a million casualties virtually eliminates any hope of a successful outcome to the intervention.

Unfortunately in the real world, decision makers cannot hold "all else constant." When evaluating options for designing a strategy of intervention, they can vary both the form of the intervention and its target. The estimation of Model 2 allows us to clarify somewhat the effect of varying the strategies for intervention when holding the characteristics of the conflict constant, more in line with the options faced by decision makers. Table 4.6 presents the results of the calculations of the probability of success derived from the interactive model, Model 2. The effect of the interactive model on the relationship between the characteristics of the conflict and successful outcomes is marginal. The probability at the base is slightly higher, and the effect of varying the type of conflict is imperceptible. Overall, however, the marginal effect of changes in the strategy for intervening do have a significantly different substantive interpretation from Model 2 than the results of Model 1. For instance, table 4.6 suggests that any strategy for intervention stands a greater chance of success than a military intervention in support of opposition forces, all things of course being equal. These increased probabilities of success range from 9 percent (military support for the government) to 22 percent (mixed support for the government). Furthermore, regardless of the target of the intervention, a mixed strategy has a considerably better chance of success than an intervention relying solely on military means. Through further calculations it can be shown that even the best strategy for intervening (mixed in support of the government) has a near-zero chance of success when the number of casualties approaches one million. The best strategy in an ideological conflict—mixed in support of the government—furthermore, has only a 40 percent chance of success, even when the number of casualties is at the low end of the spectrum. This compares with an 85 percent chance of a similar intervention policy being successful in religious conflicts. In both Models 1 and 2 a major power intervening has a considerably higher chance of bringing the fighting to an end than does a nonmajor power adopting the same strategy, though in neither case is the relationship statistically robust.

Discussion

The results of this component of the research project can be evaluated in two ways. The first is in light of the hypotheses laid out in the earlier part of this chapter, which will contribute to our understanding of conflict processes and conflict resolution. The second is in terms of what it tells the policy community grappling with the tricky questions of where and how to intervene. These two realms of understanding are of course intertwined, though to some degree they demand a slightly different focus in terms of inferences and interpretations. Both will get their hearing in this section.

Before focusing on the specific results of the hypotheses outlined earlier, some broad observations about the differences between the intense and the general cases should be explored. These differences can be quite extreme and lead to inferences that are revealing. First, the probability of success at the base conditions—to some degree the easiest case—is much greater in the intense conflicts than in the general category. For example, an intervention in an intense conflict at the base conditions has a 69 percent chance of success, yet the same intervention evaluated across the broader sample of cases has only an 18 percent probability of success. Second, the combatants' identity characteristics play a significantly greater role in determining the success of an intervention in the intense conflicts. Third, the role of a mixed intervention is much clearer in the intense conflict than in the broader population of cases. Support for the government and the power status of the intervenor have virtually the same impact across the intensity divide, and in each instance the effect of high-casualty conflicts is to reduce the probability of success to near zero, though the change in probability of success in the intense conflict is considerably more dramatic.

The different probabilities of a successful intervention at the base line between the intense and general categories serves as a useful point of comparison—and is quite remarkable in its range. This 50 percent increase in the likelihood of observing a successful intervention when the minimum threshold for the intensity is raised to 10,000 casualties per year suggests that something significant happens when the level of slaughter is extreme. The 10,000 fatality threshold requires that, on average, the conflict results in about 850 casualties per month over the course of a year and sustains this for the length of the conflict. Given that at the peak of the U.S. involvement in the Vietnam War (January through May 1968) the United States was taking casualties at a rate just twice of this figure, averaging 10,000 fatalities per year reflects a considerably hostile conflict (see Gartner and Segura 1998 for data). Interestingly enough, these are also the types of conflicts where decision makers have the most difficulty in conceiving of implementing a successful policy; that is, there is a marked decrease in the probability of observing an intervention in the first place (see chapter 3). So what is going on that leads to the most difficult cases being the most tractable and responsive to outside interventions?

We might think about this in two ways. The first is that the intensity of a conflict is difficult to sustain, and many of the interventions are of sufficient magnitude to affect the course of the conflict. In essence the intervenors do not go into the conflict lightly, and they display considerable resolve. Because the combatants cannot sustain the level of intensity, the outside intervention acts as the catalyst that helps bring the fighting to a halt—even if only temporarily. The second way to think about the effectiveness of interventions in these intense conflicts is that they are more likely to reach the hurting stalemate that some see as a necessary condition for resolution, and that the role of the intervention serves to rapidly shift the phase of the conflict (Kriesberg 1992) and contributes to the ripeness for resolution (Haass 1990).

Based on the reasoning behind an intervention that I articulated previously, where the intervenor is trying to influence the cost-benefit calculations and the expectations of the combatants, five hypotheses were specified. On the whole there is considerable support for the arguments that were put forth, though exceptions are notable and need to be explained. The results, furthermore, are considerably stronger for the more narrowly defined intense conflict than for the general case. For example, reflecting on hypothesis 4, which is possibly the easiest hypothesis to deal with, regardless of the definition of the cases or the model used to test the proposition, high-casualty conflicts have a lower probability of successful interventions than conflicts without the extreme killing. This is a reasonably intuitive result. In the intense category of cases, the upper limit for conflict casualties (990,000) has a near nil chance of a third party intervening and successfully stopping the carnage under a fixed set of conditions; a high-casualty conflict in the general category of cases still results in the lowest probability of a successful intervention. As we will see shortly, even under the best of conditions high-casualty conflicts do not lend themselves to outside interventions if the goal is to stop the fighting.

Overall, mixed strategies for intervening tend to be more successful than any single focused efforts—supporting hypothesis 1—though this is not universal across all specifications. In the intense category of cases, a mixed intervention always has a higher probability of a successful outcome than a sole reliance on military instruments. The minimum increase in the likelihood of observing a successful outcome when employing a mixed strategy is 22 percent over a purely military intervention. In the general category of cases, a mixed intervention has a mixed relationship to successful outcomes. In the additive model, Model 1, a mixed intervention is slightly less likely to be successful than a military effort, while in the interactive model, Model 2, the results get slightly more complex. A mixed strategy is always better than the base conditions—military support for the opposition—but a mixed strategy does not always get to the highest probability of success. It seems that the interaction between the instruments for intervening and the target has a discernible effect on the likely outcome. Military support for the government, for instance, has the highest probability of success, followed by a mixed intervention in support of the opposition. The evaluation of hypothesis 1, therefore, must look something like qualified support.

There is overwhelming support for the notion that ideological conflicts are less amenable to outside interventions (hypothesis 2), though under the general model our confidence in the strength of that relationship is weaker than we would like. This evidence would seem to counter the well-regarded speculations of Kaufmann (1996), who suggested that intense ethnic conflicts would be least susceptible to outside interventions. Likewise, major power interventions seem to have a higher probability of success than the same intervention by a nonmajor power. Support for the government tends to be more successful than supporting the opposition, though again, in the interactive models we see that this conclusion must be qualified based on the method of intervening. Given the framing of the outcome in terms of successfully stopping the fighting for a minimum of six months, the results seem reasonably well in tune with the theoretical logic that posits that interventions attempt to alter the perceptions and calculations of the respective antagonists. To stop the fighting, both sides must hold reasonable expectations that the intervention will lead the opposing side to calculate that an end to the fighting is in its interest; it is the intervenor's job to determine the policies that will have the greatest impact on the deliberations of the combatants. But what does all this contribute to the decision-making process unfolding in the secluded corridors of the White House, the Palace, or the Ministry of Foreign Affairs?

Policy-Relevant Implications

When designing strategies for intervening into civil conflicts, decision makers face hurdles associated with uncertainty—uncertainty over what works under which types of conditions. Most prescriptive analyses rely on a relatively small number of "similar" cases from which to draw analogies for future policies (Dorman and

Otte 1995; Kanter and Brooks 1994; and Neustadt and May 1986 for the operative logic). We know, however, from the relative frequency with which intervention policies fail that the analogical method by itself has severe shortcomings, shortcomings that could be mitigated by attention to trends developed over a large number of cases and a considerable length of time. At the end of the day the results of this analysis should be judged by what they tell us about the decision to intervene in intrastate conflicts, particularly those conflicts that often create the most difficult decisions for policymakers. A few points stand out that should give cause for decision makers to pay attention to the trends identified. A word of prudence to the policymaker is appropriate.

Just as a good argument can be made that a sole reliance on the most analogous case can be a prescription for disaster, so too can one be made about the sole reliance on statistical trends. The relationships between strategies for intervening and subsequent outcomes should be considered as a blueprint from which to begin the decision-making process rather than the Rosetta stone that might dictate the policy of choice. Even if used in broad brush strokes to identify those strategies and conditions under which interventions are highly likely to fail, this analysis could make a substantial contribution to the deliberative process. I would suggest, however, that this analysis be used in conjunction with good solid political reasoning, the incorporation of ethical considerations, and an understanding of the history and context into which the intervention is being considered. Used in this manner, "successful" policies would more likely be the norm.

With this in mind, the results point to a number of policy considerations. First, the difference in strength and direction of the results across the categories of cases would suggest that at minimum the intervention process plays out differently across some threshold of intensity, and that in designing policies this characteristic of the conflict should be factored into the evaluation of alternatives. Second, and more important, when the conflict involves large numbers of fatalities, such as those in Bosnia, Somalia, and Rwanda, characteristics of the conflict itself can play a substantial role in determining the outcome of the intervention attempt. Decision makers should pay attention to who is fighting and how bloody the conflict has been as they consider alternatives. This prescription might simply be a confirmation of what intuition tells us, but as we saw in chapter 3 certain aspects of these particularly bloody conflicts push toward interventions on humanitarian grounds. The general reluctance of any state to intervene in Rwanda in April 1994 reflects this notion that the perception that success is difficult to achieve when the level of hostility is extremely high. In general, ethnic or religious conflicts are more amenable to outside interventions than are ideological conflicts, and it is easier to stop the fighting when the total number of fatalities is at the low end of the spectrum—even though that low end may already constitute a large number of casualties. If the number of fatalities reaches upwards of a million, the chances of using military or economic instruments to bring a halt to the fighting are minisculely low, leading to the conclusion that any proposed intervention might best be tabled if something akin to stopping the fighting is the objective.

Although it is most often politics that drives decisions to intervene in ideological conflicts, using the results of Model 2 in the general case we can determine that there is a 71 percent chance of successfully bringing the fighting to an end if the intervention is carried out by a major power, is a military intervention supporting the government, and the number of casualties are low. Under the worst conditions, interventions into ideological conflicts are almost certain to be failures (high casualties, minor power, and military intervention supporting the opposition), having only a 1 percent chance of success. This poor record in these types of conflicts could be tied to two factors: (1) the intractability of the issues at stake in ideological conflicts, and (2) the frequency with which interventions in ideological conflicts lead to counterinterventions by the intervenors' ideological foe. Although the tendency for interventions to exacerbate ideological conflicts cannot be clearly discerned at this juncture, some evidence supports this interpretation (chapter 2).

If a state chooses to intervene in an ideological conflict that is quite violent, it should do so knowing that the chances of either propelling one side to victory or compelling one or both sides to cease fire and come to the bargaining table are rather small. Intervening under these conditions, therefore, is more likely to exacerbate than settle the conflict. During the cold war there are numerous examples of interventions in ideological conflicts that seemed to at best fan the flames of the struggle. In Nicaragua and El Salvador these difficulties are most evident. The Nicaraguan war was supported by both the United States and the Soviet Union, with Americans arming and funding the contra movement trying to overthrow the Sandinista government, which was supplied with weapons and money by the Soviets. Both sides were sufficiently supported to ensure a military stalemate, but the political demands were nothing short of dissolution of the opponent. The conflict continued because political compromise was unacceptable and military victory was unachievable. It took the cooling of the cold war to allow for a relaxation of patron support and the eventual development of political alternatives.

Tentative answers to the puzzling questions faced by decision makers as to how to intervene, and on behalf of whom, can be found in this analysis. In general, a mixed strategy is most often the more successful method of intervening, but this is tempered somewhat by the target of choice. It would seem from the evidence that overall support for the government is the best bet. What is unclear from this analysis—but clearly should be a topic for future research—is the relative effect of different mixes of "carrots and sticks."

The policy implications of this work are also immediate and can be applied to contemporary situations. For example, the Bosnian conflict has figured prominently in global affairs for the past few years, with substantial efforts to control the fighting undertaken by various individual states and multilateral organizations. Up until the interventions that evolved from the Dayton Peace Accords, all of these previous attempts to bring a halt to the fighting were largely unsuccessful. The results of this analysis point to some of the reasons why. First, the number of casualties was substantial—by some estimates upwards of a quarter of a million—which greatly diminished the likelihood of a successful outcome. Second, for the most part the interventions relied primarily on military means. Food aid was provided to the civilian populations, where possible, but this was more an attempt to minimize the trauma of the war than to alter the calculations of the combatants, and therefore not targeted at authority structures. And, finally, most interventions were decidedly neutral, so as to not appear to be siding with the positions of any of the combatants. The tide really changed in the war when NATO sanctioned the use of military strikes against Bosnian-Serb positions in response to the shelling of Sarajevo. The United States was largely responsible for carrying out the retaliatory strikes, and the practical effect was to stop the shelling of the city and increase the tempo of attempts to negotiate a settlement.

At the time of this writing the outcome of the post-Dayton intervention into Bosnia was still in limbo, yet the results of this study give reason to be optimistic about the effort to bring stability to the region. The intervention itself was composed of nearly 60,000 troops deployed in such a way as to separate the warring factions. And although on the surface the NATO troops attempted to be neutral, the initial phase of the intervention appeared much more heavily weighted against the Bosnian-Serbs. The overwhelming military capability of the troop deployment by NATO[4] may have been sufficient to blunt the fighting, but as it was, the military component of the intervention was coupled with a substantial redevelopment package amounting to tens of millions of dollars. Given the conditions of the conflict and the mixed intervention strategy largely favoring the Bosnian government, my analysis predicts a 77 percent probability of successfully halting the fighting. The large number of casualties works against a successful outcome, but the combination of military force and economic redevelopment aid substantially increases the chance of success over previous policies. Had the economic redevelopment money not been part of the intervention package, my analysis suggests that the probability of success would be reduced by 8 percent. As it stands today (1999) the fighting in Bosnia has largely stopped, and what exists is a divided society occupied by a large number of outside soldiers. The political and social rebuilding remains fragile, but the necessary first step of a halt to the fighting has been achieved. Talk of outside interventions into the neighboring conflict in Kosovo began in late 1998 but

---

[4] There are troops from non-NATO countries—for example, Russia has more than 1,000 troops deployed—but NATO countries contributed the bulk of these forces.

never materialized until mid-1999. Led by the United States and Britain, NATO intervened militarily in support of the Albanian opposition's struggle against the Serbs. Initially the bombing, coupled with a large occupation force, appears to have halted the fighting, though by September 1999 it is still too early to tell if the intervention is sufficient to effectively stop the fighting for six months. If it does it will have beaten the odds as determined by the results in table 4.3.

Overall, the theoretical framework in combination with the empirical analysis can be quite compelling. There does appear to be consistent empirical trends across a large number of cases that can be used to guide the policy process. These trends suggest that both the characteristics of the conflict and the design of the intervention strategy influence the outcome of the policy—at least if the intervention is carried out unilaterally and the assumed goal is to bring a halt to the fighting. These two limiting criteria, however, do not always hold. Since the end of the cold war the world has witnessed an increasing reliance on collective efforts to intervene between the combatants in internal conflicts. At times the expressed goal of these collective interventions is to stop the fighting, but just as often the goals are broadened to include a more comprehensive settlement of the dispute (Damrosch 1993). The following chapter will attempt to expand the conceptual domain by which we can understand multilateral interventions into civil conflicts and begin to take up the challenge of articulating the conditions for interventions in this post–cold war environment.

FIVE

The Effectiveness
of Multilateral Interventions

If unilateral interventions have dominated the international landscape throughout the cold war, then multilateral interventions seem to be more salient in the current political environment. An understanding of the role and success of outside interventions in internal conflicts would be incomplete without a systematic discussion of how the two forms of intervention differ and the conditions under which multilateral efforts may be more (or less) effective than their unilateral counterpart. For analytical purposes, two assumptions were adopted for the previous chapters: (1) that the interventions were unilateral, and (2) that the goal of these interventions is to stop the fighting associated with the civil conflict. Neither assumption holds under all conditions.

A cursory reading of contemporary international events suggests that the assumption of unilateral action is somewhat limiting, at least when focusing on the post–cold war era. Furthermore, many of the multilateral interventions adopt a more diverse range of initiatives. This is a result of the shifting goals of an intervention from stopping the fighting to supporting the outcome of negotiated settlements. In this chapter I relax the two earlier assumptions and in doing so refocus some of the conceptual issues, examine the role played by multilateral interventions, and consider a broader range of intervention options and their attendant consequences.

A definition of a multilateral intervention is in order. There are a number of cases where multiple states intervene on behalf of one side in an intrastate conflict with the goal of bolstering the capabilities of their client. The Greek civil war is an example of a collective effort by the "West" to help the Greek government defeat the communist insurgency. These types of cases do not fall under the rubric of what I here call multilateral interventions. By multilateral interventions I refer to those interventions that are under the leadership of an international command structure and are composed of more than a few national participants. Moreover, these interventions entail the active placement of personnel on the ground in the conflictual country, but they are not involved in the supply—or resupply—of the weapons of war. Personnel can be involved in the provision of humanitarian relief, infrastructural redevelopment, political oversight, and cease-fire monitoring, to name a few of the tasks. Troops that are associated with the intervention generally do not engage in partisan combat but rather attempt to play a neutral role in preventing the outbreak or spread of fighting.

The transition from unilateral to multilateral interventions is evident across a broad spectrum of cases. Since the end of the cold war at least 22 intrastate conflicts had begun, considerably dwarfing the 10 whose settlement seemed to coincide with the end of the cold war. Forty-five percent of those conflicts begun after 1990 have had at least one unilateral intervention—and about half of those having only one—and 45 percent of them have had multilateral interventions under the auspices of the UN. Operations by the UN were initiated in Georgia, Somalia, Iraq, Bosnia, Takjistan, Liberia, Yugoslavia, Rwanda (twice), and Angola. Between 1947 and 1990 there were a total of 12 UN peacekeeping interventions and all but two—the Dominican Republic, 1965, and the Congo, 1960—were related to interstate conflicts. The fivefold increase in the number of UN interventions does reflect a substantial shift in the propensity toward multilateral over unilateral interventions in the post–cold war period.

At first blush one might conclude that the main difference between multilateral and unilateral interventions lies in the number of intervenors and the extent to which they coordinate their actions. This, however, would be too perfunctory and neglect some of the more critical characteristics of multilateral interventions. More important, what would be missed would be the ability to determine when one type of intervention is a more viable option than the other. Discriminating between the two types of interventions will be the point of departure for the current section. It seems safe to assume that states participate in collective interventions in order to advance the prospects of regional stability. This assumption is consistent with that of the earlier chapters, though the conditions that lead to instability are quite different from those extant when unilateral interventions are more common.

The Cambodian Conflict Pre- and Post-Paris Accords

To clarify the importance of the effect of changing conditions on the prospects for multilateral versus unilateral interventions, let me start with a brief description of the conflict in Cambodia. There are at least two distinct phases to the Cambodian conflict in which outside parties intervened; the first was from 1975 to 1991, the second was during the post-1991 period.[1] These two phases clearly bridge the pre/post–cold war climate.

When the Khmer Rouge came to power in 1975, the Cambodian society was plunged into a period of immense social upheaval. Estimates of the number of deaths resulting from the purges, forced migrations, and "reeducation camps" run upwards of a million. The Vietnamese intervened to oust the Pol Pot regime and install a "stable" government in its place. The exterminations carried out by the Khmer Rouge ended, but stability was not the final result. The Chinese were the historical enemy of the Vietnamese, and so for apparent geopolitical reasons they began supporting the Khmer Rouge in their struggle to regain control of the Cambodian state. Thailand, the Soviets, and Laos all intervened with either military or economic aid in support of their respective ally. For over a decade the internal Cambodian conflict continued with four factions competing for control. Three of the groups formed a coalition government in exile: the Khmer Rouge, the party of Prince Sihanouk, and the followers of the former prime minister, Son Sann. The Khmer Rouge received Chinese aid, the Vietnamese were aided by the Soviets, and the countries in the Association of Southeast Asian Nations (ASEAN)— most notably Thailand and Laos—channeled aid to the other members of the coalition. None of the aid programs to the various groups appeared designed to contribute directly to the resolution of the issues at stake, but rather to offset the efforts of the opponent and alter the battlefield equilibrium. A military stalemate, possibly leading to negotiations, was the most likely outcome.

Mikhail Gorbachev's rise to power in the Soviet Union ushered in many changes, not the least of which involved the climate of conflict in Cambodia. East-West détente coincided with a similar easing of the Sino-Soviet relationship, which ultimately contributed to Soviet pressures on the Vietnamese to withdraw from Cambodia. Between the loss of patron support, diplomatic efforts of the ASEAN countries to broker a peace accord, and a more accommodating international environment, the Vietnamese withdrew all combat forces from Cambodia by September 1989. The Paris negotiations had achieved the general framework for a peace accord, with a final agreement signed in October 1991.

Under the terms of the agreement, the UN organized a force made up of civilian and military personnel to implement and observe an election, to help remove the myriad land mines littering the countryside, and to facilitate the redesign, repair, and reoutfitting of the infrastructure. These objectives are intricately linked to the prospects that the fragile peace accord will endure. Without some form of

---

[1] Obviously one can go back further in Cambodian history and detail other periods of internal conflicts with outside interventions—for example during the U.S. involvement in the Vietnam war—but for my purposes these two contrasting periods are sufficient.

political settlement under which most groups could feel reasonably comfortable and secure that their specific claims could be aired and resolved, the fighting would with all certainty flare up again. This was particularly crucial for the Khmer Rouge, but also for the traditional monarchy and the four-party coalition that evolved out of the peace process. Likewise, the uncertainty and fear associated with the large number of land mines strewn across the countryside would mean that the rural community would be hesitant to plow and sow their fields; with a destroyed infrastructure, the ability to produce and transport the goods and services required to build the economy would be severely crippled. All of this could contribute to a sense of disillusionment that might shatter the fragile peace accord and dash any hopes for long-term resolution. Addressing these types of threats to stability requires a broader range of implements, a longer time horizon, and a wider spectrum of outside actors. The fighting, of course, did not end immediately, and political stability was not an overnight result, but the intervention that followed the signing of the peace accord paved the way for a transition to a more peaceful environment that may endure.

The UN's mission was organized into distinct issue areas, each designed to address a specific component of the peace accord and the reconciliation effort (Frost 1993). The specific areas involve human rights, the election, military oversight, civil administration, police functions, repatriation of refugees, rehabilitation of the health and social infrastructure, and the dissemination of information. The breadth of these organizational tasks reflect the different goals evident across the pre- and postaccord period. It is difficult to imagine a unilateral intervention into a civil conflict that could undertake such a broad array of tasks, not only because most of them would require the consent of the opposing factions but also because the implementation would be monumental and the initial time projections quite long.

The contrasts between these two phases of the Cambodian conflict and the associated interventions are stark. Geopolitics dominated the pattern of interventions in the pre-1991 phase, with military and economic aid given unilaterally. The aid that was given appeared to have the goal of victory or stalemate and clearly was not focused on using the interventions to resolve the issues at stake. As the decade of the 1980s came to an end, so too had most of the unilateral actions of the patrons, and along with them the more hostile phase of the conflict. The intervention associated with this phase was multilateral, broadly designed to ensure the cessation of hostilities and to rebuild and reconcile the society. Given these wide-ranging goals, at the time of the intervention the participants had to have a reasonably long-term horizon. This latter effort by the UN was vastly different in scope and strategy from any of the individual unilateral interventions, leading us to look for the roots of these different types of interventions, an explanation of when they will be undertaken, and the conditions that increase their effectiveness.

Conceptual Differences Between Unilateral and Multilateral Interventions

A number of characteristics of multilateral interventions make them quite distinct from those generally carried out under the auspices of unilateral actions. Not only are the skills and resources required to carry out the task of maintaining a cease-fire and contributing to the rebuilding of a society more varied than those associated with partisan efforts targeted at the violent aspects of the conflict, but also the expected time frame is different, as are the political and material costs and benefits.

One of the key elements in determining who will intervene, and where, is the time frame under which the actions can be expected to achieve effective results. As we saw earlier, political imperatives often dictate that unilateral interventions be designed with a short time horizon in mind. This does not mean that the implementation phase is always short, but rather that the decision makers do not conceive of the intervention playing out over the long haul. When the United States intervened in Haiti in 1995, for instance, the president publicly proclaimed that the troops would go in, do their job, and get out in a matter of weeks. Had they stayed for a considerably longer period of time President Clinton would have begun to feel the political heat from the increased risk. However, even though the United States was constrained politically, the UN was able to deploy a peacekeeping mission to carry out the rebuilding tasks that the United States could not undertake. Part of the task adopted by the UN in Haiti was to "promote institution building, national reconciliation, and economic rehabilitation" (United Nations 1996). Efforts to rebuild a country's infrastructure or provide the types of humanitarian relief that can prevent famine cannot operate with a short-term horizon. It is estimated, for example, that more than two million land mines are strewn across Cambodia, and thousands of Cambodians have been maimed or killed in trying to carry out the daily chores of life. A similar problem exists in a number of other countries recently wracked by civil war. Removing land mines is a slow, tedious job that requires patience, persistence, and professionalism. Likewise, organizing elections, renewing water supplies, or building schools and roads take time, time that political leaders are unlikely to commit to unilaterally given their myriad other constraints.

The role of time is important in decisions over who intervenes and how, largely because of the costs of intervening. Costs increase with time, and under the best of conditions these costs increase linearly with equal increments added with each additional year or month. The material cost of keeping troops overseas might be one element, but this would be exacerbated by the increased risk associated with prolonged exposure in a hostile environment. As we saw in chapter 3 it is the political costs that are most salient to the decision makers. The risk of injury or death to the intervening forces is clearly a function of many things, but it is equally clear that time of exposure to hostile forces is one of them. And while costs are increasing with time there are generally no additional benefits to be gained as a result of the increased exposure. Likewise, economic interventions can be subject to the increasing cost functions without increased payoffs. For example, sanctions can impose constraints on markets for which the costs are cumulative over time. The loss of markets to competitors and the collapse in prices resulting from an oversupply are just two of the mechanisms. The ratio of costs to benefits, therefore, would tend to increase quite substantially the longer the time frame under which the intervention is planned. If the planning stage of the intervention suggests a long-term involvement, then the relative costs to benefits might quickly overwhelm the capabilities—or interests—of the potential intervenor. Spreading out these costs across a larger number of actors should increase the likelihood of orchestrating an interventionary force.

As important as the extent of the time horizon is in determining who intervenes, so too are the characteristics of the mission and the training required to carry it out. In a unilateral intervention, the policy may involve a group of advisers training local soldiers to be more effective at prosecuting the war. Yet once the two sides have generally agreed to settle the conflict, training soldiers how to be efficient fighters becomes much less important than supervising the fragile peace and training local people in how to rebuild their society. In Cambodia, the Paris Peace Accords of 1991 necessitated a change in the intervention strategies adopted by outside actors. No longer could an outside party contribute arms or training to the former combatants and still maintain the formal conditions of the Accords or fulfill the role of reconciling the warring factions. These varied tasks require a different mix of skills by the intervening forces, and these different tasks require a more intrusive and enduring commitment. The extent of the difference in missions between unilateral interventions—at least the military component—and their multilateral counterpart is reflected in the need to reorient and retrain the intervening troops (Fetherston 1994). Even the economic component of an intervention changes with the context of the conflict. Sanctions may give way to widely applied aid programs; partisan economic support evolves into nonpartisan redevelopment packages; and support for relief and resettlement is designed to bring people back into the country rather than to mobilize them in exile. Long-term, peacebuilding-type interventions have costs that are somewhat unconventional to state actors, require skills that generally fall outside the purview of the more conventional machinery of foreign policy, and present an increased vulnerability from the prolonged exposure in a recently hostile environment. Any one state might be able and willing to contribute to the intervention effort, but few would shoulder the burden unilaterally. In short, the strategy and implements used in the intervention must be tailored to fit the needs of the specific conflict; for instance, minesweepers and election observers might be required in Cambodia, whereas institutional support and confidence building may be the primary goals in El Salvador. But in either case the expected duration of the commitment, the tasks required of the military or civilian personnel, and the phase of the conflict are all quite distinct from those conditions that attract unilateral interventions. The ability of a decision maker to participate will be a function of the ease with which costs are distributed and benefits accrue collectively.

One way to overcome this constraint on peacebuilding-type interventions is to spread out the costs among a large number of actors. The UN serves this role well, though it is not the only multinational organization capable of such a task. The European Union (EU), the North Atlantic Treaty Organization (NATO), the Organization of American States (OAS), and the Organization of African Unity (OAU) are examples of other organizations able to orchestrate multilateral interventions. The cost of funding an intervention can be distributed by either donations or fixed dues, the operational aspects of the strategy are turned over to existing bureaucracies, and political liabilities are absorbed within an insulated organization. As with Olson's (1965) logic of collective action, the outcome may not be optimal, but the free riding of all but the largest contributors can be tolerated and still achieve a modicum of success. Political liabilities under collective interventions are often minimized by contributing to the efforts of a broader community rather than orchestrating a unilateral act. International condemnation is much less likely, and domestic political opposition can be deflected to the international organization. Furthermore, the costs of the intervention get distributed across a broader spectrum of countries, decreasing in absolute terms the burden on any one country. Oftentimes one large country pays a disproportionate share of the material cost of an intervention, though even then the political costs—those associated most directly with the risks—get distributed more widely.

Benefits also accrue collectively and are not necessarily distributed in relation to the contributions by individual states. All national leaders can claim the success of UN interventions, even if their support consisted only of voting in favor of the policy. If the intervention is only marginally effective, then distance from the policy is easy to achieve, at least for most countries; but if highly successful, then claims of active involvement in design, organization, or implementation can serve to lift the political fortunes of a national leader. Under the conditions where long-term interventions are necessary to effectively contribute to the building of a stable and functional society, this distribution of costs and benefits remains a critical component of the decision process. National leaders will be more likely to support interventions that require a long-term outlook if they can delegate responsibility beyond their national borders. Peacebuilding efforts implemented in the *aftermath* of civil conflicts generally meet these criteria of multifaceted interventions with a long time horizon.

Conditions Conducive to Multinational Interventions

As with the earlier chapters, two aspects of multilateral interventions need to be addressed: (1) when they are more likely to be undertaken, and (2) the conditions under which they are more likely to achieve their goals. One way to think about the observed changes in the character of many conflicts and any subsequent interventions is as a result of movements across phases in the conflict (Kriesberg 1994). Understanding the shift from partial to impartial, uni- to multilateral, and narrowly to broadly designed interventions requires us to come to grips with the effect of changes at the systemic level and the phase of the conflict. Although each of these factors may be independent of the others, they need not be so. Empirically we might expect them to covary in a systematic manner, even though they may independently influence the decision calculus.

System Characteristics and the Shift to Multilateral Interventions

Systemic changes have precipitated the evolution across phases of conflicts in two general ways, with subsequent intervention attempts responding in appropriate fashion. The effect of the end of the cold war has simultaneously led to a flourishing of some intrastate conflicts and the resolution of others. First, the breakdown of the bipolar system has in some instances removed the constraints imposed by the dominant member of the bloc, resulting in an increase in attempts by ethnically or religiously homogeneous groups to achieve political sovereignty. This can be most clearly seen in the sphere of influence of the former Soviet Union and shows up as an increased frequency in civil conflicts. Second, the changes at the systemic level have reduced the role played—and support offered—by the opposing ideological foes to the various sides in other ongoing civil conflicts. As the supply routes that fueled the conflicts began to constrict, the combatants had increased incentives to find alternative methods for achieving a desirable outcome. In many instances this is reflected in the movement from a more violent aspect of the conflict to a conciliatory posture. Outside interventions, under these types of conditions, must also change their focus, and as they do so multilateral efforts take on increasing importance in the resolution of intrastate conflicts.

These same systemic changes that have altered the course of civil conflicts around the globe have also led to a fundamental change in the way the global community can respond to civil strife. In the days of the tight bipolar system, multilateral interventions were often stymied by the veto power of the major powers in the UN. Certainly there were other multilateral configurations, such as the OAS, but interventions carried out under their banner were usually more consistent with unilateral missions that used the organization for political cover. The inability to marshal collective interventions in civil conflicts during the cold war was partially a result of the perception of a zero-sum environment in which the two main ideological blocs operated. A number of UN peacekeeping missions were indeed established over the years, but these were predominantly involved with holding a line of demarcation between interstate combatants.[2] As we saw in chapter 3, the cold war played a considerable role in determining when states would intervene in intrastate conflicts, with the evidence suggesting that there is a much smaller probability of a country intervening unilaterally in the post–cold war period than during it.

The evolution of the conflict resulting from changes in the international system affects the payoff structures to both intervenors and combatants from continuing the hostilities. As conflicts begin the process of settlement, the objective of interventions changes from that of influencing the course of the fighting to solidifying negotiated agreements and rebuilding an infrastructure—be it political, social, or economic—with an eye toward the eventual resolution of the issues at stake. One result of these changes is that instead of unilateral interventions in support of one side or the other, we see an increasing number of multilateral efforts that are decidedly neutral. Changes at the system level have also changed the way in which the various blocs interact with regard to regional conflicts. Without the staunch ideological incentives to constrain efforts at cooperation, multilateral efforts are considerably easier to approve and organize. The 1996 effort to organize a multilateral force to assist and repatriate refugees in Zaire was given unanimous approval in the UN, yet it is difficult to conceive of such an overwhelming consensus at the height of the cold war, when the possibility of a superpower veto would have dominated the discussion of a mission to relieve the humanitarian crisis.[3]

Conflict Phases and Multilateral Interventions

A key determinant of when and how interventions will take place is the phase of the conflict in which an intervention is considered. As you will recall from chapter 3, the probability of a conflict abating with or without an intervention was conceptually one of the crucial factors in determining the likelihood that a third party would intervene. It was argued that a unilateral decision was predicated on the

---

[2] There were a few instances of UN interventions in civil conflicts, such as the Congo crisis and the economic sanctions on South Africa, but these were relatively rare compared with the number of UN missions in interstate conflicts. Indeed Montgomery (1995) claims that the UN mission in El Salvador in 1991 was the first in an internal conflict.

[3] Some do think that geopolitics was still the driving force behind the international effort, with France seeking to protect the Rwandan Hutus from defeat at the hands of the Zairean rebel force dominated by Tutsi and apparently supported by Rwanda. France clearly played a critical role in organizing the international effort; what their motives were is unclear (see Mitchell 1996).

prospective costs and benefits of a successful outcome, as well as the probability that an intervention would succeed. We can assume that a similar logic operates when multilateral interventions are contemplated.

Multilateral interventions will more often be considered once the most violence phase of the conflict has passed, a cease-fire has been negotiated, and the contending groups are trying to find ways to reconcile their differences. In essence, the bulk of the efforts are geared toward resolving the conflict through negotiation rather than capitulation. Threats to stability would be associated with the breakdown of a negotiated settlement and the resort back to armed conflict. In many respects stability requires attention to the fragile process of reinforcing the terms of the agreement and rebuilding the society. Unilateral interventions would be less efficient under these types of conditions because their initial focus is on shifting the balance of capabilities within the struggle by biasing the intervention in favor of one side to the conflict. Multilateral interventions, on the other hand, seek to maintain a current balance at an agreed-upon level while efforts are made to reduce both the consequences of the conflict and the overall level of mobilization. Once the most violent phases of the conflict have passed it is increasingly likely that a multilateral community can achieve consensus on an intervention policy. Under these types of conditions the objective is not to weigh in on behalf of a particular combatant, but rather to use the status quo as the foundation from which to build. Not only does consensus become easier, but also risks are reduced and the probability of success increased.

A phase of a conflict generally refers to the extent of hostilities or cooperation among the antagonists (Dixon 1996; Kriesberg 1994; Pillar 1983). Phases can reflect periods of escalating or de-escalating hostilities, or resolution and reconciliation. The particular phase of a conflict can influence the character of an intervention in two ways: (1) the risks incurred by intervenors, and (2) the perception of the status quo ante at the time of an intervention. Interventions carried out under a multilateral umbrella generally attempt to reinforce a negotiated status quo at a level of hostility somewhat below peak levels. Since multilateral interventions can be thought of in terms of a decision-theoretic framework, costs, benefits, and the likelihood of being successful are important. The critical difference between the unilateral and multilateral decisions is that in the latter (a) there must be a common denominator acceptable to most members of the community, and (b) the costs and benefits are distributed across all sanctioning parties. The phases of the conflict influence the ability to cater to these collective needs.

As the conflict shifts from one of overt military confrontation toward cooperation, negotiated settlements begin to take shape. In the foreign capitals, then, decisions regarding policy toward the warring countries become less shaped by geostrategic concerns than they do by efforts to ensure the continuation of negotiated agreements. In effect, estimates of p and q (the likelihood of settlement with and without interventions, from chapter 3) become a less important part of the calculus. States are no longer concerned with stopping the fighting (even on terms favorable to their positions) but rather with supporting efforts that ensure the continued cessation of hostilities. Solidifying the gains made at the negotiating table, however, requires considerably more than a "hands-off" policy, and the policies that are required entail considerably more—and considerably more diverse—efforts than nation states are generally disposed to contribute on a unilateral basis. Once a cease-fire is negotiated, rarely would a third party prefer the reinitiation of the fighting over the reconciliation of the combatants. U.S. support for both the UNITA rebels in Angola *and* for the implementation of the Peace Accords reflects this changing preference on the part of the intervenor.

Any efforts by outside parties to ensure regional stability after the cessation of violent internal conflict have to focus on altering the physical, social, and economic infrastructure in a manner that is inclusive rather than divisive. To be effective, therefore, interventions must (1) be neutral, (2) have the consent of all parties to the conflict, and (3) have a coherently organized and implemented strategy. Next I describe the conditions under which each of these criterion hold and how each contributes to successful outcomes, followed by a series of hypotheses from which historical evidence can be judged.

Conditions for Successful Multilateral Interventions

After the conceptual differences between unilateral and multilateral interventions have been examined, it is apparent that the conditions for successful outcomes should also vary across the multilateral-unilateral divide. Surely the strategy for intervening makes a considerable difference. An ill-conceived intervention is no more likely to be effective just because a larger group of states are involved in some coordinated fashion. Somalia makes that clear. But since the goals have shifted so dramatically, and usually the phase of the conflict has transformed the observed preferences of most parties involved, the notion of what constitutes an effective program for intervening must also be reevaluated. Besides the strategy for intervening—the design of the mission, or operational criteria to use Paul Diehl's term (1993)—other factors are critical in the determination of the effectiveness of the outcome, most notably the role of neutrality and consent.[4]

---

[4] Clearly myriad other factors can influence the outcome of a multilateral intervention, ranging from aspects of the historical relationship between combatants to random events. Most of these other factors are nonmanipulable in the short term or would account for very little of the variation in the outcome and are therefore marginalized in this analysis.

Neutrality and Successful Outcomes

Neutrality is an important concept. According to Paul Diehl (1993), the concept of neutrality involves the goals, composition, and activities of the intervening forces and at times compels even-handed actions in spite of the assignation of specific blame for past events. Unilateral interventions almost always weigh in on behalf of one side in the conflict.[5] This biased intervention places the potential leverage of an intervenor into the same adversarial relationship as that between the combatants. The interventions by the United States and the former USSR in Afghanistan and Nicaragua, for instance, could not be viewed in a constructive light by the opposing sides in the conflict. Unilateral interventions are designed to alter the balance of capabilities in an effort to influence the course of the conflict. Multilateral interventions, however, can—but need not—be neutral, and neutrality has attributes that can sway the course of the resolution phase of the conflict (Diehl 1993).

Neutrality on the part of the intervenors permits impartiality when addressing short-term threats to the cease-fire, usually the result of localized disputes or misunderstandings. In this regard a neutral force allows the third party to act effectively as the "go between," or arbitrator, in efforts to diffuse challenges to the peace. Since a neutral intervenor does not disproportionately coerce any one side in the conflict, the climate should be such that the resort to violence is at best only a final option and no longer an immediately accepted tool of policy. This will increase the cooperation of all parties to the dispute. In effect, neutrality on the part of the outside party may contribute to a change in the structure of the payoffs resulting from cooperation with and defection from the status quo.

The status quo is an important part of negotiated settlements to civil conflicts. When there are changes to the status quo, one would presume that the desired direction of those changes would be toward greater cooperation rather than increased hostilities. A neutral intervenor can facilitate this movement by helping to ensure that the current relative balance of capabilities remains static. If battlefield conditions play a crucial role in determining when negotiations start and succeed (Haas 1990; Holl 1993; Pillar 1983; Zartman 1995), then maintaining that relative balance of capabilities should be important for the ultimate outcome of the intervention. By contrast, a biased intervention would have a difficult time maintaining a stable balance of capabilities, thereby shifting the status quo from the

---

[5] A biased intervention is not a necessary condition for unilateral action, though it is by far the dominant position, and should contribute to the success of the outcome. As was seen in chapter 2, of the 190 interventions, 6 were considered to be neutral, less than 3 percent. Most of these neutral interventions, moreover, were associated with the same conflicts—the civil war in Chad—and can be tied to a pan-African effort to bring peace to the region. None of the neutral unilateral interventions, it should be noted, were successful at stopping the fighting.

point at which the cease-fire was signed and giving reason to the disadvantaged party to try to restore the balance.

Although neutrality cannot guarantee that any of these conditions will prevail, it should increase the likelihood that they will. Because of this there is a much better chance that the intervention itself will be effective. Imagine for a moment the goal of repatriating refugees and reducing the trauma associated with the humanitarian consequences of the conflict. A neutral intervening force would have considerably more latitude in coaxing back refugees who left a region or a country out of fear for their personal safety. A biased intervention would either fail to alleviate the concerns that drive the fear, or if it did with that particular refugee population, it may cause the opposing populations to flee out of a reciprocated fear. Humanitarian access to refugee populations would be subject to similar constraints based on a neutral or biased intervention. To some degree this fear of the Rwandan Hutu refugee population in Zaire is what led to the initial efforts to organize a multilateral force in late 1996. Even NGO activities designed to ameliorate the consequences of the conflict and to bridge the chasms separating the opposing parties are generally easier to implement on a neutral basis than military troops sent under the auspices of a multinational organization. Doctors without Borders, the Red Cross, and numerous other church and sectarian organizations generally adopt neutral positions with regard to the issues at stake and use their professed neutrality to gain access to quarters that partisan or state-based efforts would find inaccessible.

Equally important as the effect of neutrality within the conflicting country is the role of neutrality in maintaining the coherence of the coalition and minimizing the chance that a former patron of one of the opposing groups decides to revert back to unilateral action. Maintaining the united support of the coalition and of the broader—nonparticipating—global community would be an important element in achieving an effective outcome. The ability of the accords that initially ended the Angolan conflict to be upheld after the UNITA movement abrogated the agreement is in part a reflection of the overwhelming support of the world community. Had the intervention been largely one-sided, then the short-term breakdown in the Accord may have been followed by unilateral support for either the government in Luanda or for UNITA. In any case, reverting back to nonneutral actions on the part of outside parties would have potentially scuttled any hope of reviving the Accord.

For example, one of the key aspects of the UN's mission in Cambodia was the ability of its administrators to adopt the role of a neutral caretaker that oversaw the running of the bureaucratic machinery of the government while the political infighting among the opposing groups could play itself out. The terms of the agreement specified the organization of the Supreme National Council (SNC) of Cambodia, made up of the four Cambodian factions. The SNC then delegated to the UN all powers necessary to implement the terms of the agreement (UNTAC [UN Transitional Authority in Cambodia]; Ratner 1993). No one group would countenance the idea of the interim government being run by its military foe. Without this neutral role of the UN, it is unlikely that the Cambodians would have made it to election day under conditions that might lead to a free and fair outcome. As it was, the election was relatively peaceful with a large percentage of the eligible population voting, and the outcome was certified by the international community as being essentially fair. The observation of cease-fires also requires a considerable degree of neutrality, as with the clearing of land mines or other forms of humanitarian relief that are generally nonpartisan endeavors.

Consent and Successful Interventions

As important as neutrality is to multilateral interventions, so too is the notion of consent. The effectiveness of a multilateral intervention in an internal conflict will be greatly facilitated with the agreement of all parties—or nearly all—to have an outside force impose constraints on the course of the conflicts and the behavior of the combatants (Diehl 1993). Consent and neutrality are of course mutually reinforcing components of an intervention. Neither is a necessary condition for either the development of a multilateral effort or its ultimate success, though both should have a significant impact on the outcome of the intervention. Joint consent by the conflicting parties to the actions of an outside force is a far cry from the dynamics of a unilateral intervention. In unilateral interventions the actions of the intervenor are generally biased against one side, and therefore almost by definition would not have the consent of the opposing side. In both Angola and Cambodia this shift between unilateral-biased interventions to multilateral-consensual can be clearly seen. Mutual consent of the conflicting parties was not a characteristic of the unilateral interventions; however, the multilateral initiative that resulted from the Paris Accords ending the Cambodian conflict had as its starting point a cease-fire and set out to reorganize the society along more consensual lines. The four warring factions agreed not only to the multilateral intervention under the auspices of the UN but also to form an interim coalitional governing body (SNC) and then turn over operational control to the UN (Ratner 1993).

If the goal of an intervention is to alter the balance of capabilities to the extent that the fortunes of war shift between combatants, then mutual consent for the intervention is out of the question. The side that would be relatively disadvantaged by the actions of the outside party would surely not give consent to the intervention. But if there were mutually beneficial consequences from an intervention, then consent should be more forthcoming. The most likely avenue to a positive-sum outcome from the intervention is to have the goals involve working toward a resolution, have the implementation be neutral with respect to the warring parties, and have the intervenor enjoy the mutual consent of the antagonists. Mutual consent helps ensure that all parties to the conflict see compromise as the best avenue to resolve the issues at stake. The lack of consent by one or more parties to the policies associated with an intervention would from the outset not only pit the intervenors against various factions of the opposition but also make the policy appear to be rooted in the goal of victory for one side in the conflict—violating, in essence, the need for neutrality. It becomes increasingly difficult to carry out programs generally associated with the notion of humanitarian relief and peace-building without the at least tacit consent of the participants in the conflict.

There of course have been instances of multilateral interventions without the consent of all parties; some even have been relatively successful. The UN effort to resolve the Congo crisis in the 1960s is an example of an intervention without the consent of one faction, and it was the very existence of that faction that the UN sought to eliminate. The UN also imposed a trade embargo on South Africa that clearly did not have the consent of the apartheid government, and it could be argued that the sanctions had a reasonably strong impact on the transformation of the conflict. The EU and the UN's intervention into the Bosnia conflict prior to 1995 also did not enjoy the full consent of all parties, most notably the Bosnian-Serb faction, and these efforts were largely ineffective at either halting the conflict or rebuilding the society. This was so in spite of the fact that these interventions had a very strong neutral orientation. The post-Dayton NATO-led effort did enjoy the consent of all parties and, although it employed a vastly different force structure, was considerably more effective in its mission. Cambodia, Angola, and El Salvador are examples where the consent of all parties contributed to a more effective intervention. The degree to which neutrality and consent are mutually reinforcing cannot be overstated, even though they are not necessarily coincident. For example, it is considerably easier to imagine a neutral intervention that does not enjoy the consent of all parties than it is to conceive of mutual consent given to a biased intervention.

The Strategy for Intervening and Successful Outcomes

The third critical component that determines the outcome of a multilateral intervention is the design of the intervention itself. Here I mean the strategy, or to use Paul Diehl's term the operational criteria, around which the intervention is organized. As would seem intuitively clear, a well-designed strategy should increase the probability of achieving the desired outcome. Recall that the organizing issue around which this book revolves is that decision makers do not and have not had a clear understanding of what constitutes an effective intervention strategy—what works under which types of conditions. Clearly the strategy is an important part of the policymaking process. Many will immediately reflect back on the efforts to diffuse the Somalian conflict and how the UN efforts shifted from humanitarian relief (which was reasonably effective) to restoring stability by arresting the leader of one of the warring clans (which was an abject failure).[6]

A well-designed intervention strategy does a number of things to the climate where the intervention takes place that will increase the effectiveness of the effort. First, a coherent set of operational criteria will contribute to the building of trust between the combatants and the intervenors, as well as among the combatants. In this regard the coherency of the mission is related to the degree to which it mirrors the goals of the intervention and adheres to the concepts of neutrality and consent. At this fragile stage of the conflict, trust is an important element; the more trust that can be fostered between the parties involved, the less likely it will be that minor incidents will escalate into events that threaten the stability of the peace accords. There are numerous examples of relatively minor violations—or misunderstandings—of the terms of an agreement, or the pace of its implementation, that led to serious threats to the overall framework of an agreement. For example, disagreements over the implementation of a phased withdrawal of South African troops from positions in Namibia led to the near collapse of the Namibian peace accord. The complete lack of trust between the South West Africa Peoples Organization (SWAPO) and the South African security forces was largely accountable for the rapidity with which one reasonably small incident began to spiral out of control.

A consequence of an ill-defined strategy is an inability to be sufficiently adaptable to changes in the environment, or to foresee areas that might lead to situations that threaten the viability of the intervention. When the overall plan is not clear or the tools available are incapable of addressing an evolving chain of events, then the intervenors will tend to rely on ad hoc measures, which in turn can result in challenges to the authority of the mission itself. If the warring parties do not confer sufficient authority on the intervening organization, there is an increased possibility that they will begin to question the ability to carry out the mission. If a resulting policy is cobbled together, the critical component of neutrality becomes more difficult to sustain and further threatens the effectiveness of the intervention. As the mission becomes increasingly reliant on ad hoc procedures there will most likely be an escalating number of failures of policy or tactics on the part of the intervenors. Failures of either policy or its implementation will lead to a skittishness and a lack of resolve on the part of the countries or organizations contributing to the intervention. There is not a lot of conceptual separation between an intervention "flying by the seat of the pants" and the failure of the mission. Again, Somalia serves as a poignant example, but so too does much of the early effort to maintain the cease-fires in Bosnia.

---

[6] The latter policy may have reflected U.S. preferences more closely than those of the UN community.

The question of what constitutes a coherent operational strategy is the logical follow-up, even though the answer will not get the attention it deserves at this time. Ultimately, I will venture, the answer is that it depends. The relatively small number of cases—and the even smaller number of conclusive outcomes from which to draw inferences—limits the ability to make meaningful generalizations. But the question regarding the makeup of a coherent strategy does have intuitive answers; it is these that I will explore in a rather cursory manner before going on to suggest some testable hypotheses that derive from the argument developed previously. A more systematic treatment of the implementation of an interventions will follow in a discussion of a couple of the more salient cases of multilateral efforts.

A well-designed strategy must of course be consistent with the notions of neutrality and consent. Bearing these two components in mind one can readily intuit the broad outlines of different types of multilateral interventions. For example, if the intervention is organized around the insertion of a military force into the country, then the force structure must be designed and deployed in such a way that one side is not disproportionately constrained. The use of a multilateral military force to disarm the warring factions needs to be carried out in a manner that ensures that at most points along the way all sides have been disarmed relatively equally, avoiding the impression of disarming one side to the benefit of the opponent. This to some degree is what transpired between the South African security force in Namibia and the SWAPO military, leading to a chain of events that nearly scuttled the truce. The creation, training, and implementation of a civil police force is often a critical need at the end of a civil war; helping to create this force in a way that is not unduly beneficial to a particular faction will increase the likelihood of the cooperation of all parties and ultimately contribute to the success of the intervention. Aid programs, resettlement efforts, and infrastructural redevelopment should all be developed in a manner that ensures mutual consent and reflects a neutral disposition on the part of the intervening organization. Implementing negotiated agricultural reforms, for instance, can pose a thorny problem for the intervenors. In an environment where there are appearances of taking from one group to give to the other, a coherent and well-thought-out program for doing so will increase the effectiveness of the overall mission. What that coherent structure will look like will depend to a large degree on conditions that prevail on the ground at the time of the intervention.

Equally important, though possibly more nebulous than the need to design an intervention strategy with the objectives of neutrality and consent in mind, is the requirement that the operational strategy have the needs of resolving the conflict, not the needs of the organizing unit, at the forefront of the policy. Initially this may appear so flippant and self-evident as to not warrant attention, but in terms of increasing the probability of a successful outcome it should greatly influence the articulation of a workable strategy. And of course an overarching focus on the intervenors themselves is not unheard of. The U.S. entry into Somalia under the auspices of a UN humanitarian intervention, and much of its policy at the later stages of the intervention, seemed to fail on this score. The nighttime "landing" with television crews on hand to watch reeked of a demonstration for the benefit of the American audience. The helicopter battles and the staged "raids" on suspected Aidid's hideouts also seemed more for domestic consumption than for constructive efforts to influence the course of the conflict. There were other shortcomings to that intervention, both in conceptual terms and the implementation, but the grandiose displays in pursuit of domestic recognition reflect the potential to organize an intervention with something other than conflict resolution in mind.

A strategy that emphasizes the needs of the local environment would reflect the specific challenges inherent in that conflict. In El Salvador a focus on human rights and removing the National Security Police, which was widely believed responsible for much of the physical abuse, was critical to the successful fulfillment of the peace accord. To carry out this task the UN organized not only a new civil police authority but also a police academy with training carried out by UN-supplied personnel. Without removing one of the main sources of tension in the society, the prospects for a peaceful resolution would be diminished. In Cambodia there was a need to organize the bureaucratic mechanisms of government on an interim basis, and when the policies of that caretaker bureaucracy began to operate contrary to the spirit of the accords, the UN stepped in to take over much of the operational control of the Cambodian bureaucracy. The complexity of multilateral peacebuilding-type interventions suggests that operational criteria conducive to stability in one conflict might not be the best strategy in another. The extent of the role played by nonmilitary or NGOs may need to differ depending on the situation on the ground. Posting military observers in locations that contribute to the disarming of the combatants might be the strategy of choice in one conflict, yet a more aggressive role might be more effective in another. Bosnia seemed to require a considerable display of force to ensure the terms of the peace agreement, while Angola relied more heavily on observation and intermediary involvement. In each instance, however, a most critical factor seems to be the need to define the operational criteria in terms consistent with the conditions identified by the peace accord.

Essentially the strategy, neutrality, and consent need to cohere in order to have a truly effective multilateral intervention. This is a tall order and probably accounts—at least in part—for why there have been relatively few—and relatively few successful—multilateral interventions in internal conflicts, and why changes at the systemic level—most visibly the end of the cold war—have apparently increased the frequency of multilateral efforts. These factors are obviously intertwined, and the implementation aspects can be manipulated by those organizing the intervention. Each of course suggests certain hypotheses about the conditions under which we are more likely to observe multilateral interventions and when they will be increasingly likely to succeed.

Specific Hypotheses

In this section I articulate a series of hypotheses describing the conditions under which we would expect an increased likelihood of observing an intervention and more effective outcomes. I follow these hypotheses with a discussion of two contemporary cases, though I am under no illusion that a discussion of the case histories is akin to a formal test of the hypothesized relationships. Although the number of cases is generally too small for a proper test—based on the principles of regularities in trends (Ray 1995)—the summarizing of hypotheses and a discussion of relevant cases will contribute to further theoretical development, and a concise description of what I see as a well-defined intervention policy. In short, although untested, the hypotheses will stand as the articulation of prescriptive advice disguised under the rubric of proper social science. My epistemological bias is largely convergent with Jim Ray's (1995) and would gravitate toward an understanding that policy advice should follow from well-tested and strongly supported relationships between explanatory and outcome variables; this, unfortunately, is beyond the means available at this time. That does not mean, however, that policy should remain idiosyncratic until there are enough cases to carry out sufficient tests, particularly if policy debates can be informed by sound intuition and coherent logic.

HYPOTHESIS 1

Multilateral interventions will be more likely after a negotiated settlement to a conflict than before any such agreement.

Multilateral efforts are generally ill-equipped to intervene in an ongoing conflict in a manner that biases one side to the conflict. This is both a function of tactical capabilities and organizational convergence. Multilateral interventions into ongoing intrastate conflicts are not unheard of, though they tend to be dominated by one major actor or generate the overwhelming support of the global community. Economic sanctions against South Africa are an example of the latter instance, while the 1994 intervention into Haiti under the auspices of the OAS reflects the former. Clearly the United States dominated the OAS decision process, an outcome also observed with the Grenada invasion of 1983. A negotiated end to hostilities reflects a significant shift in the phase of a conflict, making conditions more suitable for multilateral interventions.

HYPOTHESIS 2

The less the international environment is perceived in zero-sum terms, the more likely will be multilateral interventions in internal conflicts.

Two factors lead from the makeup of the system to the propensity to organize multilateral rather than unilateral interventions. First, the lower the tension among central actors in the system, the more likely it will be that conditions conducive to positive-sum outcomes will prevail. This positive-sum outlook to the solution of intrastate conflicts will lower the propensity for individual states to take unilateral action in support of one side in a conflict. Without an intense bloc or ideological component to international interactions, the tendency to see all internal conflicts in terms of the larger international dimensions will be minimized, and multilateral solutions will look more attractive. Second, a climate of cooperative interactions among the central actors in the system will make the organization of multilateral interventions considerably easier than during a more conflictual period. At the level of the UN, for instance, the threat of a veto by a member of the Security Council would significantly increase the difficulty in designing an intervention that meets the needs of the intervenors *and* those of the country in conflict. In a tight bipolar international system, spheres of influence are geostrategically important, zero-sum logic prevails, and cooperation on policies regarding regional conflicts is more difficult to orchestrate. Multipolar or collective security environments should increase the likelihood of collective interventions. Obviously to some degree this will reflect the cooling of the cold war, but these types of international environments need not emanate from such a specific historical period.

HYPOTHESIS 3

A neutral posture on the part of the intervenors will increase the likelihood of a successful outcome.

A neutral posture helps ensure that the status quo conditions in place at the time of the cease-fire hold—at least in relative terms—and that the likelihood of one side feeling aggrieved *by* the intervention is diminished. Multilateral interventions will be more likely to take place after the negotiation of a cease-fire agreement between warring parties (hypothesis 1), and a negotiated outcome to a battlefield environment generally freezes the status quo at a level agreed upon by the combatants. Trying to alter the terms of that negotiated settlement through the use of the intervention increases the likelihood that at least one of the parties will defect, ultimately leading to the breakdown of the accord. Neutrality minimizes the chances of a reversion to military hostilities and maximizes the prospects of an effective intervention.

HYPOTHESIS 4

Mutual consent by the warring parties to the intervention, and its terms, will increase the likelihood of a successful outcome.

The consent of all warring parties to the intervention ensures two critical things: (1) that all parties are onboard at the time of the intervention, and (2) that all the parties see negotiation and cooperation as the most preferred path to resolution. If an intervention is imposed on a conflicting group, then it is quite likely that they did not see the intervention as contributing to their overall security. Continued fighting may still be in their immediate interest. Having all sides agree—implicitly or explicitly—that cooperation yields the greatest payoff increases the probability that the intervention will succeed.

HYPOTHESIS 5

The more coherently an intervention is organized and implemented, the more likely that the policy will lead to a successful outcome.

This is a rather intuitive hypothesis with large implications for the ultimate outcome of the mission. By a coherent intervention I refer to one in which the strategy, or operational criteria, are consistent with the specific needs of the combatants and their environment rather than tailored to meet the political needs of the intervenors. A coherently organized intervention will increase the level of trust among the combatants and between the combatants and the intervenors, will decrease the tendency to rely on ad hoc policies cobbled together to address a deteriorating situation, and will contribute more fully to the implementation of the terms of the peace accord. All these consequences that flow from a well-organized intervention will increase the likely success of the policy.

Two Descriptive Case Histories: Zaire and El Salvador

The two case histories that follow are illustrative rather than randomly chosen and serve to detail the interplay of the effect of the international system, characteristics of the interventions, and the phase of the conflicts on the outcome of multi-lateral intervention policies. Both Zaire and El Salvador were pawns in the super-power struggles during the cold war, both had "problems" with insurgencies, and both were party to unilateral and multilateral interventions. For all their similari-ties there are also immense differences between the conflicts and the interventions. Zaire's troubles started with decolonization, with violent aspects of the conflict waxing and waning throughout its history. The latest civil war began at the end of 1996, long after the cold war ended. El Salvador's civil war pretty much played out throughout the decade of the 1980s, and the process of resolution coincided with the end of the cold war. In the Zairean conflict the notions of neutrality and con-sent were not always central to the implementation of the multilateral interven-tion during the early part of the 1960s, and yet the intervention was largely suc-cessful at ending the hostilities. In the latter part of 1996 and into 1997, neutrality, consent, and a cease-fire had become critical requirements of a proposed multi-lateral intervention. In El Salvador unilateral interventions gave way to a multi-lateral effort as the phase of the conflict shifted toward cooperation. A peace accord combined with a multilateral intervention based on neutrality and mutual con-sent contributed to what looks like a potentially stable political environment.

The Conflict in Zaire

When Belgium pulled out of what was then, and now, called the Congo (for pur-poses of clarity I will refer to it as Zaire), they left behind not only a Belgian mili-tary garrison, a nascent Zairean army staffed by Belgian officers, and a Belgium-dominated industrial sector with commercial interests in the vast resources of Zaire, but they also left a fragile political structure. Shortly after the withdrawal of the Belgian administration, there was a mutiny within the ranks of some of the mili-tary sectors against their white officers. Belgium's response to the unrest was to send in an interventionary force to secure the safety of their expatriate citizens. Many of the white officers expelled from the Zairean military teamed up with the nascent political authority in the Katanga District and declared an independent state. The Katanga District is one of the most resource rich in all of Africa and accounted for a considerable share of Zaire's income. Zaire immediately called on the UN to assist them in developing a viable military infrastructure and to reunite—by force if necessary—the secessionist regions with the central government.

Under the leadership of Dag Hammarskjöld the UN organized an interven-tion force but did not take on the task of trying to forcibly expel the Belgians and reunify the country. The UN resolution authorizing the intervention was targeted at compelling the Belgians to withdraw through the use of diplomatic condem-nation and assisting the Zairean state to organize a viable military infrastructure. And even though at the initial stages of the intervention the UN saw the secessionist problem as an internal political debate, it did help to train a Zairean force that was committed to expelling foreign forces and ending the secessionist movement. The UN mission was rather hastily organized, with a Security Council resolution supporting the effort passed on July 14, 1960, just 10 days after the mutiny began. Within a couple days of the resolution the first UN troops began to arrive in Leopoldville (Dayal 1976). The Belgian intervention, meanwhile, continued in spite of the apparent contravention of international law. In fact, Belgian officers were active in recruiting and training a gendarmerie to defend the newly claimed republic. By late 1962 it was estimated that the breakaway Katanga government had up to 40,000 troops and 400 mercenaries at its disposal (Nkrumah 1967).

The period between July 1960 and late 1962 was politically unstable and militarily tense. There were "coups" and "countercoups" within the Zairean government, eventually leading to General Mobutu's takeover of power. Patrice Lumumba, the on-again, off-again prime minister with suspected pro-Soviet leanings was assassinated under rather mysterious circumstances. Some link Lumumba's death to the CIA, who may have had a geopolitical interest in getting the charismatic leader off the stage (Kalb 1982); others to Mr. Tshombe, the leader of the secessionist state of Katanga (Nkrumah 1967). The Belgians were under increasing pressure to restrain and withdraw what remained of the Belgian officer corps and the white mercenaries hired to defend the Katanga state. After an inconclusive effort by UN forces—under code name Rumpunch—to decouple the foreign officers from the Katanga gendarmerie, the Organisation des Nations Unies au Congo (ONUC) decided to end the Katanga cessation, by force if necessary. On September 13, 1961, UN troops in Elisabethville initiated military action against Katangan troops. The attempt to forcibly expel the Belgians, however, was authorized by the UN leadership in Zaire and without the consent of the UN Secretariat (Dayal 1976). The attempt was largely unsuccessful and served to increase the tension between the Katanga government and the UN, as well as within the UN itself (James 1996).

By December 1962 the tide had changed in favor of a more active role for the UN in ending the secession. Under increasing international pressure Belgium turned its support in favor of a unified Zaire and the expulsion of the mercenaries defending the Katanga regime. With the help of U.S. military transport planes, both Zairean soldiers and Belgian paratroopers were mobilized at the front lines, with Belgian troops capturing the strategic town of Stanleyville. On December 28, UN troops attacked the Katangan defenders of the town of Elisabethville, and by January 18, 1963, the secession movement was all but over. In June 1964 the UN mission to Zaire was officially terminated after suffering nearly 250 casualties in the successful bid to end the Katangan independence movement.

The UN intervention was hastily put together with an initial mission of ensuring the withdrawal of Belgian troops and providing security and technical assistance to the fledgling state of Zaire. As the mission unfolded it also greatly expanded, leading ultimately to military efforts to maintain Zairean sovereignty over the entire territory of the former Belgian Congo. In terms of ending the civil war the mission was generally successful, even though it violated most of the conditions articulated earlier in this chapter. When the UN entered Zaire at the request of the government in Kinsasha, it did not do so with a neutral posture. The UN never viewed the secessionist movement as legitimate and always appeared to act as if its minimum objective was political unification through diplomatic pressure and persuasion. It is equally clear that the Tshombe government in Katanga did not initially consent to the UN intervention. On top of all this, the mission itself was not coherently organized, with objectives shifting with the fortunes of diplomatic efforts. At the extreme, commanders in the field ordered the use of military force against the Katangan troops without the knowledge or approval of the UN hierarchy (Dayal 1976). In spite of what seems to be a poorly organized effort, it succeeded in expelling the foreign forces and maintaining the territorial integrity of Zaire, the stated goal of the original Security Council Resolution.

The apparent success of the multilateral intervention was not the result of the conscious violation of each of the components linked conceptually to a successful outcome, but rather in spite of those factors working against its success. To understand why this case contradicts the logic outlined earlier we must look elsewhere. The Katanga secession took place near the apogee of the cold war, which had considerable implications for the role played by both the UN and other outside actors. If indeed the United States was involved in the murder of Patrice Lumumba and the coup by Mobutu, this would be consistent with the trend in cold war politics at the time. It is clear that the United States viewed Zaire as a critical player in confronting Soviet expansion into central Africa, and Lumumba as a Soviet pawn (U.S. Department of State 1994). Neutral interventions into civil conflicts were going to be difficult during this period, regardless of the expressed goal of the UN Secretariat. Furthermore, it is not clear that the UN effort to end the secession would have been successful without the individual efforts by the United States and Belgium. It was the Belgians who took the vital town of Stanleyville, which increased the pressure on Tshombe to quit the struggle after recent defeats at the critical towns of Elisabethville and Kamina. So the multilateral effort got a great boost from the Western bloc, which obviously saw a need—based on geopolitical concerns—to end the unrest (U.S. Department of State 1994). The picture, however, looks remarkably different when we shift our focus to the unrest in Zaire in the post–cold war era of late 1996 and early 1997, where an opposition force overthrew President Mobutu and the UN attempted to organize a multilateral military intervention targeted at providing humanitarian relief to refugees.

To fully understand the civil unrest that swept through Zaire in 1997 it would be useful to delve into the 1994 genocide in Rwanda, though I will avoid that excursion. The point here is not to understand the roots of the conflict but rather the attempts to organize the multilateral intervention. Sidetracking into the Rwandan civil war would add little to that understanding, though it should be mentioned that the immediate impetus for the uprising can be tied to the existence of Rwandan refugees inside Zaire. Throughout the period between 1994 and 1996 private nongovernmental relief organizations and the UN were providing humanitarian assistance to the large number of refugees who fled the conflict in Rwanda.[7] But in October 1996 the deputy governor of a southern province of Zaire issued an ultimatum to the refugees to leave Zaire or be hunted down. The threat sparked a rebellion that quickly spread throughout this region of the country. With the aid of Rwandan troops a rebel group captured the town of Uvira on October 24 and the capital of the province, Bukavu, on October 30. On November 1 the Zairean opposition, again with the aid of Rwandan troops, captured the main town of Goma in the east, sending aid workers and hundreds of thousands of mainly Rwandan Hutu refugees fleeing into the hills and forests. The Zairean military put up a pitiful defense and in retreat looted the towns and brutalized the local populations. One result of the increase in military activity between Zairean and opposition troops is that the specter of a humanitarian crisis began to take on increasing salience, and members of the world community began to call for decisive action.

France, which had been a historical supporter of the Mobutu government in Zaire, and many believed to be opposed to the Tutsi-led government in Rwanda, was at the forefront of organizing a multilateral force to assist the refugees. Britain, Belgium, Spain, Italy, Canada, and reluctantly the United States got involved in a plan to "rescue" the refugees by sending in upwards of 10,000 military troops that would ensure safe locations for the distribution of aid, and among other missions, secure a corridor between the town of Goma and the Rwandan border to allow the refugees to return home. The UN Security Council adopted a resolution that authorized, under Chapter VII of the UN Charter, the creation of an intervention force under the leadership of a Canadian officer that could use "all necessary means" to defend themselves against attack (Leopold 1996). The initial proposed operation would have an end date of March 31, 1997, and would be succeeded by an unspecified "follow on operation" that would be designed and organized by the UN.

The United States was to play a pivotal role in the implementation of the intervention force, without which it was unlikely that the proposed intervention could proceed. Ultimately the intervention never materialized, with two factors being largely responsible for it never making it past the planning stage: (1) the reluctance of the United States and the inability of its conditions to be met, and (2) the apparently spontaneous return of large numbers of refugees to Rwanda. The United

---

[7] The description of this current aspect of the conflict relies heavily on daily and weekly print media, such as *Reuters*, the *New York Times*, and the *Economist*.

States set two main conditions and predicated its support for the intervention on the continued reluctance of the refugees to return to Rwanda. The first condition was a cease-fire between the Zairean troops and the opposition forces. At one point the United States said that it would consider a "de facto cease-fire" (Aldinger 1996) and that it expected the "acquiescence and cooperation" of the opposing parties (Mitchell 1996), but such cooperation never materialized. The Zairean government, fearful of the effect of foreign forces on its territory, issued a warning to the effect that the intervention forces would perhaps have to confront Zairean troops, while the successes of the opposition forces gave them little reason to agree to a cease-fire. Another major condition involved the time line for exiting and completing the mission. The UN called for a six-month operation while the United States was only willing to commit to four months. Essentially this reluctance on the part of the United States was related to the coherence of the objectives of the mission and how the relative lack of clarity might lead to a repeat of the Somalian debacle of 1992.

Two ways to think about the proposed UN intervention are in terms of systemic conditions and phases of the conflict. System characteristics probably contributed on a couple of dimensions. First, the demise of cold war politics most likely gave Laurent Kabila a window of opportunity unavailable in prior years. Given the perceived geostrategic importance of Zaire and Western support for Mobutu during the cold war, it is likely that Kabila's movement would have met with considerable opposition from the United States and France. In the post–cold war climate Kabila was not viewed as a communist, Zaire as less strategically important, and there was no hint of other major power influence. Second, in the more cooperative post–cold war environment there was almost no resistance within the UN to the proposed intervention. The particular phase of the Zairean conflict also played a role, largely working against the UN-proposed initiative. Rather than contemplating the intervention during a phase of waning hostilities, the UN proposal was approved during a time of escalating confrontations. The conflict, if it was shifting phases, was going from a low-level disruption in the distant countryside to a full-scale civil war in which the opposition was gaining the advantage. This was not a situation in which the opposition would likely consent to a cease-fire, because any negotiated halt to the fighting would disproportionately benefit government troops.

While the debate raged among the contributing members to the proposed force, large numbers of Rwandan refugees headed for home, effectively eliminating any chance that the United States would participate in the intervention. Since the intervention never materialized beyond the stage of explorations, it seems futile to attempt to diagnose what might have happened. But the signs are all there that the rather ad hoc nature of the proposed policy, the lack of an effective cease-fire, and the inability to secure the mutual consent of the conflicting parties did not augur well for the likely outcome of the mission. The reluctance of the United States appeared to be based on a series of questions that were the "right" questions to ask. Given the logic outlined earlier, it is quite likely that the proposed intervention would have had a difficult time achieving the initial objectives.

El Salvador

The civil war in El Salvador is one that covers many of the issues associated with external interventions in internal conflicts. The revolutionary movement, the Frente Farabundo Marti de Liberacion Nacional (FMLN) was rooted in the extreme social injustice pervasive in the Salvadoran society and the abusive policies of the ruling elite in trying to control dissent (Stahler-Sholk 1994). The leadership of the FMLN, moreover, was committed to a revolution based on Marxist principles. By contrast, the ruling elite was composed of a coalition between the military and the agrarian oligarchy, to whom agrarian reform and social change were inimical. By October 1980 a coalition of five opposition groups under the banner of the FMLN took up arms in an attempt to overthrow the political system; very shortly thereafter the groups had demonstrated themselves to be a significant military force and a serious threat to the stability of the regime (Karl 1992).

A small country in a troubled region in close proximity to one of the major antagonists in the cold war was bound to attract outside intervenors, as it indeed did. President Carter granted military aid to support the Salvadoran government, but Ronald Reagan massively increased the volume of U.S. assistance and took a more active role in shaping internal politics as well as prosecuting the war against the FMLN (Karl 1992). By the mid-1980s the United States was giving the Salvadoran government more than a million dollars per day in an effort to bolster its ability to suppress the FMLN's challenge and at one point had U.S. combat advisers working alongside the Salvadoran military in training and planning roles. In spite of the considerable effort on the part of the United States, the government in San Salvador was unable to defeat the FMLN. For most of the conflict the FMLN controlled rural areas but was unable to defeat the government in the cities, but on November 11, 1989 the FMLN took the war to the capital and demonstrated that they had sufficient military capabilities to organize a "final offensive." The offensive fizzled and fairly conclusively showed that the civil war was stalemated, which opened up a series of serious negotiations aimed at resolving the conflict.

The Soviet role in the Salvadoran civil war is considerably less clear. The United States repeatedly claimed that Soviet arms—either through Nicaragua or Cuba—were fueling the capabilities of the FMLN, a charge that the Soviets repeatedly denied. Most evidence of any Soviet intervention is tenuous at best (Dunkerley 1982; Shearman 1988), though there could be little doubt that the Soviets were at least supportive of both the notion of a Marxist revolution in Central America, and the ability of the conflict in El Salvador to tie the hands of the Americans. But even the thought of a Soviet involvement in El Salvador would have had a psychological impact on policy in the United States (Shearman 1988). Clearly the Soviets were selling arms to the Nicaraguan government after the Sandinista revolution, which gave greater weight to U.S. policies against the Nicaraguan regime, but there is little to suggest that El Salvador was one of the cold war battlefields in anything but rhetoric.

By 1989 the military stalemate, the change in the U.S. presidency from Ronald Reagan to George Bush, the murder of six Jesuit priests by U.S. trained Salvadoran soldiers, and the cooling of the cold war all contributed to an increased reluctance on the part of the United States to continue its support of the regime in San Salvador. At the same time there seems to have been a recognition on the part of the leadership of the FMLN that the chances of victory were slim and negotiating a settlement presented a viable alternative. Just two days after his election in March of 1989 the new president of El Salvador, Alfredo Cristiani, called for peace talks, and in May of that year representatives of the FMLN met with UN officials to discuss the possibility of opening up a channel to the government in San Salvador. In effect the phase of the conflict was beginning to shift from one of intense hostilities to one in which cooperation was explored by both sides. The UN became the central focal point for direct negotiations between the government and opposition delegations (Montgomery 1995).

After taking on an official role as the mediator between warring sides, the UN was able to broker an agreement in July 1990 in which both sides agreed that human rights were a first priority and that a UN mission should be organized to investigate abuses as soon as a cease-fire could be arranged. Within a year the UN opened up a mission in El Salvador, Mision de Observadores de las Naciones Unidas en El Salvador (ONUSAL), with its first task to address the deplorable human rights situation. The formal cease-fire was not implemented until six months after the UN's office opened in San Salvador (Karl 1992; Montgomery 1995). The UN was not only instrumental in brokering the peace agreement between the government of El Salvador and the FMLN; some scholars see the UN's action as a pathbreaking role for the organization (e.g., Holiday and Stanley 1996; Montgomery 1995). According to Montgomery (1995), ONUSAL was the first UN mission to be established before a cease-fire agreement, was a "pilot mission" in the sense that its tasks expanded beyond military demobilization to include national reconciliation, and was the first mission to attempt to resolve an internal conflict (p. 146). Although the empirical validity of these claims can be debated (e.g., the UN's involvement in Zaire prior to a cease-fire), the novelty of the ONUSAL mission is echoed by Holiday and Stanley, who highlight its attempt to help reconstruct and strengthen domestic structures.

After the negotiation and implementation of a formal cease-fire, ONUSAL's role expanded to meet the needs of the Salvadoran society. Across distinct phases of the intervention the formal divisions associated with the ONUSAL mission included human rights, military, police, and electoral supervision. Under the human rights division, ONUSAL oversaw the development of a "Truth Commission" designed to investigate the more egregious human rights violations carried out throughout the conflict; the military division was assigned multiple tasks including monitoring the cease-fire, demobilizing forces, and clearing mines from an estimated 425 minefields. The police division's role revolved principally around organizing and training a National Civil Police (PNC) force to replace the much feared security forces blamed for much of the abuse meted out during the conflict. The ONUSAL police observers were also responsible for training the new police force and maintaining order while the transition was taking place. The electoral division was not set up until 1993, prior to the national elections, and had a mandate to organize, supervise, and certify the electoral process. In addition to these specific functions the ONUSAL mission became intimately involved in facilitating political, agrarian, and judicial reforms that were all integral aspects of the peace process. Concurrent to the ONUSAL mission other organizations, including the UN High Commission for Refugees (UNHCR), the United Nations Development Program (UNDP), and the United Nations International Emergency Children's Fund (UNICEF), were also involved in the rebuilding process, along with other private voluntary NGOs helping to repatriate and resettle refugees. At one juncture even the International Labor Organization was called in to act as a mediator when a series of negotiations over social reforms broke down (Montgomery 1995).

Although the peace process and the UN's intervention had some glitches along the way, for the entire duration of the UN mission there was never once a violation of the cease-fire agreement. By April 1995 the ONUSAL mission was formally disbanded and there is considerable hope for the future of El Salvador. The chain of events that led from unilateral interventions in support of one side in the conflict—which essentially led to a widening of hostilities and a substantial increase in the consequences associated with the conflict (Karl 1992)—to a multilateral effort designed to facilitate the peace process involved changes in the fortunes of war on the battlefield and changes in the international climate. The character of the UN intervention was such that it was (1) flexible, (2) targeted specifically at the needs of the Salvadoran society, and (3) neutral and consented to by both parties. The coherency with which the mission was organized led Montgomery to argue that it "developed *in situ* as it sought to respond creatively and positively to conditions and situations that had not been anticipated" (1995, 142). The extent to which the intervention was targeted at the expressed needs of the Salvadorans can be seen in the fact that the original negotiations were over the provisions of human rights, not a cease-fire, and that the UN would set up a mission in El Salvador without a cease-fire being in force. This was done at the request of both sides to the conflict.

The success of the intervention in El Salvador can be tied to a number of factors operating simultaneously. But in the final analysis it was a well-designed and orchestrated mission that was buttressed by the work of the NGO community, and it came at an opportune time in terms of the international climate. The confluence of good timing and coherency in organization was facilitated in part by the ability of the United States to shift from an interested unilateral party to a contributor to the multilateral effort, where, for instance, the United States began channeling economic aid through the UN in order to avoid the appearance of complicity with the government in El Salvador.

Conclusion

This chapter has shifted the discussion from unilateral interventions that generally favor one side in a conflict to the multilateral counterpart more prevalent in the current international environment. I have argued that this shift is a function of two factors, which themselves may be related: (1) changes in the international system, and (2) changes in the phase of the conflict. Both these conditions seem to influence the prospects for a negotiated cease-fire and the organization of a cohesive multinational intervention. Furthermore, there are three basic characteristics that are likely to increase an intervention's success: (1) the intervention is neutral with (2) the consent of all parties, and (3) the operational strategy is well defined and has the needs of the target country at the forefront of the policy-making process. Two brief descriptions of the conflicts in Zaire and El Salvador were used to link the hypothesized conditions to the outcome of decisions over multilateral interventions.

The arguments and evidence presented in this chapter buttress what we know from the earlier chapters. They also offer policy-relevant guidelines to those charged with deciding how and when to act in pursuit of regional stability. Multilateral interventions involve the collective organization and implementation of a complex and intrusive policy to settle an internal conflict. Costs are incurred and benefits accrue that can be distributed across the members of the participating organization. This allows for—and maybe even necessitates—a broader range of tasks to be undertaken and a longer time horizon at the time of the decision. We know, for instance, that the strategy for intervening influences the likely success of the policy. This result seems to be evident in the statistical patterns associated with unilateral interventions as well as the historical descriptions of multilateral efforts. A successful outcome from an intervention, it would seem, is not a random event. This coherency is a function of the organization and implementation of the policy and is facilitated by the mutual consent of the warring parties and a neutral posture. None of these conditions would appear to be necessary for success, but each should contribute to the probability of a successful outcome.

Given the criteria for successful multilateral interventions, linking intervention efforts to the appropriate phase of the conflict is important. Mutual consent of the warring parties and neutrality on the part of the intervenors would be difficult conditions to meet at the height of the conflict. It is considerably more likely that these conditions will be met during a nonviolent phase of the conflict. This suggests that multilateral interventions will probably be considered and implemented only after the negotiation of a cease-fire or at least a temporary respite in the fighting. The difficulty of effectively intervening without meeting these conditions could be seen in the U.S. reluctance to contribute to the multilateral efforts being organized in response to the civil war in Zaire in 1997. As a conflict begins to move toward resolution, multilateral efforts will be easier to organize, the conditions for success will be more prevalent, and the ability to develop a strategy that can address the broader needs of the society and help in the resolution process will be increased. In the following chapter I will summarize the results and inferences of this study and describe policy-relevant guidelines that might assist policymakers as they grapple with some of these tough decisions.

SIX

Conclusion

The focus of this book has been on identifying the conditions under which outside interventions into internal conflicts are likely to be successful. Since the end of the cold war there seems to be an increasing number—or at least an increasing level of visibility—of civil conflicts. Consequently, policymakers around the world have turned from an emphasis on security based largely on deterrence of threats from an ideological or strategic foe to one of ensuring regional stability through the control of internal conflicts. The academic community seems to be following suit. The theme of the book is rooted in the pursuit of an understanding of the mechanisms of conflict management. And while maintaining the standards and procedures of academic rigor it tried to explicitly speak to the policymakers grappling with these problems. One key to using social science methods in pursuit of policy-relevant inferences lies in framing the questions asked in a manner consistent with those posed by the policy community. The tricky part is to maintain the dual standard of theoretical wealth and policy relevance. Policymakers ask questions and require answers that can be framed in terms of probabilistic outcomes; scholars often need to know the extent of covariation, the effect of unit changes, and the relative explanatory power of various models. These are not—nor should they be—mutually exclusive goals. But being attentive to both requires specific analytical techniques, and at the margins, throwing away information that may be relevant if the policymaker was not an immediate audience. In this concluding section I bring together the strands of evidence offered in the previous chapters and then extend the results to draw inferences that should be useful for the policymaker and the scholar alike. I start by summarizing my central arguments and assumptions, followed by recapping the results of the empirical analysis; finally I draw it all together, developing inferences and prescriptions.

When policymakers begin asking questions about the likely prospects of formulating an effective intervention strategy, they currently have little systematic evidence from which to draw reliable conclusions. In the United States we saw this regularly in response to conflicts in Haiti, Zaire, Rwanda, and Bosnia, where in each instance prior events in Somalia served as the analogous case. One result is that policy-making becomes rather ad hoc. Analogous cases are often used to get some idea about the likelihood of achieving the desired goal, but the case selection is rarely on firm ground. Furthermore, the evaluation of the conditions and strategies that result in policy choices often result from motivational and psychological biases or a set of potentially idiosyncratic events. The results presented in this book should not eliminate a close reading of recent history from the decision process, but rather buttress it by pointing to the outcome of different strategies for intervening across 50 years of history and nearly 200 cases of outside interventions in civil conflicts. Regardless of how "closely" a particular analogy "fits," the decision community should be wary of going against the grain of strong, consistent trends. In the norm there are often more similarities than differences across conflicts, and sometimes acting as if the current conflict is unique comes with foreseeable perils.

The academic community has taken up with great enthusiasm the charge of uncovering the intricacies of civil conflicts, and we are beginning to come on line with the results of empirical analysis of when, why, and how internal conflicts flare up and can be resolved. This is not a new subject of interest (e.g., Gurr 1970), but the tempo and breadth of current academic interest is new. We are still, however, a long way from offering concrete answers to many of the thorny questions with which we are presented. Because there is so much that we do not know, this book contributes to the dialogue without addressing all the important issues; as such, it suggests as many questions as it does answers. It should be clear that we are not in the dark, but equally clear that we are not in a well-lit room. Much still needs to be understood, and shortly I will identify some of the areas to which future research could be productively targeted and from which the academic and policy communities could greatly benefit. To start this task let me briefly recant the arguments, evidence, and results offered earlier.

Internal Conflicts, Outside Interventions, and Conflict Resolution

I assumed at the outset that when states unilaterally decide to intervene, their goals revolve around stopping the fighting. Success, therefore, was conceived in terms of how effective the intervention was at contributing to this outcome. Clearly not all interventions have this as an explicit goal, though stopping the fighting may be a necessary first step for achieving alternative goals. Furthermore, if we can understand the ability of military or economic interventions to help stop the fighting, then we can push this analysis further and begin to ask questions about how a halt to the fighting can contribute to the long-term prospects for conflict resolution. For example, the initial debates over the United States contributing 20,000 troops to the NATO-led efforts in Bosnia centered on the ability of this force to contain the violence that had become a threat to security in the region. Nobody was going to be happy simply with stopping the fighting, though much of the debate turned around the ability to do so. If the fighting was stopped, it was argued, then political arrangements could be negotiated that might realign the constellation of forces in conflict. In hindsight we now know that the intervention force was effective at stopping the fighting, though we also know that something more needs to be accomplished before anyone could proclaim an end to the conflict.

If unilateral interventions seek to halt the fighting (at times on terms favorable to the intervenor; at other times simply to solidify the status quo ante on the ground), multilateral efforts have a broader range of goals. Usually undertaken after a cease-fire has been arranged, multilateral interventions often seek to solidify the gains of the negotiating table and to rebuild the social and physical infrastructure so necessary to conflict resolution. They consequently include a broader range of actors, a more diverse set of skills, and a longer time horizon at the time of the decision. Considerably more has been written about the conditions for multilateral interventions (see Diehl 1993), though we know far too little about the conditions under which they are increasingly likely to be successful. At a time when there appears to be an increased emphasis on employing the UN as peacekeepers, this becomes a serious void in our understanding.

Before asking and answering questions about the relative effectiveness of various strategies for intervening, I first needed to address the issue of when states choose to intervene. Obviously states contemplating an intervention into a civil conflict face a range of options, one of which is to do nothing—or at least do nothing with the military and economic tools at their disposal. The ability of states to substitute policy alternatives under varying conditions suggests a need for greater attention to issues of selection bias (Most and Starr 1989). Chapter 3 began the process of tackling this difficult topic. I began with the premise that intervening was a result of policy choices and that political leaders would choose to intervene only when (1) they considered an intervention to be necessary (i.e., they estimated that the conflict will continue without an intervention) and (2) they expected that the intervention would have a high chance of success. One of the key problems, of course, is that they generally do not have sufficient information to know with confidence when success or failure is likely. This subjective estimate of the likely outcome of the conflict with and without an intervention, I argued, was critical to determining whether states would intervene. But it is not the only determining factor. Since interventions are inherently political, there are also costs and benefits that derive from an intervention, and these costs and benefits are rooted in various contextual conditions. Since whether or how to intervene involves choices, I used a decision-theoretic framework to organize our thinking about the conditions under which we would expect the political leadership in one country to choose to intervene in the internal conflict in another country. The analysis resulted in a set of conditions that predict to an increased probability of observing interventions into civil conflicts. But a sense of when states are likely to intervene is not enough. For example, since we know that high subjective estimates of the probability of success are important in the decision of whether to intervene, decision makers really need to know when success is likely. This was the topic of chapter 4.

In the fourth chapter I took up the question of the types of interventions that tend to be successful under specific conditions; this, I argue, is precisely the systematic information that decision makers lack. Arguments in the literature suggest that both contextual conditions and the strategy for intervening are critical to the outcome of an intervention. For example, Kaufmann (1996) argues that the ease with which identity can be assumed or discarded will affect the effectiveness of military interventions, and Burton (1990) places cultural identity at the core of intergroup conflict. Identity patterns based on ethnicity may be more difficult to discard than those based on religious affiliation, suggesting that interventions into ethnically based conflicts would generally be less successful. Kaufmann goes as far as to argue that ethnic separation may be the only strategy to stop the fighting under some conditions. Reasons of efficiency and legitimacy also point to interventions in support of the government as being more effective than those supporting opposition groups, yet as the data described in chapter 2 made clear, outside interventions are about equally likely to side with each. This is a choice that is of course usually driven by political imperatives, but an understanding of the *ex ante* likelihood of a successful intervention is vital information to the policymaker, even if politics restrict the range of options available. Other components of the strategy involve the type of intervention itself, focusing on military, economic, or mixed strategies. Since interventions are generally trying to manipulate relative capabilities on the battlefield, who intervenes should also influence the likely success of the policy, with major powers having considerably more resources and influence than comparable interventions by less-endowed countries. Finally, it was argued that the amount of violence or the extent of the killings associated with the conflict should also influence the likely outcome of an intervention. Here again, I framed the questions from the perspective of the decision maker asking "what works under what conditions with what probability?" Using probabilistic estimates allows us to interpret the results in terms of how great is the increase (or decline) in the probability of success as we move across strategies for intervening and conditions of the conflict.

Many scholars have argued that not all conflicts (or wars) can be lumped into one category (see Goertz and Diehl 1995; Levy 1981; Organski and Kugler 1988; Vasquez 1993), with global wars differing from lesser ones and conflicts between rivals being distinct from nonrivalry-based conflicts. Some civil conflicts are considerably more intense than others, and isolating these particularly intense conflicts allowed me to examine the conditions for success across this contextual divide. Rwanda in 1994, Cambodia during the reign of Pol Pot, and the Bosnian conflict of the early 1990s stand out from those such as the Bougainville conflict in Papua New Guinea, the Dominican revolt in 1964, or the conflict in Northern Ireland. The increased visibility of very intense conflicts will attract the attention of the world community, at minimum pressuring leaders to take some type of definitive action. At the same time intense conflicts should be the ones that are least likely to be amenable to outside interventions. I used this distinction between intense and nonintense conflicts to identify changing patterns in the conditions that lead to successful outcomes.

The end of the cold war brought with it changes in the way the global community views and responds to civil conflicts. First, there seems to be an increasing number of internal conflicts, many tied to the disintegration of the Soviet empire. Although the evidence is inconclusive as to whether the late 1980s through the 1990s constitutes a new era in terms of the frequency and origins of internal conflicts, the initial trends point to the possibility of a new pattern (chapter 2). Second, the post–cold war period also appears to have ushered in a new way for the global community to respond to civil conflicts. It is now increasingly likely that collective responses to internal conflicts will be organized, either under the auspices of the UN or some other multinational organization (such as NATO). Collective interventions are different than unilateral ones on a number of dimensions, and a discussion of the conditions for successful multilateral interventions was presented in chapter 5. The basic argument was that the distribution of costs and benefits permitted the undertaking of more long-term initiatives that were required by the broad range of goals associated with multilateral interventions.

Although the number of cases of multilateral interventions is generally too small to use quantitative methods to tease out systematic trends, the anecdotal evidence does suggest that certain criteria point toward more effective outcomes. I used the contrasting examples of Zaire and El Salvador to illuminate the interplay of the role of systemic conditions and the goals, neutrality, consent, and impartiality on the outcome of debates over or the implementation of outside interventions in the respective conflicts. In the next section I summarize the results of the analysis from each chapter before moving on to examine some of the policy and theoretical inferences that can be drawn from the results.

Empirical Patterns in the Conditions
for Successful Interventions

The data on civil conflicts and any associated interventions were initially examined in terms of their distribution across a number of categories, such as who was fighting, who intervened with what types of strategies, the extent of casualties, and the relative rates of successful interventions. These data were presented in chapter 2 as a snapshot of what worked and when, without controlling for simultaneous effects of contributing factors. We could see, for instance, that the greatest percentage of the conflicts were in Asia or Africa and that Europe was considerably less conflict prone. Major powers accounted for about 40 percent of all third-party interventions, with the United States topping the list of major power intervenors, followed by the USSR/Russia, France, and Britain. Overall there were 138 conflicts, of which 89 had outside intervenors, and those 89 with interventions had a total of 190 individual intervenors. In many conflicts there were obviously multiple interventions.

Interventions were about equally likely in support of the government as in support of opposition forces, and nearly 75 percent of the interventions involved only military support. Purely economic interventions were rather rare (only 5%), with mixed interventions making up the remainder. Just under half of the conflicts were ideologically based, while groups were organized primarily along religious affiliations in only about 10 percent of the cases. Interventions supporting the government were about twice as likely to be successful as those supporting the opposition. In general, conflicts with interventions lasted considerably longer than those without outside involvement, and for the most part the larger the number of individual intervenors, the longer the conflict could be expected to last. It is not entirely clear, however, whether this is because the interventions prolonged the conflict or whether interventions are attracted to those conflicts that have been long running. There also appears to be no systematic pattern between the number of intervenors and the number of casualties resulting from the conflict, although conflicts without interventions generally have fewer numbers of casualties.

The description of the cases and the interventions lead to interesting notions about when outside actors can contribute to the end of hostilities, but at this juncture it remained simply a description—albeit one from which descriptive inferences could be derived (King, Keohane, and Verba 1994). As revealing as were the trends in interventions was the fact that over a third of the conflicts had no outside interventions. What became critical was to find a way to identify those conflicts that were more likely to attract outside intervenors. Without an understanding of when—or under what conditions—third parties will choose to intervene, our ability to draw inferences from the evaluation of the conditions that lead to successful interventions is limited. Drawing inferences only from cases in which the intervention option was chosen subjects the conclusions to a bias built into the selection of cases. This is a problem all too common in much of the analyses of interventions (see Connaughton 1992; Dorman and Otte 1995; Haass 1994; Kanter and Brooks 1994;) and derives from the inability to distinguish whether a certain set of conditions in the cases chosen augured well for success and the decision to intervene was predicated on the existence of these conditions. Very similar cases with a critical variation on one dimension might have a widely divergent outcome. Chapter 3 took up this issue of the conditions under which states choose to intervene. I hypothesized that four conditions would affect the propensity of states to intervene in internal conflicts, incorporating the role of shared borders, the intensity of the conflict, the existence of a humanitarian crisis, and the pre– and post–cold war environment.[1]

The results of the empirical analysis generally support the arguments that were presented. As an indicator of the subjective estimate of the likelihood that an intervention would be successful I used the intensity of the conflict. By intensity I mean the number of casualties per year, and as this number rises it becomes less likely that an outside actor will estimate that their intervention will be sufficient to stop the fighting. The analysis confirms that the more intense the conflict, the less likely will be outside interventions; and when the intensity is extremely high, the probability of observing an intervention drops to only 15 percent (down from 50%). Furthermore, states were 25 percent more likely to intervene unilaterally during the cold war than in its aftermath. The politics of the cold war could be used to rationalize a myriad of policies, and interventions into civil conflicts are clearly one such policy. Several factors would account for the role played by the cold war, including the decreased strategic utility derived from interventions, the increased domestic costs of trying to convince the body politic that the intervention is in its interest, and the increased ease with which multilateral interventions can be organized and implemented. As I argued in chapter 5, because of the changed dynamics of international power relationships, collective operations within the UN are considerably easier to design and organize. It also appears from the evidence that conflicts with humanitarian crises are more likely to attract outside interventions than other civil conflicts. This is consistent with the findings of survey research in the United States that demonstrate an American willingness to countenance interventions under a very limited range of conditions, relieving humanitarian tragedies being one of them.

---

1 There are undoubtedly more factors that influence the decision to intervene, though I would argue that the relative purchase that additional explanations give is marginal when compared with those identified here.

The analysis in chapter 3 provides a selection mechanism by which we can proceed to evaluate the conditions for successful interventions. It is clear from the evidence that states select themselves into some conflicts and out of others. Some of these conditions that contribute to the choice of policy, moreover, also have an effect on the likelihood that an intervention will succeed. It is from this understanding of how states self-select into an intervention that we can move on to discuss the conditions that result in interventions being more likely to contribute to the end of hostilities.

An understanding of the conditions under which interventions will be successful is at the heart of this analysis. As I have made clear throughout this work there is a certain paradox in the policy dilemma faced by decision makers. On the one hand, they generally do not want to intervene when the conditions for success are dismal; on the other, they have little systematic *ex ante* knowledge to guide their determination of when successful outcomes are likely. Chapter 4 took up this task in a manner somewhat distinct from the more traditional method of deriving policy-relevant advice on interventions. The more common approach to studying interventions has been a series of case studies on recent interventions that depict the conditions in a few select instances that are probably salient at the time. Certainly these serve a purpose in identifying some of the intricacies and potential pitfalls evident in these few select instances, but in some ways this is akin to focusing on the outlier events and arguing that they are what should drive the decision process. The approach adopted in this analysis assumes that systematic patterns in the ebb and flow of successful interventions exist and that it is these patterns that can inform both the policy and the academic communities. In framing the analysis in chapter 4 I again tried to ask questions from the perspective of decision makers contemplating an intervention. I argued that they want to know the probability that a given intervention will work under a specific set of conditions. Answers to these types of questions, I demonstrated, can be generated using rigorous social science methodologies.

The analysis in chapter 4 was broken along two lines. First I examined the conditions for successful interventions across all cases of civil conflicts in which there were interventions. It is this general case that is dealt with most often, and it is the category that affords the broadest level of generalization. But certain conflicts, those in which the level of violence is extremely high, pose particularly vexing problems for decision makers. We saw in the third chapter that very intense conflicts were considerably less likely to attract outside interventions, which I argued was because potential intervenors held very low expectations about the likely success of their efforts in these conflicts. But the results of chapter 3 also demonstrated that humanitarian crises increased the probability of an outside actor intervening, and I posited that this was a result of the political forces coming to bear on decision makers, compelling them to take some action to alleviate the carnage.

We can see these pressures playing out today with the French and the European Union in the Algerian conflict, and public disquiet was also evident in Zaire in 1996, Bosnia in 1995, Somalia in 1991, and Kosovo in 1999. These competing tensions suggest that an analytical distinction be drawn between the general case and those raging at very high levels of intensity.

The most important result that we can draw from the analysis of interventions across all cases is that the strategy for intervening has the largest influence on the outcome of the intervention; the type of conflict does not seem to matter very much. Overall, and given a fixed set of conditions, the probability of a successful outcome is rather low—less than 20 percent—and the effect of the orientation of the groups challenging the government has only a marginal impact on changes in that probability. On the other hand, supporting the government rather than the opposition increases the likelihood of a successful intervention, particularly if the intervention is a military one. It also matters considerably who is intervening. As expected, major powers have a 20 percent greater probability of success than do less powerful intervenors. The number of casualties also has an effect on the likely outcome of an intervention, where interventions into conflicts with upwards of a million casualties have a near nil chance of successfully containing the violence.

The most striking thing about the evidence pertaining to the outcome of interventions is that interventions are considerably more likely to be successful when the conflict is quite intense. Given a set of base conditions (the same as those for the general category of conflicts) an intervention into a highly intense conflict has about a 70 percent chance of successfully stopping the fighting. This is over three times the probability of success in the more broadly defined set of cases. Furthermore, the type of conflict into which an intervention is carried out now seems to matter considerably, with interventions into intense ideological conflicts having a 47 percent lower probability of success than the same intervention into a religious conflict; interventions in ethnically oriented conflicts have a 30 percent less chance of being successful. This adds considerable evidence to the argument of Kaufmann that identity patterns matter and that the ability to discard an identity influences the outcome of outside interventions. The strategy for intervening, again, has a direct effect on the outcome of the intervention, where support for the government is generally more effective than similar support for the opposition, and in these intense conflicts, mixed forms of intervention are generally better than solely military interventions. Apparently, using multiple channels to influence the distribution of capabilities is more effective when the fighting is intense.

An interesting thing about these results becomes apparent when we consider that the more intense the conflict, the less likely are outside actors to become involved in the conflict (chapter 3). So what we have is a situation where states are selecting themselves out of interventions—possibly because they hold a low expectation for success—and yet once they do intervene, the likelihood of being successful is remarkably high. The explanation for this is somewhat conjecture, but it is plausible that these intense conflicts are "ripe" for resolution (Haass 1990) or the phase of conflict is more conducive to outside efforts to facilitate conflict resolution (Kriesberg 1994). In a sense the combatants have been sufficiently brutal, the costs sufficiently high, and the war weariness sufficiently overbearing that an intervention by an outside force is enough to bring a halt to the fighting. It may be that in particularly intense conflicts the balance of capabilities is such that there is an effective stalemate in terms of the ability of either side to prevail, and these stalemate conditions exist at a very high level of violent conflict. Neither side can win, and neither side is willing to unilaterally back down. An outside intervention is sufficient to tip the scales in the favor of one of the actors, leading either to victory or the conclusion that suing for peace is the most preferred strategy at that time. The logic and the evidence are also consistent here that tipping the balance in favor of the government is more likely to lead to successful outcomes than supporting the opposition, and that mixed interventions are more effective than the solely military variety.

One of the peculiar aspects of interventions into civil conflicts is that they appear to be much more prevalent since the end of the cold war, and it seems that the public is considerably more aware of their progress. The evidence from chapter 3 demonstrates that unilateral interventions were more likely during the cold war than after it—somewhat counter to intuitive impressions—and the data presented in chapter 2 show that it is not clear that a new trend is evolving since the end of the cold war. Analysis by Ted Gurr (1994) also raises questions about the perceived increase in civil conflicts following the demise of the Soviet Union. Intuitive impressions, however, are not entirely incorrect. One interpretation of recent events is that unilateral interventions are giving way to a multilateral variant (which would account for the apparent increased prevalence of interventions), and that the immediate aftermath of the Soviet collapse did result in an upswing in conflicts, but that trend quickly tapered off. The increased use of multilateral interventions into civil conflicts suggests that we would benefit from an understanding of the conditions under which collective efforts are employed rather than unilateral ones, and the conditions that lead to successful outcomes. This was the focus of chapter 5.

Conceptually, multilateral interventions differ from their unilateral counterparts along a couple dimensions. First, the distribution of costs and benefits are quite different; second, the goals of the intervention are considerably broader in the multilateral, as compared with the unilateral, intervention. But beyond what I argue are these fundamental distinctions, a number of practical considerations are necessary for effective multilateral interventions. The neutrality of the intervening organization is critical, as is the existence of a cease-fire among the combatants, and the mutual consent of the conflicting parties. Once a cease-fire is in place and all sides consent to the role of outside actors, the goal of stopping the fighting is no longer relevant. In essence the subjective estimates of the ability of an intervention to stop the fighting are no longer important, and the focus now is on solidifying the gains made at the negotiating table. If either side thinks that the intervention is partial to its opponent, then the intervention reverts back to altering the balance of capabilities and would be increasingly prone to failure. To some degree the intervention in Somalia suffered this fate.

Case studies of the evolution of the conflicts in El Salvador and Zaire were used to tease out some of the interplay between various factors that would account for the outcome of multilateral interventions and the subsequent effectiveness of those policies. The pattern in El Salvador quite closely reflects the conditions outlined theoretically, where unilateral interventions were the norm before the end of the cold war, with the United States being the most active intervenor. The end of the cold war changed the internal dynamics within El Salvador as well as the extent of external support. After persistent jockeying for bargaining positions, a cease-fire was negotiated along with terms for a settlement of the conflict, the integration of opposing troops and political leaders, and the rebuilding of the infrastructure. A considerable multilateral intervention initiative played a key role in ushering the two sides toward a permanent resolution of the conflict, and the conditions identified as those critical for success were solidly in place at the time of the intervention.

Zaire presented a somewhat different look at the ability to organize multilateral interventions and their role in resolving conflict. The history of interventions into Zairean conflicts also spanned the cold war divide, with outside actors playing a role in ending uprisings in the 1960s. The multilateral intervention organized under the auspices of the UN in the early 1960s is one of the few instances where the UN intervened in a partisan manner to help put down an insurrection. Despite the fact that the UN's policies violated nearly all of the conditions outlined, it was generally successful at restoring the authority of the central government in Zaire. There were also unilateral interventions in the early history of the Zairean state, both by the Belgians and the Americans. Events in 1996, however, present a more nuanced view of the conditions for effective multilateral interventions and are more consistent with theoretical expectations of when they would be expected.

Under the auspices of a French and Canadian organized effort the UN tried to intervene in the Zairean civil war. The reason for the attempted intervention was ostensibly to help repatriate thousands of Rwandan refugees who were being further displaced by the conflict in Zaire. If the arguments presented in chapter 5 were to hold true, then we would only expect an intervention when there was a cease-fire, the mutual consent of the groups in conflict, and an impartially organized effort. Although the French and the Canadians were able to generate considerable support for their proposed intervention, the policy never went forward. The United States, which would have had to play a critical role in the proposed intervention, could never be brought fully onboard. It is clear from a reading of this contemporary event that the three conditions were simply never met, and it was the failure to meet these conditions that led to the decision by the United States to withdraw from the planned intervention. A cease-fire could not be negotiated between the opposition troops loyal to Laurent Kabila and those of the government. Kabila argued that since he was dominating the battlefield, he saw no reason to agree to cease-fire under terms that would assist the government of Mobutu. If he considered the proposed cease-fire to benefit Mobutu's troops, then the intervention itself must have certainly looked like a partisan attempt to support France's ally, Mobutu. The combined effect of these battlefield conditions and the perceptions of the motives behind the intervenors (rightly or wrongly) resulted in Kabila refusing to consent to the intervention, which directly increased the risks of exposure by the UN-led troops. A military victory by Kabila's opposition forces ultimately ended that phase of the conflict in Zaire.

With this brief survey of the results complete, I will conclude with a discussion about the inference and implications on two fronts. First, important theoretical implications are derived from this analysis, and I will point to ways in which this work might help inform a broader body of research. Second, I will articulate some of the policy-relevant inferences that might be important to those struggling over the decision of whether or how to intervene in specific conflicts.

Theoretical Implications and the Contribution to Peace Research

Although written as much to the policy as the academic community, theoretical implications for the study of conflict and conflict resolution should not be minimized. These implications fall into four main areas: (1) the idea of selection bias issues in studying outcomes of policy decisions, (2) the role of outside actors in shaping the course of conflicts, (3) the role of identity in conflict and conflict management, and (4) the notion of conflicts being ripe for resolution.

The selection bias problem is one that has plagued the study of intra and inter national conflict, and is an inherent problem in almost any research in world politics (Tetlock and Belkin 1996). Questions of "what would have happened if" or "who considered taking action but chose not to" often have only rhetorical answers, and yet they are questions for which the ways we derive answers have a considerable influence on the way we choose cases for analysis. Some scholars have begun to address issues of the selection effect in an attempt to understand why states might select into or out of a war, and the implications of their choice on the course of the conflict (Gartner and Siverson 1996; Smith 1996). This problem seems particularly tricky when the observable behavior is an intervention into a civil conflict. Smith (1996), for instance, focuses on the role of alliance membership on the choice for intervening in an international war, which gives him a reasonable set of criteria for determining a population of potential intervenors. Siverson and Starr (1991) use the notion of shared boundaries to develop a population of cases from which to study the diffusion of international conflict. And Gartner and Siverson (1996) argue that states select targets that they determine *ex ante* they can defeat and therefore account for the fact that most wars remain limited. Intervening in civil conflicts posed a difficult problem in establishing criteria for "relevancy" (Lemke 1996) because traces of deliberations over an intervention alternative could be found for countries that had no likely defining criterion for a potential intervenor. There is clearly a need to identify conditions for relevancy that allows the inclusion of all those states that consider an intervention option, but reject it without leaving much of a trace. The results of chapter 3 did demonstrate that clear selection criteria appear to be used to opt into and out of interventions, such that certain contextual conditions lead to greater (or lesser) probability of observing an intervention. This research project used the conflict as the unit of analysis, but if arguments are to be couched in decision-theoretic terms, then a dyadic unit of analysis would facilitate our ability to draw inferences by identifying a more valid and reliable sample of cases. The notion of relevant dyads across a broad range of political choices needs to be developed further, as does the identification of selection criteria by which foreign policymakers choose their venues. A closer articulation of the factors that lead to case selection criteria will allow us to more fully expand on the concept of substitutability in conduct of foreign policy (Most and Starr 1989).

One of the questions that has drawn the attention of considerable scholarly research involves the conditions under which international wars expand beyond the initial instigators. At the root of most of this work is the notion that third parties contribute to the expansion of the conflict, whether it be because of cross-boundary concerns that present both the opportunity and willingness for outside involvement (e.g., Siverson and Starr 1991), the role of alliances (e.g., Siverson and King 1979; Smith 1996), or systemic polarity (e.g., Wayman 1984). One of the assumptions of this study—and one that is empirically supported—is that third parties can contribute to the settlement of conflicts rather than simply their expansion. Granted that international conflicts may be different from the intranational variety, the evidence demonstrates that under certain conditions third-party interventions can contribute to the de-escalation rather than escalation of conflicts. It may be that the expansion of conflicts that result from alliance commitments serve, under some circumstances, to decrease their duration. The notion of the possible duration of a conflict in the absence of the involvement of a third party presents tricky counterfactual problems, but the results of this analysis suggest that it is one of the possible implications of the diffusion of conflict and that the conditions under which this outcome might result should be explored more fully.

At the height of the carnage in Bosnia there was considerable debate about the prospects for resolving internal conflicts involving actors with long historical religious or ethnic animosities. Burton (1990) argues that these conflicts are the result of fears over threats to communal identity. And in response to the ethnic genocide in Rwanda in 1994 at least one former diplomat has charged that the only mechanism to resolve these types of conflicts is through some form of ethnic separation. Chaim Kaufmann (1996) gave a degree of academic legitimacy to these arguments by positing that under some conditions—conditions he defined in terms of the orientation of the groups in conflict—only militarily enforced ethnic separation will be effective at ending a conflict. These are thorny issues with wide-ranging implications about the ability of diverse people to coexist under certain situations. The results of this analysis do not portend to enter the ethical debates about the movement of peoples across boundaries, but they do tentatively point toward a rather strong relationship between the orientation of the groups in conflict and the ability of outside actors to alter the course of the fighting. Obviously there are many directions to push these ideas, but clearly they deserve a more systematic treatment that helps uncover the extent to which identity patterns determine not only the onset of violence but also the way these types of conflicts can be resolved.

Finally, the idea that conflicts reach a point at which they are ripe for resolution is considered by some to be a critical determinant in our understanding of conflict resolution (e.g., Haass 1990). This concept generates considerable conceptual support in the sense that it is argued that conflicts go through phases and that particular phases are more conducive to steps toward resolution, whether those steps are a function of outside involvement or more effective bargaining (e.g., Kriesberg 1991; Pillar 1983). One of the critical problems faced by those who argue that resolution requires readiness, ripeness, or a plateau is that they have not demonstrated this systematically, nor have they identified a point at which conflicts become ripe. The results presented in this work demonstrate that the notion of ripeness may have empirical support, at least in civil conflicts, and that to some degree the point at which conflicts are increasingly disposed to settlement can be tied to the extent of the violence experienced by the society. If a "tipping point" could be identified at which combatants are increasingly amenable to resolution efforts, then the work of diplomats would be greatly enhanced. Identifying the point of ripeness requires more sophisticated data analysis using event history modeling techniques, but early efforts give reason for optimism (Regan and Stam 2000).

Implications, Inferences, and the Usefulness
to the Policy Process

How civil conflicts end is a broad question, but it is a central question in the policy community today. This study's contribution to an answer lies in offering evidence about the role outside actors can play in the process of ending civil conflicts, and it attempts to derive policy-relevant information about the conditions for successful interventions through the use of rigorous social science methodologies. After working through the logic and evidence that I could bring to bear, it is now time to pull all the pieces together and see how far we can push these results into the realm of policy implications. The place to begin is with a brief foray into expectations that we should hold for our ability to bridge this gap between social science research and policy-relevant inferences (George 1995).

It would probably be unreasonable, and most likely inadvisable, to hope that policy would be made solely on the basis of quantitative analysis of a population of cases pooled across a half century of time. Our methods, measurements, and models are simply not sophisticated enough to permit inferences that have a high enough degree of certainty to gamble on the outcome of issues like war and peace. But at the same time this particular approach does not offer any less in terms of certainty between cause and effect than does the more traditional small sample case study. In fact, one could make the argument that this approach offers considerably more policy-relevant inferences than does the analogous case approach championed by Neustadt and May (1986) or a structured case comparison. Case study analysts often choose cases based on a weak notion of scientific method, bias their findings by choosing cases and indicators that seem to be consistent with their theoretical notions, and report results that in general could be difficult to replicate. In the area of foreign policy, however, it is advice predicated mostly on case study techniques that dominate the policy debates. This is so despite the fact that may other areas of policy are informed substantially by statistical analyses identifying trends over time and space. Stock market analysts, commodity traders, and economic planners and forecasters place a considerable amount of weight behind long-term trends identified through statistical techniques and employing simplifying assumptions much as has been done in this study of interventions.

What we can draw from this study is an understanding of an overall trend in the relationship between a treatment (interventions) and an outcome (end of hostilities). If any such trend is robust and the putative causal impact substantial, then the policy community can at minimum take away a sense of guideposts along the way to desirable policy outcomes. Failure of an intervention is generally not the sought-after goal of the foreign policy community, and indicators that consistently point toward an impending failure should—and probably would—attract the attention of those responsible for the formulation and implementation of policy. The analysis here is best seen as one of a range of potential inputs upon which policy should be developed. What we can offer through rigorous quantitative analysis of political events is evidence of what works and when, qualified by the caveat that these findings hold "on average." The on-average principle is not a point estimate upon which one could necessarily stake a career—let alone the resources of a country. But the notion of estimates of outcomes around which there is some confidence interval is sufficiently entrenched in actuarial sciences used by the insurance industry and financial forecasting used by the Federal Reserve Bank to set monetary policy that foreign policy should not view this approach as anathema to the conduct of the foreign policy process. Quite the opposite should be true. The policy community should be able to begin policy deliberations with a basic understanding of what past trends reveal about the prospects for the outcome of their policy, and then use this baseline to approach specific analogous cases to identify the intricacies of special conditions and circumstances.

Given this brief foray into the role of evidence and its application by the policy community, what inferences can we draw about the role of outside interventions into internal conflicts? The first thing that must be kept in mind is that the policy choices available are the result of political conditions extant at the time of the decision. The full range of options are not equally accessible under all circumstances. For instance, supporting a government in its struggle against an opposition's challenge may be the most effective method of stopping the fighting, yet depending on the political alignments of the groups, supporting the government may not be an acceptable option. For example, the United States and the NATO countries faced this dilemma over if and how to respond to the Serbian suppression of an independence movement in the province of Kosovo in late 1998. By the time they did intervene in mid-1999, they had little choice but to support the Albanian opposition. This choice, however, generally diminished the prospects for success. The approach then—if a state decides to intervene—might be to design a strategy that is most effective given the political constraints. Equally plausible is that given the conditions of the conflict and the orientation of the groups involved, the prospects for a successful outcome is so low that in spite of political imperatives, the best strategy is to not intervene. Intervening, it may turn out, simply increases the level of conflict without any reasonable prospect of achieving a desirable outcome. In hindsight this may be the advice that should have been proffered during the early years of U.S. involvement in the Vietnam conflict.

The evidence presented in the earlier chapters points to inferences about where and how an intervention can contribute to outcomes that bring a halt to the violence in the conflicting country, with the overarching inference suggesting that unless the conflict is what some call ripe for resolution, the prospects for successful interventions is rather low. The interventions that are particularly ripe seem to be those in which the extent of the carnage is quite high, what I have identified as the more intense conflicts. Ripeness in the sense that I am using it appears to reflect the battlefield—and probably social—conditions in which the rate of casualties place a considerable burden on society, and possibly the war weariness increases the effectiveness of outside support. The intervention may be sufficient to permit victory by one side, but it is more likely to alter battlefield conditions enough to compel participation in negotiations to arrive at a peace settlement. This is consistent with those who explore the conditions that lead to successful bargaining or negotiation strategies (e.g., Morgan 1995; Pillar 1983). The apparent reluctance of states to intervene in these rather violent conflicts is offset by the high rate of success if they do so. The end of hostilities associated with an outside intervention is about four times more likely when the rate of killing is greater than 10,000 people a year than in less intense conflicts. In general, this wide gulf between the effectiveness of interventions across the intensity of the conflict holds except when the combatants are organized along ideological lines. Intervening in ideological conflicts seems to have rather dismal prospects for successful outcomes—if that outcome is defined in terms of stopping the fighting—regardless of most other conditions of the conflict.

The inference here is that where a state chooses to intervene matters in terms of its ability to affect the outcome as well, possibly, as the outcome that is desired. Early in the analysis I made a simplifying assumption that states intervene to stop the fighting, and I argued that this is a reasonable goal to attribute to outside interventions. I also argued that fighting between groups in conflict can end in a lot of ways; at one extreme is the military defeat of one side, at the other is a mutually beneficial negotiated settlement. Although states may intervene in ideological conflicts to end the fighting, to the intervenors the most acceptable method for achieving that goal is possibly through victory rather than compromise. This may be a function of political imperatives. But what seems clear is that in ideological contests the end of hostilities through victory on the battlefield is a fairly elusive goal. On the other hand, the relatively high rate of successful outcomes from interventions in intense culturally based conflicts suggests that well-placed interventions can contribute to the peaceful resolution of civil conflicts. The difficulties associated with outside interventions contributing to the end of ideological conflicts is also likely to be the result of offsetting support for the combatants. Counterinterventions that simply influence the relative battlefield capabilities by raising the level of both groups may exacerbate the conflict and decrease the chance that either side could be effective. At some level this is at the crux of ideological conflicts. Under the very best odds, if the decision is made to intervene on one side of an ideological conflict, supporting the government has a considerably higher probability of success. Again, however, the importance of political imperatives may make such options moot.

Prescriptive advice to a decision maker contemplating an intervention might be to stay clear of the rather low-level conflicts because they have a reasonable chance of settling themselves without interventions, whereas the prospects for contributing to that peaceful outcome with an intervention is rather low. In this sense the advice is to focus quite extensively on the first part of the two-staged decision process outlined in chapter 3 and resist the temptation to close too quickly on the conclusion that the conflict will continue without outside involvement. The evidence seems to suggest that the lower-level conflicts are more likely to be of shorter duration if they do not have outside interventions (chapter 2) and that the prospects for a successful outcome from an intervention is never better than 50 percent, and even then only when the intervention supports the government. Since two-thirds of the civil conflicts in the post–World War II period have had outside intervenors, there may be a tendency to prematurely close on the intervention option without letting other less-intrusive alternatives play their course. But also given that the majority of the conflicts were during the cold war there was probably a propensity to view all conflicts from some sort of lens clouded by cold war dynamics.

Beyond the context of the conflict lies the strategy for intervening. It is reasonably clear from the evidence presented earlier that how a state intervenes affects the probability of achieving a successful outcome, as does the issue of who intervenes. It is also evident that no matter how the analysis is broken down, major powers—or those with considerable resources—are more likely to be successful with their intervention policies than nonresource-rich countries.

In general, interventions that support the government are more successful than those that support the opposition. For example, military support for the government is more likely to contribute to at least a short-term respite in the fighting than military support for the opposition would, and interventions incorporating a mix of economic and military instruments are more likely to succeed than an intervention focusing solely on military means. This inference holds regardless of the target, and it makes sense. But when trying to support opposition forces struggling against the government, both a mixed and a solely economic intervention are better than simply a military intervention. If you keep in mind that one way to support an opposition economically is to impose economic constraints on the government, the results sustain the inference that sanctions can work. Government forces fighting an opposition group may be more amenable to resolve the conflict if they see the economic constraints imposed from outside to be particularly burdensome. This inference is consistent with research into the conditions under which governments will resort to repression to stifle political dissent (see Gartner and Regan 1996). If the policy debate is over using military *or* economic means to intervene, economic interventions are more effective. In the very intense conflicts (where there have been no instances of solely economic interventions) an intervention that incorporates an economic element is better than one that focuses solely on the military aspects of an intervention. Conversely, if the debate is over whether to use military *and* economic leverage to stop a civil conflict, include the economic dimension. Countries involved in internal struggles are apparently susceptible to outside economic influence, and it appears that battlefield calculations can be influenced by financial considerations.

Some of the questions about the strategy for intervening that have not been answered by this analysis, though it would be useful if answers could be forthcoming, involve issues of the timing or sequencing of interventions, and the use of the carrot and the stick. For example, does an intervention that unfolds over a relatively short time period—such as Somalia, 1990—have a greater probability of success than an incremental strategy? Similarly debates have raged within policy communities—such as over the U.S. aid to El Salvador—as to whether the sequencing of inducements and punishments are effective at altering battlefield behavior. Although further quantitative analysis might be able to offer insights into these questions, at present the use of analogous cases can possibly help guide the decision process. Another fruitful avenue for investigation is the relationship between diplomatic interventions and the military and economic variety examined here. It would be reasonable to expect that at times the conditions for successful policies would converge, yet under other conditions one form of intervention may have to precede the other.

Decision makers grappling with whether or how to participate in multilateral interventions have other criteria to keep in mind. First it seems clear that the goals of multilateral interventions differ substantially from those that drive unilateral interventions. Since multilateral interventions generally follow on from a negotiated end to the fighting, a fuller array of goals are on the agenda. Second, multilateral interventions can be, and often are, carried out by a wider range of actors. States may still be the primary participants in multilateral interventions, but they are less likely to be the organizing unit or the sole provider of the tools with which to intervene. Supranational or regional organizations are likely to be at the forefront of multilateral efforts, with individual states often contributing the resources at the disposal of the organization.

Several policy implications can be offered regarding multilateral initiatives. First, adopting a neutral posture is a prerequisite to successful multilateral interventions. This is in part because of an interaction with the second condition that leads to more successful outcomes, the mutual consent of all parties to the conflict. If the intervening community does not adopt a neutral position vis-à-vis the combatants, then almost by definition the intervention is attempting to alter the battlefield conditions—or potential battlefield conditions should the parties resume fighting. The important implication here is that if a country has a history of partisan participation in a conflict, it either needs to demonstrate convincingly that it is now playing a neutral role, or it needs to only be involved in a supplementary manner in the organization and implementation of the multilateral intervention effort.

All the good intentions, impartiality, and mutual consent, however, will not overcome the liabilities associated with a poorly organized intervention effort. Building trust and developing the conditions for conflict resolution and reconciliation are important components of any effort to capitalize on the successes at the negotiating table. A coherently organized and implemented intervention is more able to cater to the often conflicting needs of the antagonists and should be flexible enough to adapt to changing conditions. This was seen quite clearly in the case of El Salvador where recurring sticking points in the implementation of the peace accords were effectively addressed by a fluid and adaptable UN mission. Responding to breaches in a negotiated settlement should adhere to the tenets of neutrality, and the more coherently the intervention is organized, the more likely it is that responses by the intervenors will not be viewed as partial to one side and, therefore, will maintain the trust and respect of the various participants to the conflict.

In the end, intervening in civil conflicts will remain tricky business. For a host of political—and maybe ethical—reasons, political leaders will confront these decisions with some regularity. Systematic work such as this demonstrates that the policy process does not have to be idiosyncratic and that there are some policy options that will consistently lead to better outcomes. The social science community can contribute further to the management of the foreign policy process by filling in some of the gaps in my analysis. Expanding on ideas about methods of internation influence and the ability of foreign policy makers to substitute across a range of options would be particularly fruitful avenues of inquiry. Both the policy and scholarly communities can benefit from increased attention to issues of how and when outside actors can best manage internal conflicts.

Appendix: Cases of Civil Conflicts and Interventions

Time Span*	Country	Casualties	Intervenor(s)	Target	Outcome
1944–1949	Greece	200,000	US	Government	Success
			UK	Government	Success
			Albania	Opposition	Failure
			Yugoslavia	Opposition	Failure
			Bulgaria	Opposition	Failure
1946–1946	Bolivia	1,000			
1946–1950	China	300,000	US	Government	Failure
			Taiwan	Opposition	Failure
1947–1947	China	1,400			
1947–1947	Paraguay	2,500			
1948–1962	Malaysia	14,000	UK	Government	Success
			China	Opposition	Failure
			Australia	Government	Success
			New Zealand	Opposition	Success
1948–1948	Costa Rica	1,000	Nicaragua	Government	Failure
1948–Ongoing	Burma	130,000	China	Opposition	Failure
1948–1948	Yemen Arab Republic	3,000			
1948–1948	Colombia	14,000			
1949–1962	Colombia	30,000	US	Government	Failure
1950–1952	Philippines	3,000	US	Government	Success
1950–1950	Indonesia	5,000			
1953–1953	Indonesia	1,000			
1954–1954	Guatemala	2,000	US	Opposition	Success
1954–1964	India	20,000			
1956–1959	Iraq	5,000	Syria	Opposition	Failure
1956–1956	Hungary	3,500	USSR	Opposition	Success

*Ongoing refers to conflicts under way as of 1994.

(continued)

Time Span	Country	Casualties	Intervenor(s)	Target	Outcome
1956–1960	Indonesia	50,000	US	Government	Success
			China	Opposition	Failure
1958–1959	Cuba	3,000			
1958–1958	Lebanon	30,000	US	Government	Success
			UK	Government	Success
			Syria	Opposition	Failure
1959–Ongoing	China	100,000			
1960–1964	Ethiopia	300	Somalia	Government	Failure
1960–1965	S. Vietnam	300,000	US	Government	Failure
			N. Vietnam	Opposition	Failure
1960–1965	Zaire	300,000	UN	Government	Success
			Belgium	Opposition	Failure
			Belgium	Government	Success
			Algeria	Opposition	Failure
			Egypt	Opposition	Failure
1960–1962	Laos	30,000	US	Opposition	Success
			USSR	Opposition	Success
			S. Vietnam	Opposition	Success
1961–1966	Iraq	5,000	Syria	Government	Failure
1962–1963	Algeria	1,000			
1962–1991	Ethiopia	45,000	US	Government	Failure
			Cuba	Opposition	Failure
			Cuba	Government	Failure
			USSR	Opposition	Failure
			USSR	Government	Failure
			Sudan	Opposition	Failure
1962–1967	Yemen Arab Republic	100,000	Egypt	Government	Success
			Jordan	Opposition	Failure
			Saudi Arabia	Opposition	Failure
1963–Ongoing	Indonesia	15,000			
1963–1973	Laos	18,000	US	Government	Failure
			France	Government	Failure
			N. Vietnam	Opposition	Failure
1963–1964	Cyprus	3,000	UN	Neutral	Success
			UK	Neutral	Failure
			Greece	Government	Failure
			Turkey	Opposition	Failure
1963–1972	Sudan	200,000	Belgium	Government	Failure
1963–1964	Rwanda	20,000			
1964–1994	Israel	10,000	Libya	Opposition	Failure
			Saudi Arabia	Opposition	Failure
			Kuwait	Opposition	Failure
			Bahrain	Opposition	Failure
1965–1972	Chad	1,500	France	Government	Failure
			Libya	Opposition	Failure

Time Span	Country	Casualties	Intervenor(s)	Target	Outcome
1965–1965	Dominican Republic	1,000	US	Government	Success
			Honduras	Government	Success
1965–1985	Thailand	10,000	US	Government	Failure
			China	Opposition	Failure
			Malaysia	Government	Failure
1965–1965	Indonesia	5,000			
1966–1966	Uganda	1,000			
1966–1972	Guatemala	45,500	US	Government	Failure
1967–1970	Nigeria	25,000			
1967–1967	Zaire	2,000	US	Government	Success
			Belgium	Opposition	Failure
1967–1970	Nigeria	25,000			
1968–Ongoing	Spain	1,000			
1968–1980	Burma	1,500	China	Opposition	Failure
1969–Ongoing	UK	3,000	Libya	Opposition	Failure
1970–1975	Oman	2,000	UK	Government	Success
			Iran	Government	Success
			Jordan	Government	Success
			Yeman	Opposition	Failure
1970–1970	Jordon	1,500	Syria	Opposition	Failure
1970–1994	S. Africa	14,500	UN	Government	Failure
			US	Opposition	Success
			UK	Opposition	Success
			USSR	Opposition	Failure
1970–1975	Cambodia	150,000	US	Government	Failure
			N. Vietnam	Opposition	Success
			S. Vietnam	Government	Failure
1971–1972	Uganda	2,000	Tanzania	Government	Failure
1971–1971	Sri Lanka	1,000	US	Government	Success
			UK	Government	Success
			USSR	Government	Success
			India	Government	Success
			Pakistan	Government	Success
1971–Ongoing	Bangladesh	24,000			
1971–1971	Pakistan	9,000	India	Government	Failure
1972–Ongoing	Guatemala	150,000			
1972–Ongoing	Philippines	10,000	US	Government	Failure
1972–Ongoing	Philippines	50,000			
1972–1979	Zimbabwe	15,000	UN	Opposition	Success
			Cuba	Opposition	Success
			S. Africa	Government	Failure
1972–1972	Burundi	10,000	Zaire	Government	Success
1973–1977	Pakistan	9,000	Afghanistan	Opposition	Failure
1974–1974	Iraq	1,000			
1974–1974	Cyprus	3,000	Turkey	Opposition	Failure

(continued)

Time Span	Country	Casualties	Intervenor(s)	Target	Outcome
1974–1974	Cyprus	3,000	Greece	Government	Failure
1975–1988	Lebanon	125,000	US	Government	Failure
			France	Government	Failure
			Syria	Opposition	Failure
			Israel	Government	Failure
1975–Ongoing	Mauretania	1,000	France	Government	Failure
			Morocco	Government	Failure
			Algeria	Opposition	Failure
1975–Ongoing	Morocco	15,000	Algeria	Opposition	Failure
			Libya	Opposition	Failure
1975–Ongoing	Indonesia	15,000			
1975–Ongoing	Indonesia	200,000	US	Opposition	Failure
			Canada	Opposition	Failure
1975–1991	Angola	102,000	US	Opposition	Failure
			Cuba	Government	Failure
			USSR	Government	Failure
			Zaire	Opposition	Failure
			S. Africa	Opposition	Failure
1977–1985	Ethiopia	30,000	Cuba	Government	Success
			USSR	Government	Success
			Somalia	Opposition	Failure
1977–1977	Zaire	500	Morocco	Government	Success
1978–1984	Guatemala	21,000	US	Government	Failure
1978–1979	Zaire	1,000	Belgium	Government	Success
			France	Government	Success
			Morocco	Government	Success
1978–1982	Chad	1,000	France	Government	Failure
			Senegal	Neutral	Failure
			Nigeria	Neutral	Failure
			Congo	Neutral	Failure
			Zaire	Neutral	Failure
			Libya	Opposition	Success
1978–1992	Afghanistan	200,000	US	Opposition	Failure
			USSR	Government	Failure
			Iran	Opposition	Failure
			Pakistan	Opposition	Failure
1978–1979	Iran	10,000	Iraq	Government	Failure
1978–1979	Nicaragua	30,000	US	Government	Failure
1979–1991	Cambodia	25,300	USSR	Opposition	Failure
			China	Opposition	Failure
			Thailand	Opposition	Failure
			Laos	Opposition	Failure
			N. Vietnam	Government	Failure
1979–1992	El Salvador	60,000	US	Government	Failure
			Honduras	Government	Failure
1979–1993	Mozambique	122,000	USSR	Government	Success
			Tanzania	Government	Failure

Time Span	Country	Casualties	Intervenor(s)	Target	Outcome
1979–1993	Mozambique	122,000	Zimbabwe	Government	Failure
			Malawi	Government	Failure
			S. Africa	Opposition	Failure
1980–1981	Nigeria	1,000			
1980–Ongoing	China	2,000			
1980–1988	Zimbabwe	1,500	S. Africa	Opposition	Failure
1980–1986	Uganda	250,000	US	Opposition	Failure
			S. Korea	Government	Failure
1981–1982	Iran	4,000			
1981–1981	Gambia	800	Senegal	Government	Failure
1982–Ongoing	Peru	27,000	US	Government	Failure
1982–1990	Nicaragua	10,000	US	Opposition	Failure
			Honduras	Opposition	Failure
			USSR	Government	Failure
1982–Ongoing	Sri Lanka	24,000	UK	Opposition	Failure
			Norway	Opposition	Failure
			India	Government	Failure
1982–1991	Somalia	20,000	US	Government	Failure
			US	Opposition	Failure
			Ethiopia	Opposition	Failure
1983–1992	Burma	6,500			
1983–1986	Chad	1,500	France	Government	Failure
			France	Government	Success
			Zaire	Government	Failure
			Libya	Opposition	Failure
1983–1983	Grenada	200	US	Opposition	Success
1983–Ongoing	Sudan	990,000	Libya	Opposition	Failure
			Iran	Government	Failure
1984–Ongoing	Colombia	11,000	US	Government	Failure
1984–1984	Nigeria	1,000			
1984–Ongoing	Turkey	15,000	Germany	Opposition	Failure
1985–1989	Ecuador	2,000			
1985–Ongoing	India	30,000	Afghanistan	Opposition	Failure
			Pakistan	Opposition	Failure
1985–1993	Iraq	180,000	UN	Opposition	Success
			US	Opposition	Success
			Iran	Opposition	Failure
1986–Ongoing	Nigeria	11,000			
1986–1986	Yemen	2,000			
1986–1988	Uganda	10,000			
1987–1989	Sri Lanka	25,000			
1987–1991	Ethiopia	45,000	USSR	Government	Failure
1988–1991	Papua New Guinea	1,000			
1988–1990	Lebanon	1,500	Syria	Government	Success
			Israel	Opposition	Failure
1988–1988	Burundi	20,000			

(continued)

Time Span	Country	Casualties	Intervenor(s)	Target	Outcome
1989–1989	Romania	1,100			
1989–Ongoing	Chad	1,000	France	Government	Failure
1989–1990	Liberia	20,000	Ghana	Government	Success
			Nigeria	Government	Success
1990–Ongoing	Niger	1,000	Liberia	Opposition	Failure
1990–Ongoing	Mali	1,000	Liberia	Opposition	Failure
1990–Ongoing	S. Africa	14,000			
1990–1994	Rwanda	500,000	France	Government	Failure
1991–1993	Georgia	10,000	USSR	Government	Success
1991–1993	Djibouti	1,000	France	Government	Success
1991–Ongoing	Azerbaijan	7,000	Armenia	Opposition	Failure
			Turkey	Government	Failure
1991–1992	Rwanda	2,000			
1991–1992	Yugoslavia	500,000			
1991–Ongoing	Somalia	300,000	UN	Neutral	Failure
			US	Neutral	Failure
1991–Ongoing	Iraq	500,000	UN	Opposition	Success
			US	Opposition	Success
			UK	Opposition	Success
1992–Ongoing	Zaire	15,000			
1992–Ongoing	Moldova	1,000	USSR	Opposition	Success
1992–Ongoing	Kenya	1,500			
1992–Ongoing	Afghanistan	10,000			
1992–Ongoing	Egypt	1,000			
1992–Ongoing	Ethiopia	2,000			
1992–Ongoing	Bosnia-Herzegovina	200,000	UN	Neutral	Failure
			Yugoslavia	Opposition	Failure
1992–1994	Tajikistan	40,000	Russia	Government	Success
			Afghanistan	Opposition	Failure
1992–1993	Liberia	15,000	Ghana	Government	Success
			Nigeria	Government	Success
1992–1994	Angola	50,000			
1993–Ongoing	Algeria	20,000			
1993–1994	Rwanda	10,000			
1994–Ongoing	Mexico	1,000			
1994–1994	Yemen	2,000	Saudi Arabia	Opposition	Failure
1994–Ongoing	Russia	1,000			

Bibliography

Acharya, Amitav, Pierre Lizee, and Sorpong Peou, eds. 1991. *Cambodia—The 1989 Paris Peace Conference: Background Analysis and Documents*. Millwood, NY: Kraus International Publications.

Adelman, Howard, and Astri Suhrke. 1996. *The International Response to Conflict and Genocide: Lessons from the Rwanda Experience, Study #2: Early Warning and Conflict Management*. United Nations: Steering Committee of the Joint Evaluation of Emergency Assistance to Rwanda.

Aldinger, Charles. 1996. "U.S. Wants Zaire Cease-Fire Before Sending Force." *Reuters,* November 14, 1996.

Amer, Rames, Birgen Heldt, Signe Langron, Kjell Magnusson, Erik Melander, Kjell-Ake Nordquist, Thomas Ohlson, and Peter Wallensteen. 1993. "Major Armed Conflicts." In *SIPRI Yearbook 1993, World Armaments and Disarmaments*. Stockholm.

Andreopoulos, George. 1993. *Genocide and Democracy in Cambodia: The Khmer Rouge, the United Nations and the International Community*. New Haven: Yale University Press.

Baldwin, David. 1985. *Economic Statecraft*. Princeton: Princeton University Press.

Bennett, D. Scott, and Allan C. Stam III. 1996. "The Duration of Interstate Wars, 1816–1985." *American Political Science Review* 90 (2): 239–57.

Best, Edward. 1987. *US Policy and Regional Security in Central America*. New York: St. Martin's.

Blechman, Barry M. 1995. "The Intervention Dilemma." *Washington Quarterly* 18 (3): 63–73.

Borton, John, Emery Bursset, and Alistair Hallam. 1996. *The International Response to Conflict and Genocide: Lessons from the Rwanda Experience, Study #3: Humanitarian Aid and Effects*. United Nations: Steering Committee of the Joint Evaluation of Emergency Assistance to Rwanda.

Boulding, Kenneth. 1962. *Conflict and Defense: A General Theory*. New York: Harper & Row.

159

Boutros-Ghali, Boutros. 1992. *An Agenda for Peace: Preventive Diplomacy, Peacemaking, and Peace-Keeping.* New York: United Nations.

Brogan, Patrick. 1989. *World Conflicts: Why and Where They Are Happening.* London: Broomsbury.

Bueno de Mesquita, Bruce. 1985. *The War Trap.* New Haven: Yale University Press.

Bull, Hedly. 1984. *Intervention in World Politics.* Oxford: Claredon Press.

Burton, John W. 1990. *Conflict: Resolution and Provention.* London: Macmillan.

Carment, David. 1993. "The International Dimensions of Ethnic Conflict: Concepts, Indicators, and Theory." *Journal of Peace Research* 30 (2): 137–50.

Carment, David, and Patrick James. 1995a. "Internal Constraints and Interstate Ethnic Conflict: Toward a Crisis-Based Assessment of Irredentism." *Journal of Conflict Resolution* 39 (1): 82–109.

———. 1995b. "Explaining Third Party Intervention in Ethnic Conflict: Theory and Evidence." Unpublished manuscript, Iowa State University.

Carment, David, Dane Rowlands, and Patrick James. 1997. "Ethnic Conflict and Third Party Intervention: Riskiness, Rationality and Commitment." In *Enforcing Cooperation,* ed. Gerald Schneider and Patricia Weitsman, 104–31. London: Macmillan.

Chandler, David P. 1992. *A History of Cambodia.* Boulder: Westview.

Clark, Jeffery. 1993. "Debacle in Somalia: Failure of the Collective Response." In *Enforcing Restraint: Collective Intervention in Internal Conflicts,* ed. Lori Fisler Damrosch, 205–40. New York: Council on Foreign Relations.

Clutterbuck, Richard. 1985. *Conflict and Violence in Singapore and Malaysia 1945–1983.* Boulder: Westview.

Connaughton, Richard. 1992. *Military Intervention in the 1990s: A New Logic of War.* London: Routledge.

Cooper, Robert, and Mats Berdal. 1993. "Outside Interventions in Ethnic Conflicts." *Survival* 35 (1): 118–42.

Cortright, David, and George A. Lopez, eds. 1995. *Economic Sanctions: Panacea or Peacebuilding in the Post–Cold War World?* Boulder: Westview.

Daalder, Ivo H. 1996. "The United States and Military Intervention in Internal Conflicts." In *The International Dimensions of Internal Conflict,* ed. Michael E. Brown, 461–88. Cambridge: MIT Press.

Damrosch, Lori Fisler, ed. 1993. *Enforcing Restraint: Collective Intervention in Internal Conflicts.* New York: Council on Foreign Relations.

Damrosch, Lori Fisler, and David J. Scheffer, eds. 1991. *Law and Force in the New International Order.* Boulder: Westview.

Davis, David R., and Will H. Moore. 1997. "Ethnicity Matters: Transnational Ethnic Alliances and Foreign Policy Behavior." *International Studies Quarterly* 41 (1): 171–84.

Dayal, Rajeshwar. 1976. *Mission for Hammarskjold: The Congo Crisis.* London: Oxford University Press.

de Silva, K. M. 1991. "Indo-Sri Lankan Relations, 1975–89: A Study in the Internationalization of Ethnic Conflict." In *Internationalization of Ethnic Conflict*, ed. K. M. de Silva and Ronald J. May, 76–106. New York: St. Martin's.

Diehl, Paul F. 1993. *International Peacekeeping.* Baltimore: Johns Hopkins University Press.

Dixon, William. 1996. "Third-party Techniques for Preventing Conflict Escalation and Promoting Peaceful Settlement." *International Organization* 50: 653–81.

Dorman, Andrew M., and Thomas G. Otte, eds. 1995. *Military Intervention: from Gunboat Diplomacy to Humanitarian Intervention.* Aldershot: Dartmouth.

Dowty, Alan, and Gil Loescher. 1996. "Refugee Flows as Grounds for International Action." *International Security* 21 (1): 43–71.

Dunkerley, James. 1982. *The Long War: Dictatorship and Revolution in El Salvador.* London: Verso Publishers.

Eriksson, John. 1996. *The International Response to Conflict and Genocide: Lessons from the Rwanda Experience, Synthesis Report.* United Nations: Steering Committee of the Joint Evaluation of Emergency Assistance to Rwanda.

Esman, Milton J., and Shibley Telhami, eds. 1995. *International Organizations and Ethnic Conflict.* Ithaca: Cornell University Press.

Feith, David. 1989. "The Tamil Struggle: A Brief Historial Survey." In *The Tamil Question and the Indo-Sri Lanka Accord*, ed. N. Seevaratnam, 73–88. New Delhi: Konark Publishers.

Feste, Karen A. 1992. *Expanding the Frontiers: Superpower Intervention in the Cold War.* Westport, CT: Praeger.

Fetherston, A. Betts. 1994. *Toward a Theory of UN Peacekeeping.* Basingstoke, UK: Macmillan.

Freedman, Lawrence. 1994. "Introduction." In *Military Intervention in European Conflicts*, ed. Lawrence Freedman, 1–13. Oxford: Blackwell Publishers.

Frost, Frank. 1993. *The Peace Process in Cambodia: Issues and Prospects.* Working Paper No. 69. Queensland, Australia: Centre for the Study of Australia-Asia Relations

Gartner, Scott S., and Patrick M. Regan. 1996. "Threat and Repression: The Non-Linear Relationship Between Government and Opposition Violence." *Journal of Peace Research* 33 (3): 273–88.

Gartner, Scott S., and Gary M. Segura. 1998. "War, Casualties, and Public Opinion." *Journal of Conflict Resolution* 42 (3): 278–301.

Gartner, Scott S., Gary M. Segura, and Michael Wilkening. 1997. "All Politics Are Local: Local Losses and Individual Attitudes Towards the Vietnam War." *Journal of Conflict Resolution* 41 (5): 669–94.

Gartner, Scott S., and Randolph Siverson. 1996. "War Expansion and War Outcome." *Journal of Conflict Resolution* 40 (1): 4–15.

George, Alexander. 1995. *Bridging the Gap.* Washington, DC: United States Institute of Peace.

Goertz, Gary, and Paul F. Diehl. 1993. "Enduring Rivalries: Theoretical Constructs and Empirical Patterns." *International Studies Quarterly* 37 (2): 634–64.

Greene, William H. 1993. *Econometric Analysis,* 2nd ed. New York: Macmillan.

Gurr, Ted Robert. 1970. *Why Men Rebel.* Princeton: Princeton University Press.

———. 1993. *Minorities at Risk: A Global View of Ethnopolitical Conflicts.* Washington, DC: United States Institute for Peace.

———. 1994. "Peoples Against States: Ethnopolitical Conflict and the Changing World System." *International Studies Quarterly* 38 (3): 347–78.

Gurr, Ted Robert, and Barbara Harff. 1994. *Ethnic Conflict in World Politics.* Boulder: Westview.

Haass, Richard N. 1990. *Conflicts Unending: The United States and Regional Disputes.* New Haven: Yale University Press.

———. 1994. "Military Force: A User's Guide." *Foreign Policy,* no. 96 (fall): 21–37.

Hampson, Fen Osler. 1996. *Nuturing Peace: Why Peace Settlements Succeed or Fail.* Washington, DC: United States Institute for Peace.

Hanushek, Eric A., and John E. Jackson. 1977. *Statistical Methods for Social Scientists.* New York: Academic Press.

Hensel, Paul, and Paul Diehl. 1994. "It Takes Two to Tango: Nonmilitarized Response in Interstate Disputes." *Journal of Conflict Resolution* 38:479–506.

Holiday, David, and William Stanley. 1996. "Building Peace in El Salvador." *Journal of International Affairs* 46 (2): 415–38.

Holl, Jane E. 1993. "When War Doesn't Work: Understanding the Relationship Between the Battlefield and the Negotiating Table." In *Stopping the Killing: How Civil Wars End,* ed. Roy Licklider, 269–91. New York: New York University Press.

Horowitz, Donald. 1985. *Ethnic Groups in Conflict.* Berkeley: University of California Press.

Howe, Jonathan T. 1995. "The United States and United Nations in Somalia: The Limits of Involvement." *The Washington Quarterly* 18 (3): 49–62.

Hufbauer, Gary C. and Jeffrey J. Schott. 1983. *Economic Sanctions in Support of Foreign Policy Goals.* Washington, DC: Institute for International Economics.

Irving, David. 1986. *Uprising: One Nation's Nightmare: Hungary 1956.* Australia: Veritas Publishing.

Iyer, Justice V. R. Krishna. 1989. "The Sri Lanka Accord." In *The Tamil Question and the Indo-Sri Lanka Accord,* ed. N. Seevaratnam, 96–110. New Delhi: Konark Publishers.

James, Alan. 1996. *Britain and the Congo Crisis, 1960–63.* New York: St. Martin's.

Jones, Daniel, Stuart A. Bremer, and J. David Singer. 1996. "Militarized Interstate Disputes, 1816–1992: Rationale, Coding Rules, and Empirical Patterns." *Conflict Management and Peace Science* 15 (2): 163–213.

Kalb, Madeleine G. 1982. *The Congo Cables: The Cold War in Africa—From Eisenhower to Kennedy.* New York: Macmillan.

Kanter, Arnold, and Linton F. Brooks. 1994. "Final Report to the 85th American Assembly." In *U.S. Intervention Policy for the Post-Cold War World: New Challenges and New Responses,* ed. Arnold Kanter and Linton F. Brooks, 227–42. New York: W. W. Norton.

Kanza, Thomas. 1979. *The Rise and Fall of Patrice Lumumba: Conflict in the Congo.* Boston: G. K. Hall & Co.

Karl, Terry Lynn. 1992. "El Salvador's Negotiated Revolution." *Foreign Affairs* 71 (2): 147–64.

Kaufmann, Chaim. 1996. "Possible and Impossible Solutions to Ethnic Conflicts." *International Security* 20 (4): 136–75.

Keashly, Loraleigh, and Ronald J. Fisher. 1990. "Towards a Contingency Approach to Third Party Intervention in Regional Conflict: A Cyprus Illustration." *International Journal* 45 (2): 424–53.

Kennan, George F. 1993. *Around the Cragged Hill: A Personal and Political Philosophy.* New York: W. W. Norton.

Kennedy, Peter. 1987. *A Guide to Econometrics.* Cambridge: MIT Press.

King, Gary, Robert O. Keohane, and Sidney Verba. 1994. *Designing Social Inquiry: Scientific Inference in Qualitative Research.* Princeton: Princeton University Press.

Klintworth, Gary. 1993. *Cambodia's Past, Present and Future.* Working Paper No. 268, Strategic and Defence Studies Centre. Canberra: Australian National University.

Kodikara, Shelton U. 1991. "Internationalization of Sri Lanka's Ethnic Conflict: The Tamil Nadu Factor." In *Internationalization of Ethnic Conflict,* ed. K. M. de Silva and Ronald J. May, 107–14. New York: St. Martin's.

Kohut, Andrew, and Robert C. Toth. 1994. "Arms and the People." *Foreign Affairs* 73 (6): 47–61.

Kriesberg, Louis. 1991. "Introduction: Timing Conditions, Strategies, and Errors." In *Timing the De-escalation of International Conflicts,* ed. Louis Kriesberg and Stuart J. Thorson, 1–24. Syracuse, NY: Syracuse University Press.

———. 1992. *International Conflict Resolution: The US-USSR and Middle East Cases.* New Haven: Yale University Press.

———. 1994. "Conflict Resolution." In *Peace and World Security Studies: A Curriculum Guide,* ed. Michael Klare, 176–88. Boulder: Lynne Rienner.

Kumar, Krishna, and David Tardif-Douglin. 1996. *The International Response to Conflict and Genocide: Lessons from the Rwanda Experience, Study #4: Rebuilding Post-War Rwanda.* United Nations: Steering Committee of the Joint Evaluation of Emergency Assistance to Rwanda.

Lemke, Douglas. 1995. "The Tyranny of Distance: Redefining Relevant Dyads." *International Interactions* 21 (1): 23–38.

———. 1996. "Correlates of Great Power Intervention." Unpublished manuscript, Florida State University.

Leopold, Evelyn. 1991. "U.N. Chief Proposes Peacekeepers for El Salvador." *Reuters*, September 30.

———. 1996. "U.N. Security Council Set to Okay Troops in Zaire." *Reuters*, November 15.

Leslie, Winsome J. 1993. *Zaire: Continuity and Political Change in an Oppressive State*. Boulder: Westview.

Levy, Jack S. 1981. "Alliance Formation and War Behavior: An Analysis of the Great Powers, 1495–1975." *Journal of Conflict Resolution* 25 (4): 581–613.

Licklider, Roy. 1993. "How Civil Wars End: Questions and Methods." In *Stopping the Killing: How Civil Wars End*, ed. Roy Licklider, 3–19. New York: New York University Press.

———. 1995. "The Consequences of Negotiated Settlements in Civil Wars, 1945–1993." *American Political Science Review* 89 (3): 681–90.

Little, David. 1994. *Sri Lanka: The Invention of Enmity*. Washington, DC: United States Institute for Peace.

Lowenthal, Abraham F. 1972. *The Dominican Intervention*. Cambridge: Harvard University Press.

Mersheimer, John. 1990. "Why We Will Soon Miss the Cold War." *Atlantic Monthly* 266: 35–42.

Miller, Nikki. 1989. "The Impact of US Policy in Central America." In *The Superpowers, Central America and the Middle East*, ed, Peter Shearman and Phil Williams, 121–31. London: Brassey's Defence Publications.

Mitchell, Alison. 1996. "Clinton Offers US Troops to Help Refugees in Zaire." *New York Times*, November 14, Section A, p. 1.

Mitchell, Christopher, and Michael Banks. 1997. *Handbook of Conflict Resolution: The Analytical Problem-solving Approach*. Pinter: London.

Montgomery, Tommie Sue. 1995. "Getting to Peace in El Salvador: The Roles of the United Nations Secretariat and ONUSAL." *Journal of Interamerican Studies and World Politics* 37 (4): 139–72.

Morgan, T. Clifton. 1995. *Untying the Knot of War: A Bargaining Theory of International Crises*. Ann Arbor: University of Michigan Press.

Morganthau, Hans. 1967. "To Intervene or Not to Intervene." *Foreign Affairs* 46 (3): 425–36.

Most, Benjamin A., and Harvey Starr. 1989. *Inquiry, Logic, and International Politics*. Columbia: University of South Carolina Press.

Nachmani, Amikam. 1990. *International Intervention in the Greek Civil War: The United Nations Special Committee on the Balkans, 1947–1952*. Westport, CT: Praeger.

Neustadt, Richard E., and Ernest R. May. 1986. *Thinking in Time: The Uses of History for Decision Makers*. New York: The Free Press.

Nkrumah, Kwame. 1967. *Challenge of the Congo*. New York: International Publishers.

Nzongola-Ntalaja, Georges. 1986. *The Crisis in Zaire: Myths and Realities*. Trenton, NJ: Africa World Press.

Olson, Mancur. 1965. *The Logic of Collective Action.* Cambridge: Harvard University Press.

Organski, A. F. K., and Jacek Kugler. 1988. *The War Ledger.* Chicago: University of Chicago Press.

Otte, Thomas G. 1995. "On Intervention: Some Introductory Remarks." In *Military Intervention: From Gunboat Diplomacy to Humanitarian Intervention,* ed. Andrew M. Dorman and Thomas G. Otte, 3–15. Aldershot: Dartmouth.

Patchen, Martin. 1988. *Resolving Disputes Between Nations: Coercion or Conciliation?* Durham, NC: Duke University Press.

Pearson, Frederick S. 1974. "Foreign Military Interventions and Domestic Disputes." *International Studies Quarterly* 18 (3): 259–89.

Pearson, Frederick S., and Robert A. Baumann. 1993. "International Military Intervention, 1946–1988." Computer File, St. Louis, MO: University of Missouri, Center for International Studies, distributor, Inter-University Consortium for Political and Social Research.

Pillar, Paul R. 1983. *Negotiating Peace: War Termination as a Bargaining Process.* Princeton: Princeton University Press.

Ratner, Steven R. 1993. "The United Nations in Cambodia: A Model for Resolution of Internal Conflicts?" In *Enforcing Restraint: Collective Intervention in Internal Conflicts,* ed. Lori Fisler Damrosch, 241–73. New York: Council on Foreign Relations.

Ray, James Lee. 1995. *Democracy and International Conflict: An Evaluation of the Democratic Peace Proposition.* Columbia: University of South Carolina Press.

Reed, Laura W., and Carl Kaysen, eds. 1993. *Emerging Norms of Justified Intervention: A Collection of Essays from a Project of the American Academy of Arts and Sciences.* Cambridge: American Academy of Arts and Sciences.

Regan, Patrick M. 1996. "Conditions of Successful Third-Party Intervention in Intra-State Conflicts." *Journal of Conflict Resolution* 40 (1): 336–59.

Regan, Patrick M., and Allan C. Stam. 2000. "In the Nick of Time: Conflict Management, Mediation Timing, and the Duration of Interstate Disputes." *International Studies Quarterly* 44 (2): forthcoming.

Reuters. 1997. "Key Events in Zaire's Rebel War." March 15.

Roncek, Dennis W. 1991. "Using Logit Coefficients to Obtain the Effects of Independent Variables on Changes in Probabilities." *Social Forces* 70 (2): 509–18.

Rosenau, James N. 1968. "The Concept of Intervention." *Journal of International Affairs* 22:165–76.

———. 1969. "Intervention as a Scientific Concept." *Journal of Conflict Resolution* 13 (2): 149–71.

Rupesinghe, Kumar. 1987. "Theories of Conflict Resolution and Their Applicability to Protracted Ethnic Conflicts." *Bulletin of Peace Proposals* 18 (4): 527–39.

Schraeder, Peter, ed. 1992. *Intervention into the 1990s: US Foreign Policy in the Third World.* Boulder: Lynne Rienner.

Scott, James M. 1996. *Deciding to Intervene: The Reagan Doctrine and American Foreign Policy.* Durham, NC: Duke University Press.

Sellstrom, Tor, and Lennart Wohlgemuth. 1996. *The International Response to Conflict and Genocide: Lessons from the Rwanda Experience, Study #1: Historical Perspective: Some Explanatory Factors.* United Nations: Steering Committee of the Joint Evaluation of Emergency Assistance to Rwanda.

Shearman, Peter. 1988. "The Impact of Soviet Policy in Central America." In *The Superpowers, Central America and the Middle East,* ed. Peter Shearman and Phil Williams, 132–41. London: Brassey's Defence Publications.

Shearman, Peter, and Phil Williams, eds. 1988. *The Superpowers, Central America and the Middle East.* London: Brassey's Defence Publications.

Singer, J. David. 1963. "Internation Influence: A Formal Model." *American Political Science Review* 57 (2): 420–30.

Singer, J. David, and Melvin Small. 1972. *The Wages of War 1816–1965: A Statistical Handbook.* New York: John Wiley and Sons.

Siverson, Randolph M., and Joel King. 1979. "Alliances and the Expansion of War." In *To Augur Well,* ed. J. David Singer and Michael D. Wallace, 37–49. Beverly Hills, CA: Sage.

Siverson, Randolph M., and Harvey Starr. 1991. *The Diffusion of War.* Ann Arbor: University of Michigan Press.

Small, Melvin, and J. David Singer. 1982. *Resort to Arms: International and Civil Wars, 1816–1980.* Beverly Hills, CA: Sage.

Smith, Alastair. 1996. "To Intervene or Not to Intervene: A Biased Decision." *Journal of Conflict Resolution* 40 (1): 16–40.

Smith, James D. D. 1995. *Stopping Wars.* Boulder: Westview.

Smith, Tony. 1994. "In Defense of Intervention." *Foreign Affairs* 73 (November/December): 34–46.

Solarz, Stephen J. 1986. "When to Intervene." *Foreign Policy* 63:20–39.

Stahler-Sholk, Richard. 1994. "El Salvador's Negotiated Transition: From Low-Intensity Conflict to Low-Intensity Democracy." *Journal of Interamerican Studies and World Politics* 36 (4): 1–60.

Stam, Allan C. III. 1996. *Win, Lose, or Draw: Domestic Politics and the Crucible of War.* Ann Arbor: University of Michigan Press.

Tetlock, Philip, and Aaron Belkin. 1996. *Counterfactual Thought Experiments in World Politics: Logical, Methodological, and Psychological Perspectives.* Princeton: Princeton University Press.

Tillema, Herbert. 1989. "Foreign Overt Military Intervention in the Nuclear Age." *Journal of Peace Research* 26 (2): 179–95.

———. 1991. *International Armed Conflict Since 1945: A Bibliographic Handbook of Wars and Military Interventions.* Boulder: Westview.

Touval, Saadia, and I. William Zartman, eds. 1989. *International Mediation in Theory and Practice.* Boulder: Westview.

Tsbelis, George. 1990. "The Abuse of Probability in Political Analysis: The Robinson Crusoe Fallacy." *American Political Science Review* 83 (1): 77–92.

UN High Commission for Refugees. 1993. *State of the World's Refugees: The Challenge of Protection*. New York: Penguin.

United Nations. 1990. *The Blue Helmets: A Review of United Nations Peacekeeping*, 2d ed. New York: United Nations.

United Nations, Department of Public Information. 1996. *United Nations Mission in Haiti [UNSMIH]*. New York: United Nations.

United Nations, Office of Internal Oversight Services. 1966–1994. "In-depth Evaluation of Peacekeeping Operations: Start-up Phase." New York: United Nations.

U.S. Committee for Refugees. Annual. *World Refugee Survey.* New York: U.S. Committee for Refugees.

U.S. Department of State. 1994. *Foreign Relations of the United States, 1961–63. Volume XX, Congo Crisis.* Washington, DC: U.S. Government Printing Office.

Vasquez, John. 1993. *The War Puzzle.* New York: Cambridge University Press.

Väyrynen, Raimo. 1996. "The Age of Humanitarian Emergencies." University of Notre Dame typescript.

Vertzberger, Yaacov Y. I. 1993. "The International Environment and Foreign Military Intervention When and How Much Does it Matter?" Meetings of the American Political Science Association, September 2–5, Washington, DC.

Vickery, Michael. 1984. *Cambodia: 1975–1982.* Sydney: Allen and Unwin.

Wagner, Robert Harrison. 1993. "The Causes of Peace." In *Stopping the Killing: How Civil Wars End*, ed. Roy Licklider, 235–68. New York: New York University Press.

Wallensteen, Peter, and Karin Axell. 1993. "Armed Conflict at the End of the Cold War, 1989–92." *Journal of Peace Research* 30 (3): 331–46.

Waltz, Kenneth N. 1979. *Theory of International Politics.* Reading, MA: Addison-Wesley.

Wayman, Frank W. 1984. "Bipolarity and War: The Role of Capability Concentration and Alliance Patterns Among Major Powers, 1816–1965." *Journal of Peace Research* 21 (1): 61–78.

Williams, Colin H., and Elenore Kofman. 1989. "Culture, Community and Conflict." In *Community Conflict, Partition and Nationalism*, ed. Colin Williams and Elenore Kofman, 1–23. New York: Routledge.

Wriggins, Howard. 1968. "Political Outcomes of Foreign Assistance: Influence, Involvement, or Intervention?" *Journal of International Affairs* 22:217–30.

Yarmolinsky, Adam. 1968. "American Foreign Policy and the Decision to Intervene." *Journal of International Affairs* 22:231–35.

Young, Crawford, and Thomas Turner. 1985. *The Rise and Decline of the Zairian State.* Madison: University of Wisconsin Press.

Zartman, I. William. 1989. *Ripe for Resolution: Conflict and Intervention in Africa.* New York: Oxford University Press.

———. 1995. *Elusive Peace: Negotiating an End to Civil Wars.* Washington, DC: Brookings.

Index